CANTERBURY
A HISTORY SINCE 1500

CANTERBURY
A HISTORY
SINCE 1500

the story of a city and its people

DOREEN ROSMAN

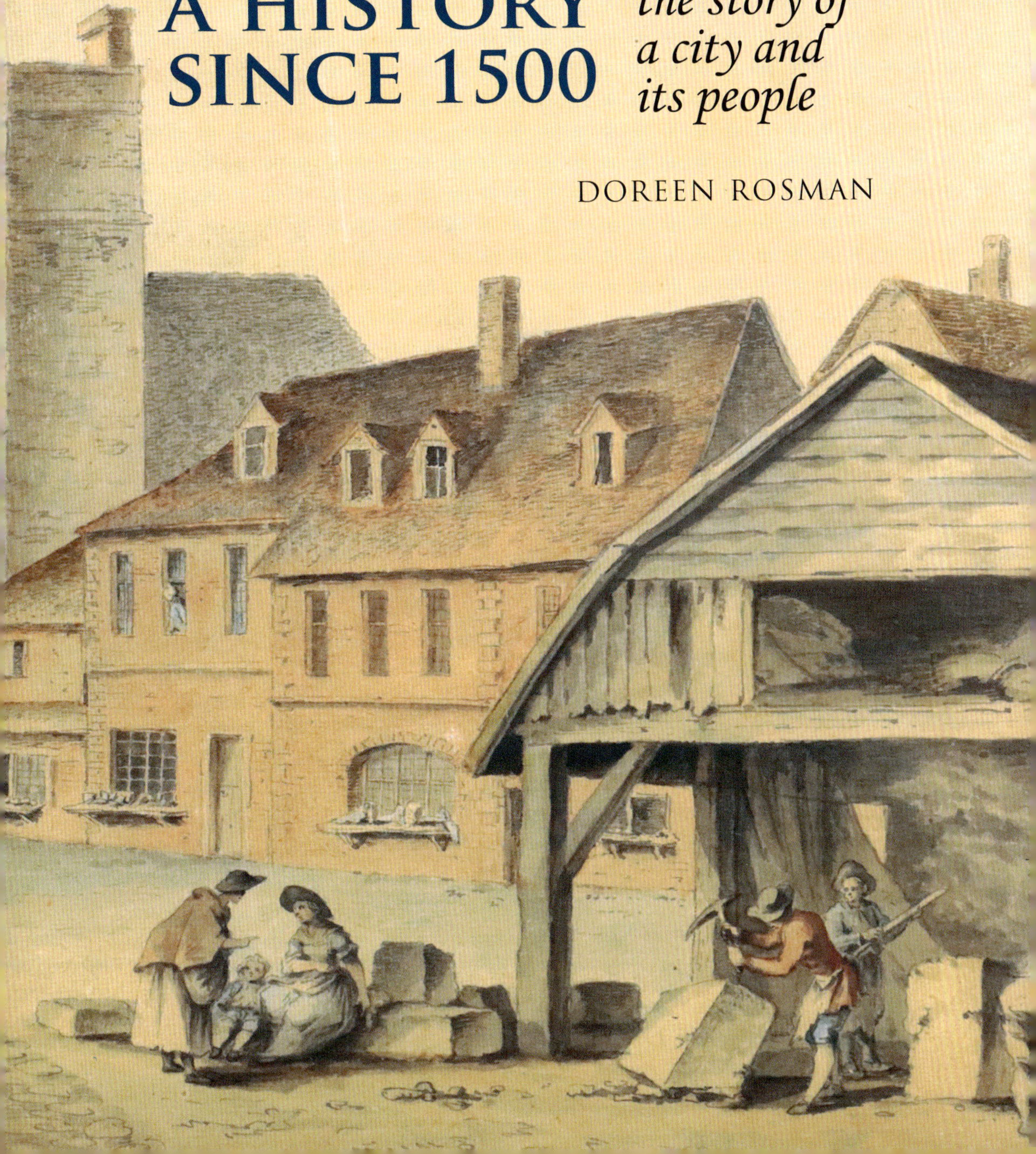

In memory
of
Clare Nicholson
and
Joy Sharman

First published in 2022

by Palatine Books
Carnegie House
Chatsworth Road
Lancaster LA1 4SL
www.palatinebooks.com

Copyright © Doreen Rosman

The right of Doreen Rosman to be identified as the author of this work has been asserted
in accordance with the Copyright, Designs and Patents act 1988

British Library Cataloguing-in-Publication data
A catalogue record for this book is available from the British Library

Every effort has been made to trace copyright holders.

Paperback ISBN 13: 978-1-910837-43-6

Designed and typeset by Carnegie Book Production
www.carnegiebookproduction.com

Printed and bound by Cambrian Printers

Halftitle page image © *ONE POUND LANE* (onepoundlane.co.uk)
Title page image courtesy of the Chapter of Canterbury Cathedral

ACKNOWLEDGEMENTS

In 2007 I trained as a Canterbury city guide – and realised that most general histories of Canterbury said little about the centuries after 1500. Plugging that gap has taken me far longer than I anticipated, and during that time I have incurred debts of gratitude to far more people than I can mention by name. I have gained many nuggets of fascinating information from fellow guides and from local University of the Third Age members, to whom I gave talks based on the chapters of this book. David Lewis, who collated much historical material for the Canterbury Historical and Archaeological Society website, responded readily to my queries and provided long-term loans of books. Ron Waters, who worked at the Market Way factory, told me about Sindy doll production. The Williamson family sought out family photographs, and Derek Butler looked through his vast postcard collection to find pictures I wanted. I received further assistance in sourcing illustrations from Craig Bowen of Canterbury Museums and from Karen Brayshaw and Clair Waller of the University of Kent, who willingly reproduced material from Paul Crampton's extensive photographic collection. Cressida Williams, Daniel Korachi-Alaoui, Toby Huitson, and Fawn Todd of Canterbury Cathedral Archives and Library gave generously of their time and expertise – and were as delighted as I was when they located material we thought had been lost. Fellow historians Hugh Cunningham, Grayson Ditchfield, Jackie Eales, Kenneth Fincham, and Sheila Sweetinburgh have kindly read chapters of this book and I have benefited from their suggestions. I am particularly grateful to two people. David Birmingham read through the entire text several times at various stages of production and has been a constant source of encouragement. At the end of the process, my brother Peter read the book from the perspective of a non-historian and non-resident of Canterbury, and ensured it was accessible not only to people who know and love the city but also to visitors interested in learning more about its history. Thank you all very much for your help.

CONTENTS

BECKET'S CITY

c. 1513

A Dutchman, Desiderius Erasmus, stands on a hill above Canterbury, gazing down at the great cathedral. He turns to his companion: 'Even at this distance,' he says, 'it fills one with awe.'

Early sixteenth-century Canterbury enjoyed a status it has long since lost. By modern standards it was tiny, with some four or maybe five thousand inhabitants, but at the time it was seen as a substantial place. It could not compete with the great provincial centres of Bristol and Norwich, which had populations of over ten thousand, but it was one of the ten biggest towns in the country and by far the largest in Kent. It also had the privilege of being one of a small number of 'county boroughs', which had greater independence than other towns: a royal charter of 1461 had decreed 'that Canterbury should henceforth be a county for ever, entirely and utterly separate from the county of Kent'. The city's importance derived both from its location, on the main London to Dover road, and from its religious heritage. People travelling between the capital and the channel ports would often stay overnight at one of its substantial inns. The archbishop was 'Primate of All England', and the cathedral was one of the most important pilgrim sites in western Europe. The murder of Archbishop Thomas Becket in December 1170 had sent shock waves across the continent: pilgrims from many lands came to visit the place where the saint had been martyred and where his bones were preserved. These sacred relics had been 'translated' or moved in 1220 from a tomb in the crypt to a great jewel-encrusted gold shrine, one of the most awe-inspiring in Europe.

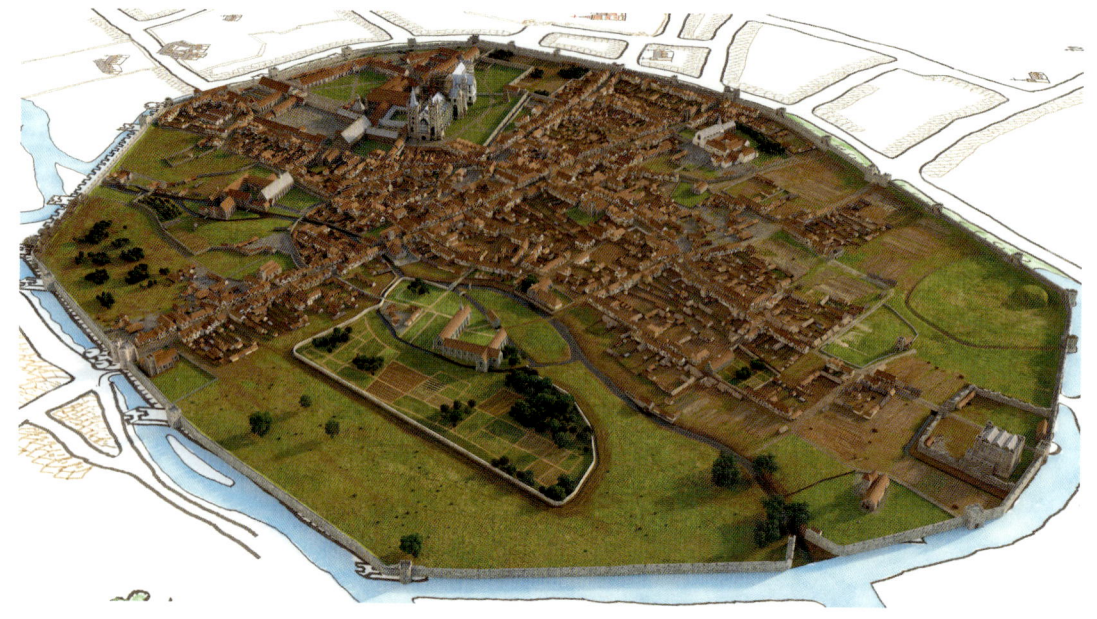

At the peak of its popularity Becket's shrine attracted vast numbers. In 1420, the bicentenary of the translation, 'a hundred thousand' people visited Canterbury, a figure that should not be taken literally but which certainly denoted a very large number. Innkeepers, souvenir makers, and the city at large benefited from the pilgrims, whose prayers at the shrine were often followed by sightseeing, shopping, dining, and drinking. In later decades, the popularity of pilgrimage as a form of devotion declined, but the shrine at Canterbury continued to attract visitors, albeit fewer

Pilgrims on the road, detail from a medieval stained-glass window. *By kind permission of the Chapter, Canterbury Cathedral.*

than in earlier centuries. Many pilgrims left gifts, which the monks of Christ Church Priory, the monastery surrounding the cathedral, carefully recorded. The monastic accounts reveal that pilgrimage, like tourism today, was a seasonal trade. The busiest months were, predictably, those between March and September, but it was rare, even in the cold, dark weeks from November to February, for a day to pass on which no offerings were made at Becket's shrine. Its importance to Canterbury was reflected in the city seal, which bore the saint's image.

Eminent people from home and abroad were among those who passed through Canterbury, and the city was sometimes chosen as the venue for royal meetings. One of the most prestigious visits took place on Whit Sunday 1520, when the Holy Roman Emperor, Charles V, was received in great state by King Henry VIII, the first occasion when the emperor met his aunt, the king's wife, Catherine of Aragon. The people of Canterbury were no doubt entertained by the spectacle of such visits, but they were a drain on city resources, not least because convention demanded that important visitors receive gifts. At her 'first coming to Canterbury' some years before, Queen Catherine had been given a silver cup containing thirteen pounds-worth of gold coins. Other visitors were presented with high-class gifts of food: Cardinal Wolsey received a supply of capons, pears, walnuts, cockles, and marzipan. Visits by the reigning monarch were particularly costly since he and his huge retinue had to be appropriately accommodated. To this end, a 'tentorium', a temporary tented town, was erected in the Forest of Blean, a couple of miles outside the city. Here the king was entertained in the style to which he was accustomed. A recurrent refrain in the city accounts concerned expenses incurred 'ayenst the kynges comyng to Canterbury'.

Canterbury was a magnet not only for national and international visitors but also for people from neighbouring towns and villages. It was the economic hub of its region, with markets for every kind of produce: live beasts, meat, poultry, fish, dairy foods, salt, wine, bread, textiles, and rushes to cover the floors of houses. City shops offered a wider range of wares than rural visitors could get from itinerant pedlars at home. One of the tasks of the city council, the Burghmote, was to regulate trade. Like councils elsewhere, it sought to prevent extortion by setting the prices that could be charged for goods such as meat, bread, ale, eggs, and candles. It also tried to protect city residents by enabling them to buy what they wanted before visitors from outside: the council accounts record that people from the countryside were fined for purchasing wheat before the permitted hour of eleven o'clock.

The rights enjoyed by people who lived in Canterbury varied according to their position in a very hierarchical society. The most privileged were freemen, who were entitled to vote in elections and to run their own businesses. People from outside the city who wanted to set up shop faced a yearly charge for the right to do so. Freedom of the city was hereditary, but newcomers could apply to become freemen on payment of a lump sum. Anyone who married the daughter of a freeman could hope to acquire the status on payment of a fee, as could men who completed a seven-year apprenticeship in the city. In 1524 John Ambrose, who had served as a grocer's apprentice, paid six shillings and eight pence for his freedom, the equivalent of some eleven days' wages, but others chose not to follow this path. On finishing their apprenticeship they remained journeymen, employed by others. Their training and skills, however, placed them above neighbours who had no such qualifications and who worked as unskilled labourers or servants. Below them on the social scale was a floating population of beggars, at whom the authorities looked askance. The city accounts record payments to a carter 'that ledde vacabunds about the towne to be whypped and for cords and whyppys for the same'.

While many Canterbury residents gained their livelihoods from one of the city's numerous trades, this was not true of all. There were professional men, notably lawyers, and a number of people belonging to different religious orders. In the sixteenth century many towns had one or two religious houses, but Canterbury was exceptionally well endowed. It had two big Benedictine monasteries: Christ Church Priory, linked to the cathedral, and St Augustine's Abbey just outside the city walls, a mere stone's throw away. Nearby, at St Gregory's, a residential community of priests followed the rule of St Augustine, while the road now known as Nunnery Fields commemorates the existence of a nunnery, St Sepulchre's. There were also three friaries. Like monks, friars took vows of poverty, chastity, and obedience but, unlike monks, they went out into towns and villages to preach. Grey-clad Franciscans, Dominicans or 'black' friars, and Augustinians (whom later generations inaccurately dubbed 'white' friars) were familiar sights on the streets of Canterbury. But what would have struck visitors most were the great buildings associated with the various orders, not just the cathedral but also a cathedral-sized church at St Augustine's Abbey and another very substantial one at St Gregory's Priory. Another massive building was the hall in the archbishop's palace. The palace itself stretched the length of what is now Palace Street, and its hall was second in size only to the great hall at Westminster.

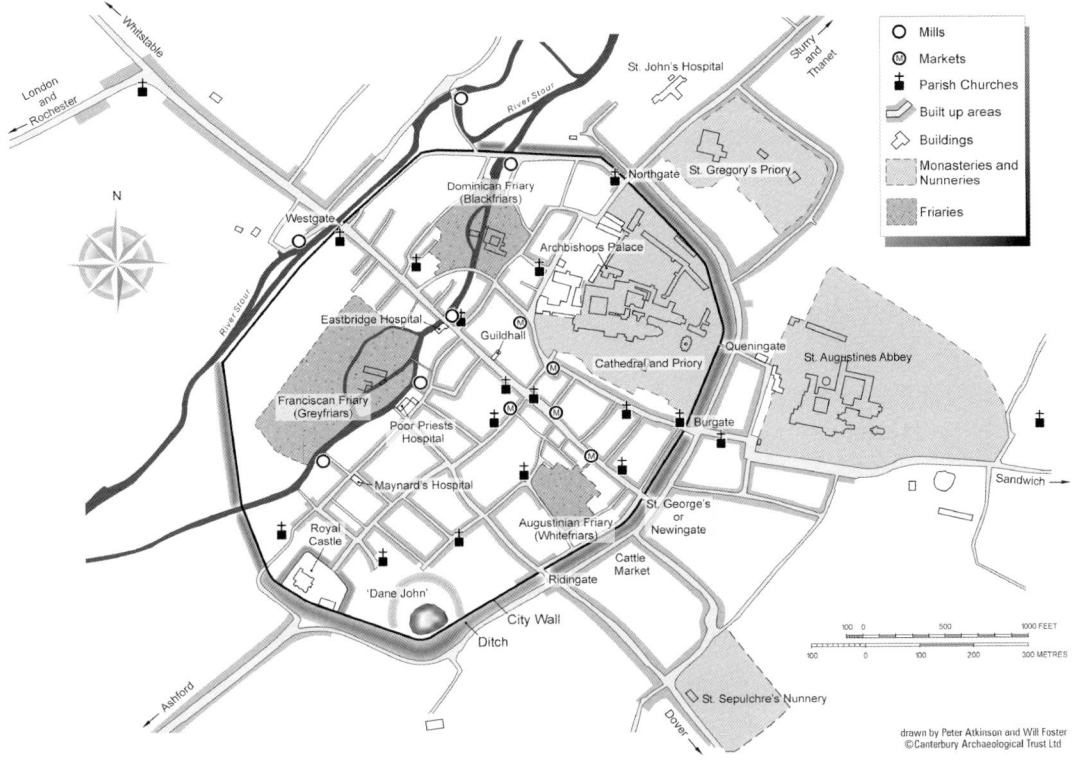

Canterbury *c.* 1500. Much land was occupied by religious houses and there were numerous markets and mills. ©*Canterbury Archaeological Trust.*

The presence of so many religious houses had a profound effect on the lives of Canterbury people. Traders – grocers, vintners, and others – depended on them for much of their business. Some local residents had regular jobs as servants of the various orders, and further employment was generated, often on a long-term basis, by the erection of new buildings. Bell Harry, the great tower in the centre of the cathedral, was completed around the start of the sixteenth century. Shortly afterwards work began on another major project: the construction of the Christ Church Gate, which was to give the cathedral priory an even more magnificent entrance than the Fyndon Gate, erected at St Augustine's two hundred years before. Other work opportunities were provided by parish churches. Surviving churchwardens' accounts for St Dunstan's and St Andrew's include payments to carpenters, joiners, pavers, and smiths, who kept the buildings in good repair and provided new fitments. Candles, which flamed before numerous

saintly images in churches, were supplied in vast quantities by the city's wax chandlers.

The two big religious houses impacted on life in other ways, too, since they owned much of the property in Canterbury. In 1504 St Augustine's Abbey received rent from 132 city tenants, along with the proceeds of Abbot's Mill (after which the Miller's Arms pub is named). Christ Church Priory was the largest landholder in the town, with over four hundred properties: these included several inns as well as shops and houses. Religious institutions exercised considerable power within the city, and there were repeated disputes between civic and monastic authorities over boundaries and jurisdiction. There was nothing unusual in this: similar conflicts occurred in other towns with powerful monasteries, such as Bristol, Exeter, York, and Norwich, but one of the most violent altercations took place in Canterbury. On 16 July 1500 some two hundred townsmen, armed with bows, arrows, and swords, attacked Christ Church Priory servants who were busy constructing a new watercourse through the Rosier meadows just outside the city's West Gate. The fight appears to have been part of an ongoing dispute over the provision of water to mills, in which both sides sought to realign ditches to their own benefit. The townsmen beat the servants up, imprisoned nine of them in the city gaol, and destroyed the new dyke. According to the enraged prior, these 'evil disposed persons' even assaulted a convalescent monk 'late afor sore

syke' (sick) who was 'walking in the ffeldes for hys recreation'. This was no spontaneous outburst by local roughs. It was led by William Atwode, a lawyer, whose family had long played a leading role in civic life. Atwode subsequently diverted water away from Barton Mill, which belonged to the priory, towards the city-owned King's Mill. The day after the Rosier attack, he caused the monks further offence by dismantling a fish market in the Burgate, a street bordering Christ Church, and moving it to the centre of town. Such actions hit the priory hard, reducing the value of the shops it owned in the Burgate and giving the tenants grounds to demand rent reductions. While the city sought to prosecute the priory servants, the prior brought a series of charges against Atwode and the mayor, some of which were heard in courts in London. The pleas made by the opposing sides reveal the bitterness of long-standing grievances and resentments. Some were decidedly petty (the townspeople had deprived the prior of his dinner by seizing a halibut purchased for that purpose); others were more substantial (the priory had befouled the city ditch with sewage). Townspeople raised £23 7s. 6½d. to help finance the legal battles between the priory and 'us', but William Atwode did not live to see the outcome. He died in the autumn of 1501, during an outbreak of the plague which periodically ravaged the city. The disputed meadows were eventually divided equally between the priory and the town, but the dispute rumbled on for some time.

The people of Canterbury combined resentment against powerful religious foundations with affection for them. The religious houses were, after all, a familiar and time-honoured part of local life. Lay neighbours sometimes worshipped in friary churches and some asked to be buried in them, a sure sign that these were places in which they

The main entrance to St Augustine's Abbey, the Fyndon Gate, dates back to 1309. *Author's photograph.*

felt comfortable. The 1518 ordinances of the 'Shoemakers', Curriers', and Cobblers' Guild' required all members to attend Mass on three feast days a year in the church of the Augustinian friars. Guilds such as this existed to protect the interests and 'mysteries' of their crafts, and to provide support for their members – both in this life and the life to come. It was believed that before proceeding to the bliss of heaven, the dead had to be cleansed of their sins in purgatory. Since the time spent in this place of pain could be reduced by the prayers of the living, the shoemakers paid the friars to pray for the souls of deceased members. Some people left money in their wills to this end: Elizabeth Hale, an alderman's wife who died in 1506, gave the Augustinian friars three shillings and four pence a year for ten years to pray for her eternal well-being, and also made bequests to the other two friaries. Other testators similarly left specified sums to the various hospitals and almshouses with which Canterbury was well endowed. Many of these were religious foundations built centuries earlier to house the old, the sick, and the poor. Inmates reciprocated by praying for the souls of benefactors such as Joane Bakke, who in 1500 left three shillings and four pence a year for three years to the brothers and sisters of St John's Hospital in Northgate.

Townspeople enjoyed access not only to the friaries and hospitals but also to parts of the two great monasteries. Over the centuries Canterbury had acquired the right to hold eight fairs a year, six of which took place in monastic grounds. St Augustine's Abbey was, predictably, the location for the fair named after that saint from 8 to 13 September, as well as for one dedicated to St Peter and St Paul at the end of June. The Whitsuntide Fair, St Thomas' Fair in July, St Michael's Fair in late September, and Holy Innocents' Fair at the end of December were all held in the lay cemetery of the cathedral priory.

The fun of fairs was matched by other recreational activities linked to religious institutions. In the early sixteenth century sacred and secular were still inextricably intertwined. 'Holy days' were 'holidays', frequently marked by feasting, revelry, games, and bonfires, as well as by religious observances. Some of these festivities took place in the fourteen parish churches which played a central role in the lives of Canterbury people. Parishes commonly had their own fraternities or guilds dedicated to particular saints. Like the craft guilds, these combined religious, philanthropic, and social activity by means of meetings, processions, and feasts. Churchwardens' accounts reveal that St Dunstan's had at least three fraternities. In 1520 the wardens found a 'booke of Abraham and Isaacke' in the church chest, which suggested that theirs may have been one of a number of Kent churches which sometimes put on plays. Another regular form of dramatic entertainment was the performance by craft guilds of 'mystery plays' (which may have taken their name from 'mestier' meaning 'trade' or 'job'). These took place each year in towns throughout England around the time of the feast of Corpus Christi. Mounted on wagons so that they could be seen, guild members enacted familiar Bible stories in a heady mix of piety and bawdy humour. Very little information survives about Corpus Christi celebrations in Canterbury, but more is known about other spring and summer processions. On 23 April, the feast of St George, an image of the saint, attended by the mayor, aldermen, and their wives, was paraded around the city in honour of God and the king. A 'Marching Watch', a feature of many towns' midsummer celebrations, took place in Canterbury on 6 July, the eve of the translation of Becket's bones. Gunners, pikemen, and archers marched through the town to the sound of drums and trumpet. They were preceded by 'gyantes' (probably large puppets) and accompanied by the mayor and aldermen, resplendent in their official robes. Gunpowder explosions added excitement to the spectacle, and the parade was followed by shooting and wrestling matches. There were religious pageants in this procession too, including one in celebration of St Thomas, introduced – or maybe reintroduced – in 1505, in which four boys dressed as knights mimed the attack on the archbishop. Gusto and verisimilitude were added to the display by the release, at the moment of the murder, of a carefully hidden bag of pig's blood. Over the years further spectacles were added, such as a mechanical 'vyce' (device), a spinning angel which flapped its wings in all directions. City accounts record the cost of constructing, painting, and storing the wagon on which the pageant took place, along with props such as the altar at which Becket was killed. Tuppence was paid 'to hym that turned the vyce', food and drink were provided for the children who played the knights, and there were occasional purchases such as 'a payer of new gloves for Seynt Thomas' or 'a new leder bag for the blode'.

The inclusion of a St Thomas pageant, financed by the city council, in the annual Marching Watch may have been designed to help restore relations with Christ Church Priory after recent legal battles. City and monastic authorities may also have hoped to raise their saint's profile in the years running up to 1520, the tercentenary of the translation of his bones. A hundred years before, the Pope had granted a plenary indulgence (i.e. exemption from time in purgatory) to anyone who made a pilgrimage to Canterbury in the jubilee year, but his successor in 1520 refused to follow suit unless Christ Church Priory agreed to donate half the pilgrim offerings to the rebuilding of St Peter's in Rome. The absence of major celebrations in 1520 reflected the declining importance of pilgrimage to the city. There was growing criticism in some intellectual circles of the whole practice of making such journeys. Erasmus, the leading scholar of the age, objected to the excessive display of wealth in pilgrim churches such as Canterbury Cathedral. John Colet, the dean of St Paul's who visited St Thomas' shrine with him, was so opposed to the veneration of saintly remains that he declined to kiss the sacred relics. Erasmus and Colet were leaders of a new humanist movement within the Church which suggested that much contemporary religious observance was far removed from the faith of the first century. Neither they, however, nor the people of Canterbury, happily celebrating the story of Becket's dramatic death, would have predicted that within a few years the pilgrim trade would cease altogether and the jewel-laden shrine be smashed to smithereens.

Digital reconstruction (based on evidence from historical documents and artefacts) of Becket's shrine c. 1408. ©University of York. All rights reserved. This work was supported by the Arts and Humanities Research Council grant number AH/L015005/1, AH/R008094/1.

2

DISSOLUTION AND DEMOLITION

Sunday 7 December 1533

A crowd gathers in the lay cemetery of Christ Church Priory. People stare with curiosity and compassion at a nun who stands on a raised platform before them. They listen as a visiting preacher denounces her: she has 'counterfeited trances' and claimed that her 'false, forged, and feigned revelations' come from God. Some shake their heads, unconvinced by his words, but most keep their thoughts to themselves. The authorities have decided what is right and what is wrong, and there is little ordinary people can do but acquiesce.

In the early 1530s Elizabeth Barton, a young nun from Canterbury, attracted nationwide attention by speaking out on 'the king's great matter', his desire to divorce his wife of twenty years and marry again in the hope of producing a legitimate male heir. Elizabeth was a visionary. A few years before, as a teenage servant girl, she had fallen into long trances, during which she spoke in a deep, unnatural voice about heaven, hell, purgatory, and the importance of praying to the Virgin Mary and other saints. To the excitement of her neighbours she showed uncanny perception into matters she could not possibly have known about (such as what a hermit was having for dinner), and some of her predictions about future events came true. 'Holy maids' of this kind were an accepted part of the religious world of the day, and the Church had standard procedures for investigating them. Seven learned commissioners were dispatched to Aldington, the village some twenty miles south of Canterbury in which Elizabeth lived. Here they witnessed a trance and heard her speak. What she said was perfectly orthodox, and the commissioners concluded that she was genuinely inspired by God. Soon afterwards Elizabeth entered St Sepulchre's convent.

Elizabeth Barton appears to have been an extraordinarily self-confident and charismatic young woman. Despite her lack of education, she gained the respect of people of status and learning, including senior churchmen. Aristocratic ladies sought her counsel and her prayers. Had she confined her strictures to matters of personal spirituality her reputation might have remained unblemished, but after a few years she moved into politically sensitive territory. She described visions which demonstrated God's disapproval of the king's proposed divorce. According to different accounts she predicted that, if Henry contracted a new marriage, God would no longer recognise him as king;

Portrait of Henry VIII from the endowment charter of the cathedral (23 May 1541), which granted the Dean and Chapter property formerly owned by Christ Church Priory. *Courtesy of the Chapter of Canterbury Cathedral.*

he would die within a month; he would go to hell. It appears she may even have met the king on a couple of occasions and told him that what he was planning was wrong.

What caused the authorities particular concern was the publicity Elizabeth's visions received. Opponents of the royal divorce seized on them with alacrity. Her spiritual director, Dr Bocking, a senior monk at Christ Church Priory, had seven hundred copies of a 'Great Book' printed, recording her revelations. The consternation of royal officials was reflected in their memoranda and correspondence which, for nearly a year, contained numerous references to 'the Nun'. Once Anne Boleyn was crowned queen in June 1533, Elizabeth had to be silenced and discredited. Anne was pregnant, and the populace had to be convinced that the forthcoming baby was a legitimate heir. The staging of two open-air sermons, the first at Paul's Cross in London and a repeat performance at Canterbury a fortnight later, were part of a defamation campaign. The preacher accused Elizabeth of treason, falsehood, and heresy, and even hinted that her relations with Dr Bocking might not have been as pure as they should have been. Two months later a special act was passed through Parliament, indicting her and some of her supporters for high treason. On 20 April 1534 Elizabeth Barton was hanged at Tyburn and her severed head was impaled on London Bridge. Dr Bocking and another monk from the cathedral priory, along with the warden of Canterbury Greyfriars, were put to death with her.

The execution of two of their number cast doubt on the loyalty of the whole Christ Church community. The prior had already written grovelling letters to the chief minister, Thomas Cromwell, claiming that he barely knew the nun and that Dr Bocking had acted 'against my will and knowledge'. In the end, official investigators concluded that only a few young monks had accepted Elizabeth's revelations, but the priory still feared reprisals. The monks apparently offered the king two or three hundred pounds as a way of begging his pardon. Meanwhile, every man and every boy over the age of twelve throughout the country was required to swear that he accepted Anne Boleyn's children as lawful heirs to the crown. Two Canterbury Franciscans refused to do so. Since their house was already tarnished by the Elizabeth Barton affair, the rest of the community was placed under house arrest.

Sir Thomas More plaque in St Dunstan's Church. More was named a saint in 1935. *Photograph by Martin Ward.*

Clergy and public officials faced a second oath. They had to swear that the king was head of the Church in England. During the years in which Henry had waited, hoping the Pope would annul his marriage to Catherine, scholars had drawn his attention to ancient documents which implied that popes had no rights over the English Church. This gave grounds for the archbishop of Canterbury, rather than officials from Rome, to preside over the divorce hearing and for Parliament to proclaim that the king was supreme head of the Church in England. The most notable figure who refused to acknowledge this ruling was the former lord chancellor Sir Thomas More, whose daughter Margaret had married William Roper of Canterbury. More was beheaded on 6 July 1535. His head is believed to be in the Roper vault in St Dunstan's church. Another person who challenged the new order was the prior of the city's Dominican friary. He preached a sermon against royal supremacy and then presumably fled abroad, since nothing more is known of him.

Religious communities harboured some of the most vocal opponents of the new order, and this may have contributed to the suspicion with which the authorities viewed them. But there had been complaints about such institutions long before the 1530s, and a few houses had been closed in the previous decade. Some communities were so small they were barely viable, while others were regarded as unacceptably lax. The Augustinian friars in Canterbury were among those who appear to have fallen short of their calling: in 1499 a city court fined 'Alice the prostitute' twelve pence for going to the friary at night, something she was said to have done on many occasions. A few decades later the friars were accused of playing dice, cards, and ball games, and even of eating and sleeping at local inns. Another long-standing complaint was that too much of the nation's wealth was in ecclesiastical hands. In 1535 commissioners were sent to 'every diocese, shire and place in this realm' to assess just how extensive ecclesiastical possessions were. Two of the richest monastic houses were in Canterbury: St Augustine's had an annual income of over £1,700, a vast sum in those days, while Christ Church was valued at a staggering £2,493 6s. 2¾d. A few months later government officials descended on the monasteries again. This time they came armed with questionnaires and new rules: instructions about the conduct of worship and the practice of community life. The visitation was an obvious demonstration that religious houses were now under state control. Even people inclined to reform jibbed at such heavy-handed intervention. John Foche, the abbot of St Augustine's, who sympathised with the views of Erasmus, objected mildly that some of the injunctions were 'very hard'.

Worse was to follow. Several of the king's key advisers were sympathetic to the new religious ideas emanating from Germany: they maintained that monasticism was based on false conceptions of faith, and they wanted to abolish it altogether. Their antagonism was clearly shared by Richard Layton, the commissioner who inspected the Canterbury houses: Layton aimed to root out 'all coloured sanctity, superstitious rules of pretended religion and other detectable abuses'. In 1536, on the basis of reports which Layton and his colleagues presented, Parliament authorised the dissolution of religious houses which had fewer than a dozen inmates or which were worth less than £200 a year. Two of the Canterbury houses, St Sepulchre's and St Gregory's, which had only eight inhabitants each, were shut down in February 1537.

The following year, 1538, was traumatic for the people of Canterbury. By this time the king had agreed to close not only small and possibly corrupt institutions but every religious house in the land, some nine hundred in all. Henry was not opposed to monasticism as such, but he needed to quash any possible disaffection. He also feared attack from

Modern depiction of the destruction of St Augustine's Abbey by Ivan Lapper. ©*Canterbury Museums and Galleries.*

countries loyal to the Pope. The sale of huge monastic assets secured the allegiance of new landholders as well as providing money for the defence of the realm. In the strange, alien world in which they now lived, most religious communities realised that they had no option but to surrender their property 'voluntarily' to the Crown. On 30 July 1538 the abbot and the thirty monks of St Augustine's signed a deed handing over the oldest abbey in England to the king. Monastic offices had been recited there every day for over nine hundred years, but now the plaintive notes of the psalms echoed round the vast church for the last time. For monks who had spent most of their lives within the abbey and who had expected to be buried in its grounds, it was an ending beyond their worst nightmares.

A further nightmare materialised a few weeks later when the great shrine, which had drawn so many pilgrims to the city, was brutally demolished. Like Erasmus and Colet, King Henry objected to practices such as the veneration of saintly relics. He issued an injunction against 'wandering to pilgrimages, offering of money, candles or tapers to images or relics, or kissing or licking the same'. Shrines throughout the country were demolished, often in the face of angry protests, but there were no such demonstrations in Canterbury, maybe because the king himself was present. Becket's shrine was dismantled during his visit in September 1538. On 8 September, while he was in the city, the king watched a play written by a former Carmelite friar, John Bale, possibly *On the Treasons of Becket*, of which no copies survive. It is likely that Henry was particularly pleased to get rid of a shrine which honoured a churchman who had stood up to a royal master. He certainly benefited financially from its demolition.

Fragment from Becket's shrine.
Courtesy of the Chapter of Canterbury Cathedral.

According to popular legend twenty-six cartloads of jewels were transported from Canterbury Cathedral to the Tower of London, but this story derives from a questionable source. A more reliable record suggests that the gold and precious stones from the shrine filled two large chests, each of which had to be carried by six or eight strong men. Rumours quickly began to circulate round Catholic Europe that the heretic king had compounded his sacrilege by burning St Thomas' bones and had 'scattered the ashes to the winds'. What actually happened to the bones remains a subject of conjecture, but 'St Thomas of Canterbury' was certainly discredited. This made it impolitic for the city to retain a picture of the martyrdom on its official seal. A payment was made to William Oldfeld, a bellfounder, 'for puttyng out of Thomas Bekket in the comen seale, and gravyng agayn of the same'. The annual pageant in honour of St Thomas was discontinued. Disconsolate citizens were compensated by a new show featuring giants and twice as much gunpowder as before.

The shock of the destruction of the shrine was followed three months later by the closure of the city's three friaries. One of the departing Augustinian friars, John Stone, 'rudely and traitorously' proclaimed that the king could not be head of the Church since 'yt must be a spyrytual father adpoynted by God'. Stone was interrogated by Cromwell and held in the Tower of London before being returned to Canterbury, where local magistrates tried him for treason. The penalty was an automatic death sentence. In December 1539 Friar Stone was hanged and then 'drawn and quartered'. His execution was staged not, as was usual, outside the walls but on the prominent Dane John mound. City accounts record that a horse was hired to drag him there on a hurdle from the West Gate gaol. Payments were made to the carpenter, to the men who set up the gallows, and to the two men who parboiled his organs, which were removed from his body before he was fully dead. Money was also paid to the woman who had the job of scouring the kettle after its gory use and to three men 'that caryed hys quarters to the gate and sett them up', a clear warning to citizens of the dangers of opposing their lord and king.

By this time only one religious house survived in Canterbury, Christ Church Priory. The events of recent years had taken their toll, and the community was demoralised and divided. In 1535 a group of monks had complained to Cromwell about their prior, Thomas Goldwell: 'he is avaricious and pretends to be poor'; 'he is backed up by the subprior and six or seven others, who would affirm the crow was white if he said so'. As news came of the closure of other houses, any faint hope of saving their

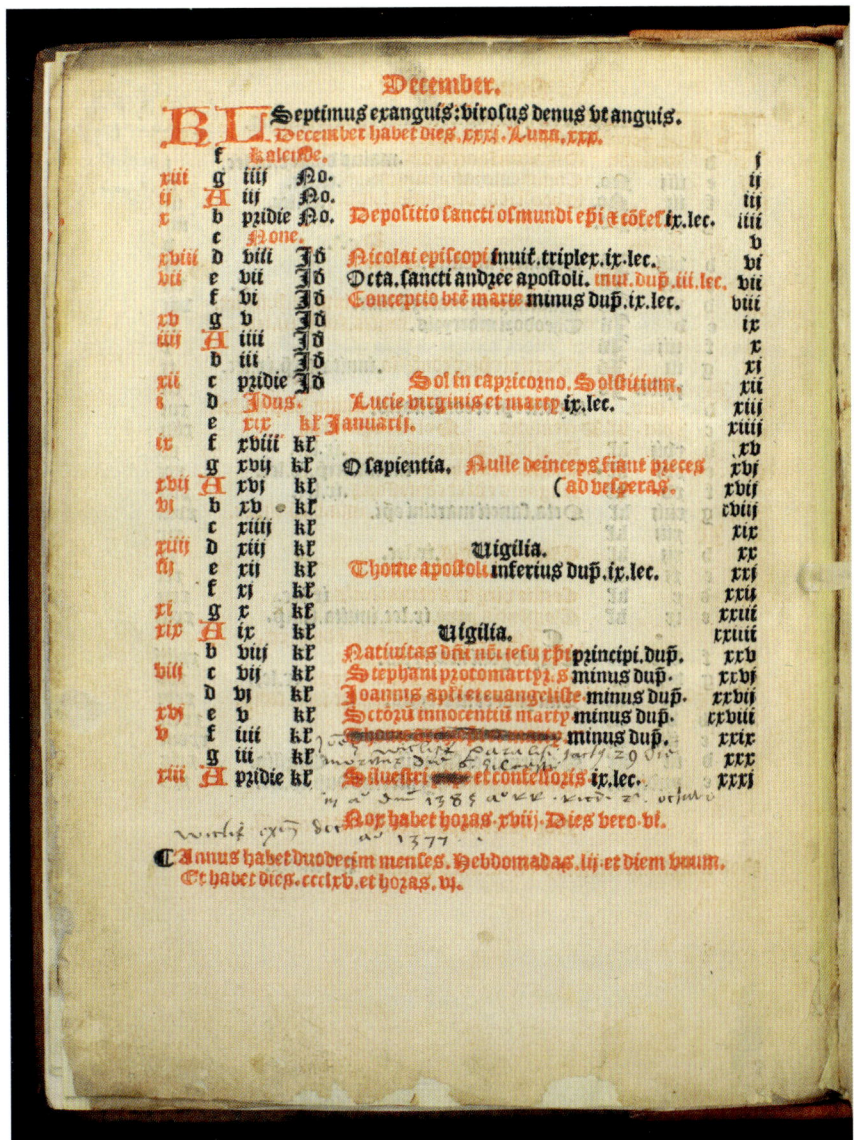

A 'Custumal' from the neighbouring town of Fordwich. Following government orders, the reference to Becket's feast day on 29 December was deleted. *Courtesy of the Chapter of Canterbury Cathedral.*

community by getting rid of an inadequate and unpopular superior faded. In the spring of 1540 the Christ Church community, too, succumbed to the inevitable. The priors of other cathedral monasteries were all appointed deans of their cathedrals, but Thomas Goldwell was not given this option: he was pensioned off at eighty pounds a year. Half of the monks, like their counterparts elsewhere, received annual pensions, ranging from forty shillings to thirty pounds. The remaining twenty-eight stayed on as members of the new cathedral foundation. Living and working together as a community on the same site, offering a regular round of religious services (albeit no longer through the night), they suffered less upheaval than members of other religious houses.

The dissolution changed the lives of other people in Canterbury besides monks, nuns, and friars. Big religious institutions employed lay men and women in a multiplicity of roles: as grooms, porters, bakers, brewers, cooks, barbers, laundresses, cleaners, and errand boys. Abbots, priors, and other senior figures often had their own individual servants. Some of the people who had worked at Christ Church Priory were probably immediately re-employed to serve the cathedral chapter, but others, including those who had worked at St Augustine's, had to seek new ways of providing for their families. Tradesmen who had supplied the religious houses lost major customers, while others suffered from the collapse of the tourist trade, as did city innkeepers. The mayor and aldermen, anxious to secure some benefit for local people, were quick to capitalise on the situation. In December 1538 they begged Cromwell to grant the town 'the watermill and all messuages, lands, and rents within the city which belonged, of late, to the monastery of St Austen's'. They pointed out that much of the money owed to the government each year 'used to be paid by victuallers and innholders, who made their gain out of the pilgrims which heretofore came to the said city, but do not now continue'. Without income from visitors Canterbury would not be able to pay its dues. The corporation clearly hoped to compensate for a reduction in tourism by acquiring money-making monastic possessions. The request for the watermill was granted, and four years later the council made a down payment for many city tenements previously managed by St Augustine's Abbey. But these probably did not compensate for what had been lost. The financial impact of the dissolution on Canterbury was acknowledged by its inclusion in a parliamentary list of 'decayed towns'.

Some people benefited from the changes. Religious houses had occupied around half the land in the city; when they were closed, desirable estates became available for lease or purchase. There were several contenders for buying the Greyfriars site, but it was acquired by one of the officers responsible for disposing of former church property. A few years later it was

The Greyfriars Guest House survived demolition. *Author's photograph.*

converted into private accommodation and was subsequently purchased by relatives of the Elizabethan poet Richard Lovelace. Some aldermen were keen to bring a manufacturer, Thomas Bathurste, to the city to set up a weaving factory. Having failed to obtain Greyfriars, Bathurste established his factory on the old Blackfriars site. It was not only the well-to-do who benefited. The new cathedral foundation was required to institute a grammar school, with scholarships for 'fifty poor boys, both destitute of the help of friends, and endowed with minds apt for learning'. The King's School was thus designed as a 'public' school. The major beneficiary of the dissolution was, of course, the person after whom the school was named. Much monastic land was sold to replenish the king's coffers, but some belonging to St Augustine's Abbey was turned into a royal deer park. The abbot's quarters were transformed into a palace and a new 'Queen's Wing' was built, in which the king's prospective fourth wife, Anne of Cleves,

The surviving Blackfriars buildings. *Author's photograph.*

The royal deer park (on land formerly owned by St Augustine's Abbey) as depicted on Map/49 (probably late sixteenth century). *Courtesy of the Chapter of Canterbury Cathedral.*

could spend her first night in England. No one knew precisely when the new queen would be able to cross the Channel, and so three hundred workmen laboured night and day from 5 October to 21 December 1539. Charcoal was burnt in earthenware braziers to dry the plaster, ensuring that the rooms were fit for use when Anne eventually arrived on 29 December.

While some buildings were refurbished for alternative use, others were simply dismantled or left to fall into ruin. Royal officials were instructed to ensure that monastic buildings could no longer be used for monastic purposes. They were told to confiscate anything of value, such as bells and lead from roofs which could be recast for military use, but vast quantities of stone remained for recycling. Huge slabs which had once formed the walls of the church at St Augustine's were transported across the Channel to help fortify the English-owned town of Calais against the French. Some nine cartloads were used to repair one of Canterbury's city gates, the Burgate. In due course some of the remaining stone from the site was sold to residents of Canterbury and the surrounding villages. A cartload of good Caen ashlar (cut stone) cost four shillings (two shillings if the stones were broken). The price of a cart of flint ranged from four to twelve pence. Stephen Thornhurst, a local property developer, paid £15 8s. 10d. for over

Pots recovered during the 'Big Dig' at the Augustinian Friary 1999–2004.
©*Canterbury Archaeological Trust.*

228 cartloads of different kinds of stone. Other buyers included one of the archbishop's relatives, three mayors, two vicars, a baker, a grocer, and a printer. One enterprising innkeeper transformed a Romanesque stone capital into a sign for the Fleur de Lys inn.

Stone was not the only commodity to be recycled; some fifteen years after St Augustine's had closed, vestments and church furnishings from the abbey church were put up for sale. Not everyone, however, paid for what they got. In 1535 a visiting commissioner had reported that during a fire at Christ Church, 'such bedding as was cast into the cloister was embezzled by poor folks'. When the religious houses were finally dissolved, people no doubt took advantage of the havoc to pick up whatever they could: loose pieces of lead, iron, glass, windows, doors, bedding, and crockery which demolition agents had thrown casually aside. Nearly five hundred years later, an archaeological dig on the site of the Augustinian friary uncovered pieces of over a hundred pots which had apparently been dumped in a cesspit when the friary was pulled down.

Over the years that followed the dissolution, the inhabitants of Canterbury saw their city change before their eyes. They watched as major landmarks such as the churches of St Augustine's and St Gregory's were pulled down, leaving just the cathedral's Bell Harry Tower to dominate the skyline. They witnessed the building of grand new houses on old religious sites and the planting of gardens and orchards around them. At the same time, however, they could still see the remains of much that had once been familiar. New owners did not demolish everything at once, and some old buildings remained standing for decades to come. The Blackfriars church was probably not pulled down until the early Stuart period. Throughout the city, stone from dismantled buildings could be seen lying around long after the monasteries had closed down. As late as 1621, 180 cartloads from St Augustine's were used to mend the House of Correction in Stour Street, previously a hospital for poor priests. Not until the bombing raid of 1942, four hundred years later, would the people of Canterbury witness such a marked change to their landscape – or see so much rubble.

3

From Catholic
to Protestant

1540

Water Lyedes, one of the churchwardens of St Dunstan's, stares at the Bible which lies open on the lectern before him. It is very large and very thick. The writing is in English and there are little woodcut pictures. He has never seen anything like it before.

Woodcut of Adam and Eve from the 'Great Bible' which was placed in every church. *Courtesy of the Chapter of Canterbury Cathedral.*

In 1538, the year that Becket's shrine was destroyed and four religious houses closed, the inhabitants of Canterbury witnessed the first of many changes within their parish churches. Like Erasmus, the king believed that people should be able to read the scriptures in their own language. He ordered that a complete Bible in English be placed in every parish church so that parishioners might 'resort to the same and read it'. At the same time churchwardens were told that they must remove any images which were treated as objects of veneration. How far royal orders were implemented varied from place to place, but the archbishop of Canterbury, Thomas Cranmer, appointed loyal reformers to key posts in his diocese. The wardens of St George's church were loath to part with the popular image of their patron saint, behind which generations of citizens had processed every St George's Day, but the archbishop's representative insisted that St George should not only be removed but 'cut in pieces', 'disfigured', 'nothing to remain'. For some parishioners who had often prayed before statues of their favourite saints, their removal was a serious deprivation. So too was the disappearance of parish fraternities, which had provided much communal recreation. Their primary purpose, however, was to keep candles alight before images of the saints after which they were named. References in parish records to the three St Dunstan's guilds ceased after 1539.

Changes such as these were imposed from above, but there was some support for them at grassroots level. As a market town situated on key trading routes, Canterbury was well placed to pick up new ideas from the continent. In the 1520s the abbot of St Augustine's had sponsored a discussion group for people sympathetic to the thinking of Erasmus. One member of this group, John Twyne, a schoolmaster and scholar, translated some of the writings of a German reformer, Melanchthon. It was unusual for a provincial town to have a permanent printing press, but Twyne's neighbour, John Mychell, established one in Canterbury. This gave local people access to a range of printed materials, including works which promoted the new modes of thought. By the middle of the 1530s there was an embryonic group of 'Protestants' in the city. One of the most ardent was John Toftes, a city councillor and lawyer. Toftes hated images and in 1542 was accused of removing 'a picture of Our Lady' from his parish church to his own home, where he 'did hew her all in pieces'. His wife and daughter-in-law were equally dismissive of the 'abominable idolatry' of old devotional practices. The latter claimed that 'her daughter could piss as good holy water as the priest could make any'.

The varied responses to religious reform led to disputes in a number of city churches. The Toftes family worshipped at St Mary Northgate, whose parish priest, William Kempe, was deeply wedded to the old ways. He refused to read out royal injunctions in church, as he was required to do, and he ignored new orders. Although he was at odds with the Toftes and their circle, he had the support of other parishioners. According to a dossier compiled by the archbishop, they thought that 'the doctrine that was taught twenty or thirty years ago was as good as the doctrine that is set forth these days'. There was conflict, too, at the neighbouring church of St Alphege. The congregation criticised their reforming rector, Humphrey Cherdayn, for speaking against the old beliefs. In the early 1540s a group of Kentish county gentry conspired to stop religious innovation. Their abortive attempt became known as the 'Prebendaries' Plot' because cathedral clergy (prebendaries) were involved and much of the planning took place in their homes. But the cathedral functionaries were not of one mind. Following the dissolution of the priory, the new foundation had been required to appoint six clerics who became known as 'Six Preachers' to deliver sermons both in the cathedral and in east Kent parishes. The king insisted that three of these should be 'of the new learning and three of the old'. In his dossier the archbishop noted that one of the six, Robert Serles, 'preacheth no sermon but one part of it is an invective against the other preachers of Christ Church'.

The discordant messages preached from the cathedral pulpit reflected the confusion of the day. There was no longer any consensus over what was deemed orthodox. John Bland, a visiting preacher at St Mary Northgate, maintained that the traditional liturgy contained 'both heresy and treason'. By contrast, William Gardiner, a cathedral prebendary, accused reformers of turning 'good wine into water'. Gardiner complained that 'the spirit of newfangles hath brought in the spirit of error'. By the 1540s the government was inclined to agree, and it sought to impose brakes on the pace of change. New measures from Westminster contradicted those issued only a year or so before. This was partly a result of the king's ever-volatile thinking, partly due to the ascendancy of different advisers, and partly fear that they had released forces they could not control. When Henry made the Bible available in English, he had not anticipated that lay enthusiasts would interpret the scriptures in new, even bizarre, ways. He complained that 'the most precious jewel, the word of God, is disputed, rhymed, sung, and jangled in every ale-house and tavern'. To counter this, restrictions were imposed on who might read the Bible – in private or in public. The king was at heart an Erasmian Catholic: he wanted some reform but was anxious to preserve many traditional beliefs and practices. The continuation of old rites aggravated those who wanted more radical change, such as a Canterbury barber, Thomas Makeblyth. In 1543 Makeblyth refused to join in the Palm Sunday procession and instead ostentatiously 'read the Bible in procession time'. On Easter Day he 'went into a corner at the Resurrection time and went not a procession as others did'. Like Makeblyth John Toftes wanted the old processions and liturgies to be replaced by simple Bible reading. He 'openly and with loud voice read the Bible in English in the church to his wife, Starkey's wife, George Toftes's wife, to the midwife of the same parish, and to as many other as then were present'.

The changes for which Bland, Makeblyth, and Toftes yearned came about when Henry VIII was succeeded by his young son, Edward VI. The boy king was a convinced Protestant, and during his six-year reign religious reform went much further than his father had ever countenanced. Church services which had hitherto been in Latin were now to be conducted in English. Parishes were instructed to get rid of any remaining objects of Catholic devotion and to expunge images of saints from murals and stained-glass windows. These orders caused local churches considerable

Frontispiece of the 1552 book of Common Prayer, featuring the young Edward VI. *Courtesy of the Chapter of Canterbury Cathedral.*

From Catholic to Protestant

expense. In 1549/50 the churchwardens of St Andrew's paid five shillings for a copy of Cranmer's new English service book. Three years later the archbishop produced a revised, much more explicitly Protestant version, which cost them six shillings. The wardens gave a poor man two pence 'for carryng owt of ye ymagys out of the chyrche' and paid three shillings to have the church walls limewashed so that the old pictures were obscured. New glass to replace the stained glass which had been removed cost £3 17s. 4d. As a result of these changes churches were less colourful than they had been before, with little to engage the eye. Processions were banned, and services relied just on the spoken word, rather than communicating through all the senses. Organisations which had existed to provide prayers for the dead were outlawed, depriving people of the consolation that they could aid their loved ones after death.

The divisions caused by religious reform should not be overemphasised. However they may have felt about the changes, people acquiesced in them. There was little else they could do in an age in which it was widely accepted that governments had the right to dictate what citizens did and believed. Some modes of thought which had been part of their mental landscape all their lives persisted but, as old practices were banned and new ones introduced, traditional faith may well have merged with some of the newer ideas. Many people probably adhered to a mixture of beliefs from different sources. Even those who held starkly opposed religious views co-operated with each other in day-to-day life. A population of a few thousand was too small for people to avoid those with whom they disagreed, and people who had worked side by side before the religious turmoil of the 1530s and 1540s continued to do so. The names of men of contrasting religious persuasions even appear together as witnesses on wills. There was certainly contention on the city council but, as members were appointed for life, religious reformers had to work alongside colleagues who upheld a more traditional faith. Each year one of the aldermen (senior councillors) was elected mayor. The office of 'first citizen' was held by traditionalists as well as by reformers even during Edward's reign.

As a body, the council had upheld royal authority throughout the previous two decades, and it continued to do so when Edward was succeeded in 1553 by his Catholic half-sister, Mary. A few months after her accession there was a popular uprising in west Kent, led by a county gentleman, Sir Thomas Wyatt. The newly elected mayor of Canterbury was John Twyne, one of the city's early Protestants, but he and his colleagues refused to have anything to do with Wyatt's insurrection. They repaired the city walls to withstand an attack, and a band of citizens led by Twyne marched to Dover to oppose the rebels. Afterwards Canterbury received letters of thanks from the queen for the 'trouthe and fydelitie borne unto her Grace in the tyme of the rebellyon'. It may be that by this time Twyne was reacting against the vigorous version of Protestantism promoted under Edward VI, but it is also possible that his support for the queen was determined by factors other than religion. Mary was the legitimate heir to the throne, and even convinced reformers hesitated to plunge the country into civil strife. This was the position adopted by Sir James Hales, an eminent Protestant lawyer. When Edward died, Sir James resolutely refused to support attempts to stop Mary inheriting the crown. A disputed succession might all too easily revive the horrors of the Wars of the Roses.

Mary's priorities were to restore allegiance to the Pope and to reintroduce Catholic worship. The return to traditional ways was clearly welcomed by some people in Canterbury: Catholic Mass was celebrated at the cathedral within weeks of Mary's accession, well before orders were issued for its restoration. The vast majority of citizens acquiesced in these changes as they had in those that preceded them, but Sir James Hales suffered for his convictions. The holder of a national office, he was committed to prison in London, where he was urged to recant his Protestant faith. The strain was so great that Hales tried to commit suicide with a penknife. The queen ordered his release but his mental disturbance continued, and on 4 August 1554 he succeeded in drowning himself in the River Stour, near his home on the outskirts of Canterbury.

Protestants who refused to renounce their convictions and attend Mass were liable to be brought before the courts and, if they still failed to conform, could face death by burning. The likelihood of prosecution varied according to locality. Kent, with its proximity to the capital and the continent, had always been an area which governments needed to control. People who lived in less sensitive regions could get away with religious irregularity more easily than those who worshipped in the archbishop's own diocese. More burnings took place in Canterbury during Mary's reign than anywhere else in England except London. Young – and not so young – men and women from neighbouring towns, villages, and the Kentish Weald, who might have survived had they lived elsewhere, were brought to Canterbury Castle to await their fate. The conditions were so bad that five of them died in gaol, escaping the pain of the flames.

There is no evidence that any of the forty-one people who were burnt to death in Canterbury were actually residents of the city. James Hales' daughter-in-law Joyce fled to the continent, as did three of the Six

Preachers, but most people of Protestant sympathies could not afford to do this and presumably conformed, at least outwardly, to Catholic worship. Some may have decided to lie low, trusting that neither neighbours nor officials would inform against them. But two clergymen who had strong Canterbury associations were put to death under Mary. One of these was Archbishop Cranmer, who was burnt at Oxford. John Bland, the radical vicar of nearby Adisham, was one of the people who suffered in Canterbury itself. Bland had preached regularly in the city and was also tried there. So many spectators crammed into the Chapter House on 21 May 1554 to witness his initial examination that there was standing room only. After a protracted trial and a nineteen-week imprisonment in the West Gate gaol, Bland was put to death on 12 July 1555. Three others suffered with him. This was the first of the Canterbury burnings, but more followed later that

year, as well as in January 1556 and on two occasions in 1557. The last victims were burnt at the stake just a week before Mary died, in November 1558. As the acrid smell of roasting flesh rose above the city, the people of Canterbury could not but be aware of the cost of religious nonconformity.

The accession of Mary's sister, Elizabeth, was followed by yet another change of religion, a reversion to Protestantism, albeit a less extreme form than that favoured by her half-brother Edward. In May 1559 loyal Catholics expressed their disapproval by processing through the city – along the route traditionally used for the St Thomas pageant. This prompted a

The Chapter House of Canterbury Cathedral where John Bland was tried. *Michael D. Beckwith, Wikimedia Commons.*

counter-procession past the homes of people known to be sympathetic to Catholicism, a mocking depiction of 'the Pope's taking farewell of his friends at Canterbury'. On Midsummer Eve 1561 a group of citizens followed the traditional practice of lighting bonfires to mark the vigil of the feast of St John. This incensed John Bale, the fiercely Protestant ex-friar whose play had been performed before Henry VIII. He feared that the lighting of bonfires on such a significant date was undertaken 'in contempte of the Christen relygon, and for upholdynge the olde frantyck supersticyons of papistrye'. Bale was now a member of the cathedral chapter, but his protest had little effect. A week later even more bonfires were lit to mark St Peter's Tide. In a deliberate act of provocation, Richard Borowes ('Railing Dick') supervised the building of a huge fire at the Bullstake (now the Buttermarket), just outside the main entrance to the cathedral. Armed with a drum, he led a procession of a hundred boys who sang 'most fylthie songes of baudrye' and mocked Protestants. To Bale's disgust, civic officials failed to heed the sermons which had been preached in the cathedral against bonfires. The sheriff even helped stoke the fire, prompting Bale to pray 'God sende that cytie better, and more godly governours'.

The Burghmote, which comprised twenty-four common councillors and twelve aldermen, was already changing. This was partly due to natural causes. At least seven – and probably eleven – of the men who were members in 1557 died in the course of the next two years, some perhaps as a result of a nationwide flu epidemic. In 1561 the Privy Council deemed half the city's aldermen as 'unworthy to govern or bere publyke office' and ordered their dismissal. By 1562 only fifteen of the men who had served on the Burghmote in 1557 were still in post.

One of the aldermen who lost his seat was John Twyne. A council member for over twenty years, Twyne had also held the offices of sheriff, mayor, and MP. In 1541 he had become the first headmaster of the King's School, but now he was regarded with suspicion. When Archbishop Matthew Parker conducted an official visitation in 1560, Twyne was told he should 'utterly abstain from ryot and drunkenness'. It is impossible to know whether the headmaster really did have a drink problem or whether the charge of drunkenness was simply a way of discrediting a man who was suspected of Catholic loyalties. Twyne's history serves as a reminder that, then as now, people's thinking changed through their lives: an Erasmian Catholic in the 1520s, he had become a central figure in the city's Protestant network in the 1530s and 1540s before upholding the rights of Queen Mary in the 1550s. After her death he was eased out of his post at the school in favour of a man more clearly committed to the reformed faith.

There were changes amongst the clergy too. Several city livings were vacant when Elizabeth came to the throne, and this provided scope for the appointment of men who accepted the new religious settlement. Some reformist ministers who had lost their positions under Mary were reinstated: Humphrey Cherdayn as rector of St Alphege and his colleague, Thomas Panton, to St Dunstan's. Other parish clergy, such as Ralph Prescott, who had been appointed rector of St Mildred's in 1555, felt unable to conform to the new requirements and had to give up their livings. Archdeacon Nicholas Harpsfield, who had worked hard to restore Catholicism under Mary, was one of five members of the cathedral chapter who refused to acknowledge Elizabeth as 'Supreme Governor' of the church. Others, including a former Christ Church monk, John Mylles, may well have remained sympathetic to the old ways but agreed to take the required oaths and retained their posts.

The change of religion under Elizabeth, like those that preceded it, was reflected in the fittings of parish churches. Churchwardens who had paid to reinstate statues and other objects of Catholic devotion during Mary's reign now faced the expense of their removal. The rood loft in St Andrew's, which separated the nave and the chancel, had been restored in the mid-1550s, but on Elizabeth's accession it had to be taken down. The wardens clearly attempted to minimise their financial losses: they sold some of the wood for six shillings and eight pence and, years later, reused some pieces to repair pews. But they incurred many other expenses. Goodman Johnson received tuppence 'for puttyng owt ye payntyng on ye walls' and an unnamed workman thirteen shillings and four pence for inscribing the Ten Commandments in their place. The removal of the high altar cost twelve pence and the purchase of a communion table, which had no associations with the Catholic Mass, four shillings and seven pence. In addition the wardens had once again to buy new service books.

It is hardly surprising that amidst all this upheaval, some people continued to yearn for the past. Images were discovered under the floorboards at St Alphege, presumably put there by parishioners who hoped that Catholicism might one day be restored. In 1561 'Mother Wells' of Northgate was charged for speaking derisively about the new faith and saying that she hoped they would soon have Mass back again. But, unlike her brother and sister, Elizabeth ruled for decades: her longevity ensured that England gradually became a Protestant country and Canterbury a Protestant city. As the years passed, the streets were increasingly filled

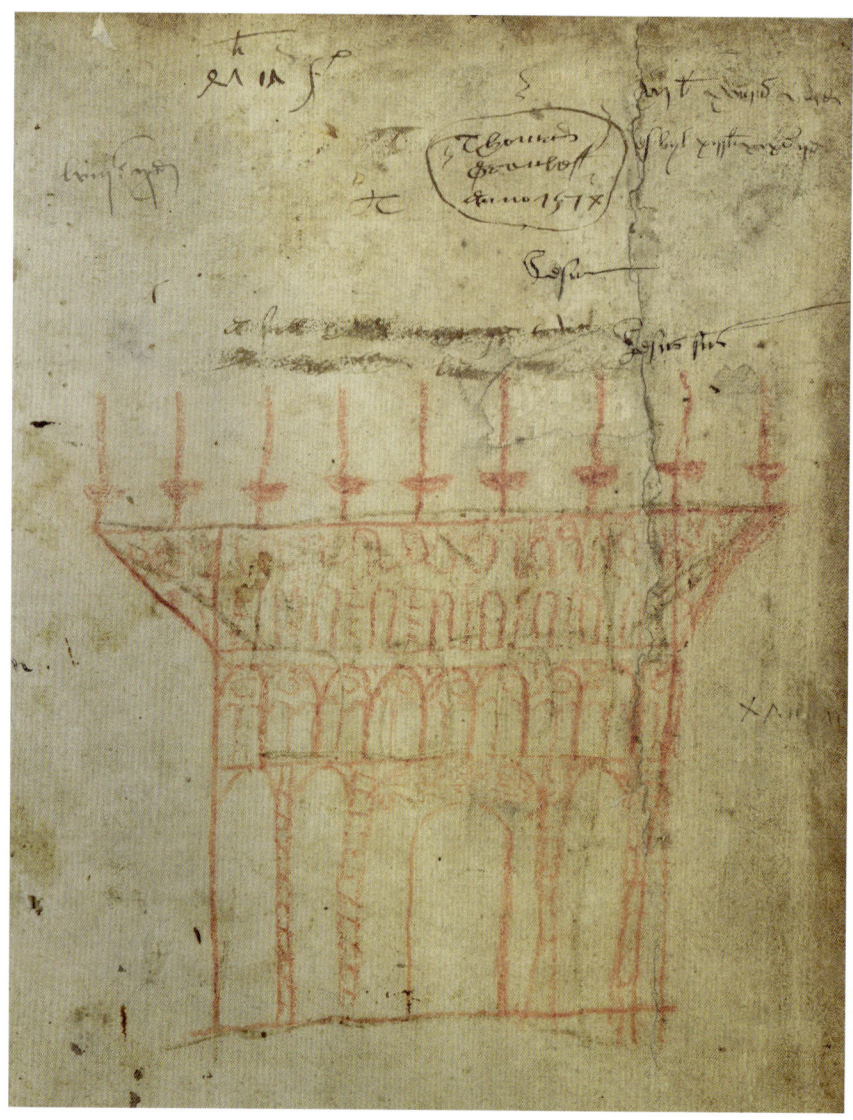

Sketch of Rood Loft, which was taken down when Elizabeth came to the throne, from the inside back cover of St Andrew's churchwardens' accounts. *Courtesy of the Chapter of Canterbury Cathedral.*

with young people who had no recollection of the Catholic rites of the past. Over time even older generations got used to the new ways.

Familiarity with Protestant practices grew alongside a radically changed perception of Catholicism. As early as 1560 John Bale arranged for boys from the King's School to perform an anti-Catholic play which he had written: this may have been an *Enterlude concernying Thre Lawes*, which featured the characters of 'Hipocrisy', a friar, and 'Sodomy', a monk. Anti-Catholic feeling was given a powerful boost by a man with whom Bale had shared lodgings during his 1550s exile. John Foxe was a brilliant propagandist, and his popular 'Book of Martyrs' provided a vivid depiction in words and pictures of Protestants who suffered for their faith under Mary. A woodcut entitled 'The Burning of Foure Martyrs' featured the first victims of the Canterbury burnings, one of whom was John Bland. According to the Privy Council, the book was 'very profitable for bringing her majesties subjects into good opynion', and churchwardens throughout the land were encouraged to purchase copies. Foxe's images informed popular sentiment, which came to regard Catholicism as a false, cruel, and essentially un-English faith.

The burning of John Bland and three other martyrs in Canterbury, from John Foxe, *Actes and Monumentes. Courtesy of the Chapter of Canterbury Cathedral.*

In 1570 the conviction that Catholics were not – and never could be – loyal citizens was reinforced by a rebellion in the north by men of Catholic sympathies. Shortly afterwards, the Pope proclaimed that 'the pretended queen of England' was a heretic, and he absolved her Catholic subjects from oaths of allegiance they had sworn to her. As suspicion mounted, Parliament ruled that any priest ordained abroad who dared to set foot in England would be deemed guilty of high treason. In 1588, the year in which Spain dispatched a fleet to invade England, three Catholic priests were hanged in Canterbury.

The threat of the Spanish Armada reinforced England's growing Protestant identity. Two hundred men from Canterbury were among those recruited into citizen armies to save the country from foreign, Catholic

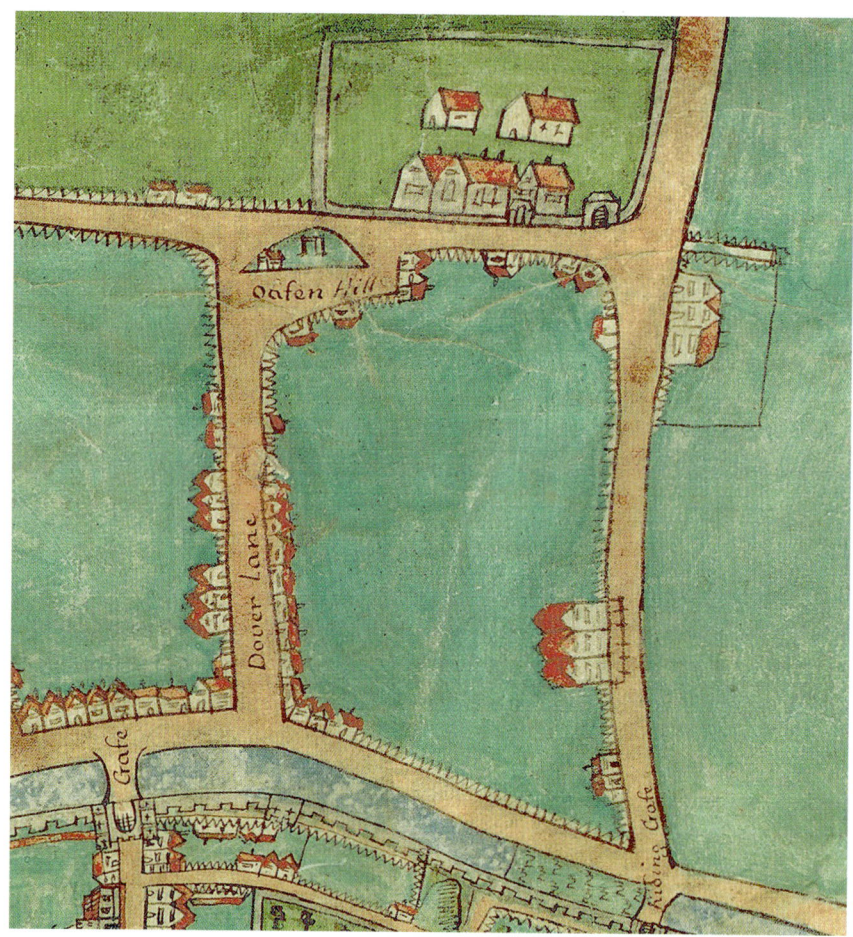

Oaten Hill gallows, on which the Catholic priests were probably hanged, as depicted on Map/123 *c.* 1642. *Courtesy of the Chapter of Canterbury Cathedral.*

rule. Arrayed in yellow coats, they marched south-east to help defend the vulnerable Kent coast. The Canterbury unit was accompanied by a drummer who belonged to a community of 'Strangers', men and women who had fled to England to escape Catholic persecution on the continent. Their presence demonstrated how much times had changed. Half a century before, Canterbury had housed one of the most famous shrines in Catholic Europe; now it was a haven for Protestant refugees.

4

CITIZENS, STRANGERS, AND COMMUNITY LIFE

Late 1575

A Walloon woman stands outside her house in Turnagain Lane watching her children play. She smiles at her neighbour, recalling the hardships they have been through together. Now she feels safe and secure. It is a big relief.

'Strangers' occupied some of these Turnagain Lane houses. The bottom storeys date from *c.* 1475. The top-storey weaving loft with great windows either side was added later. *Author's photograph.*

In June 1575 a large party of 'Strangers' arrived in Canterbury at the invitation of the city council. They were not the first continental Protestants to seek refuge in the city, since there appears to have been a short-lived French congregation during the reign of Edward VI. Some eighteen French families had relocated from Winchelsea (near the south Kent coast) in 1574. The people who joined them the following year were Walloons, who spoke a French patois, and Flemings from French Flanders. These new arrivals had fled vicious persecution in their native Low Countries, which were under Spanish control, and had lived for several years in Sandwich, the port at which they had landed. But the government was loath to allow too many aliens to congregate in one place and sought to disperse them to other towns. The Canterbury Burghmote agreed to take a hundred households and on 15 March 1575 signed an agreement granting the newcomers 'full and free exercise of their religion'. It also promised them 'sure dwelling without being constrained to departe'. For the first time for years the refugees could hope that their children would grow up undisturbed in a place they could call home.

The mayor and aldermen welcomed the Strangers in the hope that they might benefit the city, which had still not fully recovered from the loss of its religious houses and shrine. Poorer parishes had empty properties in which they could be accommodated, hence the offer of a hundred houses, but the corporation was anxious to ensure that the immigrants contributed to the economy. The Burghmote informed the Privy Council that it did not want people 'of the meanest sort, but ... such as be makers of bayes, grograines etc'. These fabrics, which became known as 'new draperies', were much lighter and softer than English broadcloth. The city dignitaries anticipated that the skilled Walloon and Flemish weavers would provide training and jobs for unemployed English people, but they did not want them to threaten the livelihoods of native citizens. The 1575 agreement specified very precisely the boundaries within which the Strangers could operate. They were allowed to make cloth 'after the fflanders ffashion' but not 'cloth or kersies such as the English doe make'. The Strangers were permitted to sell their goods wholesale but not directly to consumers, since this would bring them into competition with city traders. They were also barred from becoming freemen of the city.

The Strangers operated as a separate unit within the wider community. Unlike everyone else who lived in Canterbury, they were not expected to attend parish churches but were permitted to hold services in French according to their own rites. Initially they were allowed to use St Alphege's

Cartouche from the French church chapel in the cathedral crypt probably dating from the sixteenth century. The quotation from Ecclesiastes is in old French, the patois spoken by some of the refugees. *By permission of the Consistoire of the Église Protestante Wallonne et Huguenote de Canterbury.*

church (at times that did not clash with parish worship), but within a year, as their numbers increased, they moved into the crypt of the cathedral, at that time a coal and wood store. The French church has held a service in the crypt every week since then – for more than four hundred years. The Strangers were also required to provide for the education of their own children and the care of their own poor. Each month twelve deacons called on every member of the congregation to collect contributions to a poor fund, which was distributed to those who were out of work, sick, or in need of nursing; on one occasion a special collection was made for a member 'afflicted with the stone' to have an operation. Others received help in the form of clothing – shirts, chemises, drawers, corsets, petticoats, stockings, shoes. Aid was also given to members of French-speaking churches who passed through the city, one night's supper and lodging, and sometimes a gift to help them on their way: two shillings and sixpence was given 'to Jasper, son of the widow Pouchin, having a hand disabled, both going into Holland', and three shillings and sixpence to 'Pierre du Champgaillard, formerly a Capuchin monk, who has made profession of the Reformed Religion and resolved to live and die therein'. Poor though many members were, the French church provided generously for fellow Strangers in need. Their position as a separate and distinctive community was reinforced by an arrangement unique to Canterbury and Norwich. In both towns the congregation elected twelve 'Politic Men', whose role was to maintain order, prove wills, settle legal matters, and to liaise on behalf of members with the city authorities. The Politic Men were sworn into office by the mayor.

The existence of a community within a community, speaking a different language and operating outside the normal parish system, inevitably gave rise to some tension. Within a few months, the Privy Council had to warn the corporation to 'use such straingers as do inhabite in the saide towne charitablie and favourablie and to punishe all suche as go about to misuse them'. The 1575 agreement specified that Strangers should not be taxed more than the English, but five years later the community petitioned the Privy Council against 'impositions which they saie the Maiour and his brethren laie uppon them and they are not hable to bear', notably a charge of £14 19s. 8d. towards the rebuilding of the West Gate, for which there is no record of English contributions. The city authorities were instructed 'to use some good moderation towardes them … so as they maie have no cause to thincke themselves overburthened'.

Walloons and Flemings were not the only new arrivals in Canterbury. The late sixteenth century saw widespread migration from rural to urban areas, as smallholders who could no longer make a living from the land sought their fortunes in towns. Some people used urban contacts to obtain apprenticeships for their sons. One of the men attracted to the city was John Marlowe, who was born a few miles away in Ospringe, near Faversham. He moved to Canterbury around 1556, became a freeman some eight years later (about the time his more famous son, Christopher, was born), and opened his own shoemaker's shop. Like Marlowe, many newcomers came from the surrounding region – Thanet, the Downs, the Weald, mid-Kent – but some were from further afield. Court records reveal the existence of Welsh speakers in the city. A Shropshire man, William Watmer, arrived around 1590, joining his sister and his wool merchant brother-in-law, Robert Wynne. In due course both Wynne and Watmer served as mayor. Over two thirds of the men appointed to the Burghmote in Elizabeth's reign had been born outside Canterbury.

The city which became home to these immigrants had much in common with other towns throughout England and northern Europe. It was

An archaeologist's impression of Tudor Canterbury. ©*Canterbury Archaeological Trust.*

predominantly made up of timber-framed buildings, some large and stately, others small, dark, and ramshackle. In the narrower lanes, overhanging upper storeys, so characteristic of the age, nearly touched those of buildings opposite, shrouding the thoroughfares below. Sanitation was a problem in all early modern communities. Where space was at a premium, cesspits were often situated perilously close to wells and sometimes overflowed: John Marlowe's friend and neighbour, Lawrence Applegate, allowed the contents of his privy to pour into Iron Bar Lane. The main streets had gravel surfaces, but on wet days other roads easily became quagmires of mud, churned up by horses which inevitably deposited piles of manure. The council did what it could to keep the city clean, paying night workmen to collect detritus and arranging for huge quantities of rubbish to be removed through the Riding Gate. By modern standards the Elizabethan city might seem smelly and insanitary, but its residents enjoyed easy access to open land and fresh air. Some parishes merged into the surrounding countryside, and there were cultivated plots and pasture land in the very heart of the town, with animals grazing on the site of the future Dane John Gardens.

The earliest known map of Canterbury, published around 1588 in an atlas compiled by Georg Braun and Frans Hogenberg. *Courtesy of the Chapter of Canterbury Cathedral.*

The earliest known maps of Canterbury, which date from this period, reveal many green spaces within the city walls.

Many poorer inhabitants lived outside the walls, congregated in large residential suburbs in parishes such as St Dunstan's, St Mildred's, St Paul's, and St Mary Northgate. Houses were often partitioned to meet the need for cheap accommodation, and attics were floored to create more sleeping room. Widows, the poorest of the poor, often rented cheap property in back lanes. They struggled to make ends meet by taking in lodgers or parish orphans, by spinning and helping with the harvest, and maybe by prostitution. Visitors who had been turned away at the city gates also took refuge in these outer suburbs, often men who tramped from place to place seeking work or poor relief of a type more likely to be found in towns than the countryside. Those deemed to be vagrants ran the risk of being whipped, branded, or deported, and the council tried hard to limit their

Citizens, Strangers, and Community Life

numbers. Providing lodging or letting tenements to people who could not sustain themselves was prohibited. Overseers of the poor in each parish were required to produce monthly lists of new arrivals and of anyone, migrant or resident, who was not working. Able-bodied loiterers were taken to a 'House of Correction', where they were set to work.

The city elite disciplined the wilfully unemployed, but they also took pains to provide for local people in genuine need. Some medieval almshouses, such as St John's in Northgate, St Nicholas at Harbledown, and Maynard's near the castle, had survived the upheavals of the 1530s, but more provision for the old and infirm was needed. An eminent lawyer, Sir Roger Manwood, spent £500 on a new almshouse opposite St Stephen's church, while a fellow lawyer, Sir John Boys, founded the more substantial Jesus Hospital on the other side of the city. Leonard Cotton, a wealthy pewterer and former mayor, left money in his will for an extension to the old Maynard's Hospital, which became known as the Maynard and Cotton Spital. Other well-to-do citizens were similarly concerned to aid the less fortunate. Among the bequests made by Alderman Richard Furner was £100 to be shared equally between a hundred 'poore maydens ... which shall happen to be married after my decease', the same sum for a hundred 'poore widowes', and £50 for a hundred orphans 'borne within the cytty'. Thomas Stransham, who had served three times as mayor of Faversham,

Plaque on the Maynard and Cotton Hospital. *Author's photograph.*

LEONARD COTTON ESQUIR SOME TIME MAIRE OF THIS CITYE DID PLACE IN THIS HOSPITAL 1 BROTHER G 11 SISTERS W YEARLY STIPEND FOREVER ACCORDING TO HIS LAST WIL G ESTAMENT MADE IN Y YEARE 1605 WHOSE CHARITY IS HERE REMEBRED BY JOSEPH COLF M. OF THIS SPITAL

moved to Canterbury in later life; he ordered that income from his substantial city properties should be used to help the poor of St Dunstan's. The Streynsham Trust still provides small grants to residents of the parish.

Endowments were insufficient to meet the needs of all the poor. With the disappearance of friaries and monastic almonries, which had traditionally helped provide for the needy, the council played an increasingly prominent part in relieving the poor and destitute. It levied parish rates and sometimes, in hard times, imposed other taxes: in 1563 householders who kept dogs were charged tuppence a week as a means of aiding the poor. The fines from people convicted of wrongdoing and the fees paid by new councillors and aldermen were sometimes devoted to poor relief. Compulsory beneficence was an accepted part of holding office. From time to time mayors instructed members of the council to provide wheat for the market at subsidised prices or told them to donate money for the relief of the sick and the poor: in July 1564 each alderman was asked to give three shillings and each member of the common council one shilling and sixpence.

The years 1563 to 1565 were particularly difficult since Canterbury was hit by plague, a recurrent problem in sixteenth-century England. Strenuous attempts were made to prevent infection entering the city by banning merchants who arrived from plague-infested places. In 1563 a Canterbury grocer, Simon Brome, was fined for bringing wares from London. Early seventeenth-century accounts record payment for a watch on the gates 'to kepe them of Sandwich out, by reason of the infection of the plague there'. Other regulations sought to stem transmission within the city. In 1564 people from infected houses were forbidden to use their normal communal washing places. They could only do their washing after ten o'clock at night in an area below Abbot's Mill, normally used by butchers to wash cattle entrails. For forty days after a house had been infected, inhabitants had to carry a white rod half a yard long. In the 1580s further precautions were taken when four cottages, in which people could be quarantined rent-free, were built outside St Mildred's churchyard. Plague was no respecter of persons. In April 1594 Simon Brome, by now an alderman, lost three of his children. Fifteen years later, in September 1609, ex-mayor Robert Wynne and his wife died within days of each other. A watch was set on their house to ensure that no one entered it between 26 September and 7 November, and two maids, a joiner's wife, and another woman who had nursed the patients were confined inside. But notwithstanding all these attempts to limit infection, death rates escalated when epidemics struck. In the six months from September 1563 there were five or six times more burials

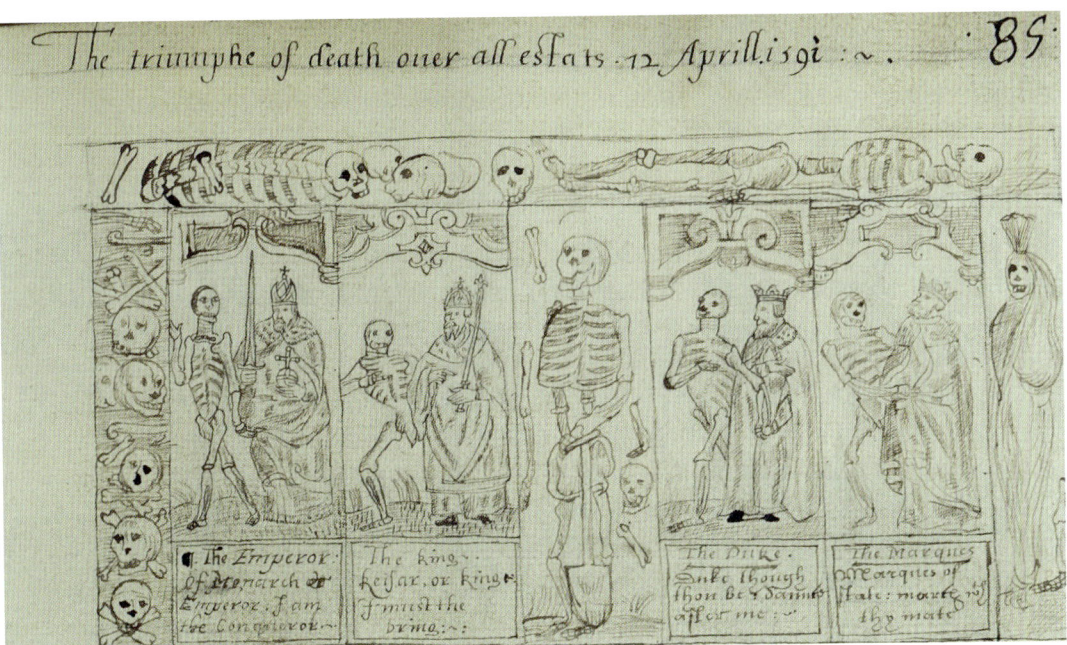

'The Triumph of Death over all Estates' by William Burch (1591), a graphic reminder that status was no protection against plague. *Courtesy of the Chapter of Canterbury Cathedral.*

than normal in St Dunstan's. The Walloon registers for 1595 record 229 burials in six months as against 34 the previous year.

Plague was not the only natural disaster to afflict the residents of Elizabethan Canterbury. In May 1576 the city was hit by storms and floods; eighteen months later the highways were blocked by heavy snowdrifts, and there were even earthquakes in April and May 1580. The most devastating affliction, however, was harvest failure. There was a series of bad harvests in the mid-1590s, and by the winter of 1595–96 grain was in very short supply. There were rumours, however, that some was still being exported. On 2 February 1596 poor men obstructed grain wagons passing through St Dunstan's on their way to the coast, and a Justice of the Peace ordered the drivers to turn back. But food remained scarce, and the mayor lamented that the poor were likely to starve.

Life may have been precarious, but people enjoyed themselves while it lasted. Elizabethan Canterbury provided a good range of recreations. The number of licensed alehouses in the city rose with the population, from twenty-two in 1577 to forty-two by 1596. There was also an unquantified number of unlicensed 'tippling houses', run by poor householders who sought to supplement their incomes by illicitly selling food and drink. Alehouses were hubs of local life, providing opportunity not only for communal drinking but also for cockfighting, gaming, and dancing. Men played dice, shove-groat, and football, and shot at butts with longbows. Local residents gathered round the bullstake to watch bulls being baited. Occasionally they may even have seen a dancing bear, whose owner was fined for taking the beast onto the city wall. Street parades offered another form of popular entertainment. People who violated communal norms were subjected to 'rough music': wearing placards inscribed with their various crimes – such as sexual misdemeanour, seditious speech, or witchcraft – they were carried round the town on horse-drawn carts, past jeering neighbours banging metal canisters. Militia bands and the town drummers sometimes marched through the city, and musicians wearing official livery – the waits – played their cornets, shawms, and sackbuts in the streets as well as for civic functions and ceremonies. The most impressive ceremonial occasion was the celebration of the queen's fortieth birthday in 1573. Elizabeth's arrival was delayed because of measles and smallpox in the city, but she eventually set up court in the royal quarters which her father had built at St Augustine's Abbey. Her birthday feast was held in the archbishop's palace – at the archbishop's considerable expense. As in the past, the city was expected to give presents to the royal visitor and her servants. It also incurred the cost of removing (or covering up) 'all dung and filth' in the streets. But the reward was spectacular: fascinated citizens watched as the queen, civic dignitaries in their glowing red robes, and visiting nobles made their way to the cathedral. In 1579 Elizabeth came to Canterbury again, and people had another opportunity to gaze at their monarch.

The queen was not the only visitor to cause a stir in the city. Companies of travelling players came to Canterbury, maybe around eighty times in the course of Elizabeth's reign. They performed before the mayor in the Guildhall but also entertained wider audiences in the courtyards of some of the larger inns. As a pupil at the King's School Christopher Marlowe may well have seen some of their performances. After leaving school Marlowe wrote four outstanding plays, but he died in 1593, at the age of only twenty-nine, in a London pub fight. Had he lived as long as his exact contemporary William Shakespeare, it is conceivable that Canterbury might eventually have become another Stratford-upon-Avon. Marlowe was not the only Elizabethan playwright to pass his formative years in the city. John Lyly,

Canterbury's theatre, erected 2011, is named after Christopher Marlowe whose memorial stands in the foreground. *Author's photograph.*

who lived in Sun Street, was to become a celebrated poet and dramatist. A decade before Marlowe, he too probably attended the King's School, as did Stephen Gosson, who wrote plays in his youth. Later, however, Gosson became a leading opponent of the theatre. Coincidentally, this virulent critic and one of the great playwrights of the age were born and bred in the same Canterbury parish.

In the closing years of the century the Burghmote took steps to curtail drama in the city. In 1595 travelling troupes were limited to performances on two consecutive days in any calendar month, and a nine o'clock curfew was imposed on their plays. Innkeepers who infringed this rule or who accommodated players for more than two days faced a forty-shilling fine. Such measures were part of a widespread attempt by Elizabethan councils to maintain public order at a time when the population of the country was growing and the proportion of people under twenty was escalating. Three years before, King's School pupils had been caught going 'abrode in the cuntrey to play playes contrary to lawe and good order'. At the same time radical Protestants, or 'Puritans', were anxious to transform England into a 'godly' land. Puritans believed that strict Sabbath observance was one of the hallmarks of true godliness, and so plays were banned on Sundays. New regulations introduced restraints on other activities on 'the Lord's Day' too. Fines were imposed on people caught trading on the Sabbath since this was deemed to be 'againste the glorie of god and the good government of this Cittie'. The Canterbury Burghmote did not go as far down this road as some towns, but it did try to control personal behaviour in the interests of both orderliness and godliness. Measures were passed against drinking and dancing as early as the 1560s, officers were appointed to watch out for people who haunted taverns, and in 1588 a Puritan mayor, Adrian Nycholls, ordered the removal of the maypole round which citizens danced in the Dane John fields. May Day festivities were seen as both disorderly and licentious.

The council's concern for public order reflected the fact that there were far more people in Canterbury at the end of Elizabeth's reign than at the beginning. There are no records of population as such, but estimates based on a variety of sources suggest that by the time the queen died in 1603 the city had around six thousand inhabitants. Its growth in the course of her reign was primarily due to substantial British migration and the arrival of the French-speaking Strangers. According to Canterbury French church records, the congregation in 1597 numbered 2,068. Its members did not all live within the bounds of the city, but Strangers clearly constituted a significant proportion of the population. They were still a distinct and segregated group, but relations with the host community seem to have been good, not least because by this time the Strangers had proved their economic worth. Skilled weavers employed local people to spin for them, and Canterbury tradesmen profited from supplying them with materials. By the early seventeenth century the people who had arrived as refugees twenty-five years before were an accepted part of city life. Their children, now adults themselves, had never known any other home. These English-born 'Strangers' had grown up in close proximity to neighbours whose origins lay elsewhere in Britain, as well as to long-established city families. Together they constituted Canterbury's varied and expanding community.

5

DISPUTES, DEPARTURES, AND DISCORD

c. 1622

Edward Wotton gazes with pride and delight at his Canterbury garden: at melons and mandrakes, at white hellebores and purple cranesbill, rare and delicate flowers with evocative names. His gardener, John Tradescant, shows him a new acquisition: 'This is a pomegranate, my Lord. No other garden in England has one.'

Tradescant's Garden (top left) Map/123 *c. 1642. Courtesy of the Chapter of Canterbury Cathedral.*

Bird and fruit depicted in the margin of the 1608 city charter. *Courtesy of the Chapter of Canterbury Cathedral.*

One of the creatures from the margin of the 1608 charter. *Courtesy of the Chapter of Canterbury Cathedral.*

By the early seventeenth century Canterbury was becoming an attractive location for gentry families who wanted houses in town in addition to their country estates. Baron Edward Wotton, a former lord lieutenant of Kent, acquired the palace at St Augustine's in 1612 and a few years later employed John Tradescant to design a magnificent garden. Tradescant and his son, who was educated at the King's School, were to become the greatest plant collectors and botanists of the age. The garden Tradescant created has long since disappeared, but images of fruit, flowers, and wildlife can still be seen on a city charter which was issued in 1608. Its text is surrounded by a wealth of glowing illustrations which create an impression of fertility, abundance, and well-being. There are birds of all kinds – a robin, a bluetit, a wren, a bullfinch; luscious fruit such as raspberries, strawberries, cherries, and mulberries; delicately depicted flowers – wild daffodils and wild roses, wallflowers and irises, heart's-ease and campion. Colourful butterflies flit around the margins and there are even tiny creatures – a snail, a frog, a rat, and a cricket. The charter can be seen as an expression of civic pride.

Beneath this confident surface, much was amiss. The charter was itself a product of festering antagonism. During the previous few years opposition had mounted throughout the country to self-perpetuating, oligarchic town councils, and the Canterbury aldermen faced a legal challenge to their right to serve as magistrates. They decided to apply for a new charter to clarify and codify the rules. It cost them £379 13s. 4d., a huge sum which, along with the expense of the lawsuit, plunged the city into debt.

Another potent, perennial source of disagreement was of course religion. While most people had got used to the Elizabethan church settlement, some were secretly sympathetic to Catholicism. Others protested, not so secretly, that the Church of England was but 'halflie reformed'. One of the most vocal religious radicals in Canterbury was a young apprentice, Robert Cushman, who was prosecuted for failing to attend his parish church (he claimed that he did not find it edifying) and for posting libellous notices on church doors. On completion of his apprenticeship Cushman became a freeman, entitled to run his own grocery business in the city, but within a few years he and his family emigrated to Leiden in the Low Countries, where they joined an Independent or Separatist church of fellow English exiles. Cushman became one of its leaders. When members of the group decided to make a new life for themselves in the Americas, he negotiated with shipping companies for their passage. He was not the only 'Pilgrim Father' with connections to Canterbury. James Chilton was born in the city but moved in late middle age first to Sandwich and then to the Low Countries. By the time the *Mayflower* set sail in 1620 Chilton was over sixty, and he died at sea. Cushman too never settled in America. He travelled to New England on the *Fortune* the following year with his son, but came straight back to conduct further negotiations on behalf of the colony. He died before he could return to the new Plymouth Colony. His son Thomas, however, and Chilton's daughter Mary spent the rest of their lives there. So too did Hester Mahieu, whose Walloon family had belonged to the city's French church, and her husband, Francis Cooke. Phillipe de la Noye, who was probably Hester's nephew, was an ancestor of Franklin Delano Roosevelt.

While Separatists sought to establish a new, unblemished church and society in America, many Puritans threw their energies into reforming existing English institutions. One of these was Thomas Scott, a country

Model of the *Mayflower* in which James Chilton and other 'Pilgrim Fathers' sailed to America. *Wikimedia Commons.*

gentleman from the village of Godmersham who moved to Canterbury around the same time as Edward Wotton. The grandson of Sir Thomas Wyatt, who had been executed for leading the 1554 rebellion against Queen Mary, Scott maintained his family's radical Protestant tradition. One of the attractions of Canterbury in his eyes was the presence of Thomas Wilson, a respected Puritan writer and preacher, as rector of St George's.

Thomas Scott became a leading campaigner against the misuse of power by the city council. The Burghmote often told the freemen electors which candidates to vote for in general elections. In 1626 it gave its backing to James Palmer, a protégé of the lord lieutenant of Kent of whose favour, the mayor insisted, 'we have great need'. Technically Palmer was not eligible to stand since, years before, the council had ruled that parliamentary candidates must be 'dwellers within the city and free of the same by half a year at the least'. Palmer was not a freeman and lived over a hundred miles away, in Buckingham, but the aldermen quickly granted him his freedom and ignored both his non-residence and the six-month rule. Their support for a candidate who knew nothing of the city and whom electors did not know provoked widespread anger. 'None but a Canterburie man', Scott proclaimed, should represent Canterbury. Four days before the polls he agreed to stand as one of two candidates against the council's nominees.

The 1626 election was particularly contentious. 'There is a company of you,' the exasperated mayor told a hatter, John Lee, 'that do always oppose the government of the city and the magistrates.' Scott for his part recorded in his journal the underhand methods the mayor and his colleagues employed against him, 'entreating, persuading, threatening' his supporters. It was nearly 250 years before secret ballots would be introduced, so at this time electors had to announce out loud whom they were supporting. This meant pressure could easily be put upon them. Six of the aldermen were brewers. They warned Thomas Curle of the Black Boy alehouse that he could lose his beer supply and maybe even his licence if he insisted on voting for Scott. When election day came the sheriff refused to allow a poll, ostensibly because the crowd was too large for him to identify those who were entitled to vote. He declared the two candidates favoured by the council to be elected by acclamation. Scott was outraged, maintaining that he would have been returned had a poll been held. He claimed that he was 'lawfully elected by the Free Comons and injuriously rejected by the Tyrannical Sheriffe'. He petitioned the House of Commons to order a fresh election, but Parliament was dissolved before a ruling was made.

The radical Puritan group around Scott was critical not only of autocratic aldermen but also of the king. Soon after Charles I came to the throne in 1625, he levied a 'forced loan', effectively a tax to cover the costs of war. Scott reluctantly paid £8, fearing that if he refused he might be imprisoned or even pressed to join the army. But when the dean of Canterbury, Isaac Bargrave, proclaimed that obedience to the king was a religious duty, Scott retaliated that 'yt is Against Conscience to yeald obedience to Tyrannicall and Lawlesse commaunds'. In his opinion, religious citizens had a duty 'to reprove our king, in all loyal and dutiful manner … saying wherefore hast thou not obeyed the voice of the Lord?' Such views were directly contrary to the king's own conviction that as a divinely appointed monarch he was answerable to God alone.

One of the royal practices Scott particularly deplored was an attempt to save money by billeting soldiers in private houses. Many troops passed through east Kent, and in the autumn of 1627 some were billeted in Canterbury homes. Scott condemned this as 'against the liberty of a free Englishman'. Maybe as a result of this stance he was elected in preference to Palmer in the 1628 general election. But the city paid a price for going against the lord lieutenant's will. Within weeks Irish soldiers were billeted on its householders, particularly, it seemed to Scott, on people who had supported him in the election. He instructed his wife to lock the doors to stop soldiers entering their house, but two 'lusty Irish popish soldiers' nevertheless forced their way in. The fact that the troops were Irish Catholics added to the tension. They may have been employed to fight Spaniards but in the eyes of ordinary citizens they were themselves the enemy. As more and more people refused to house them, the hungry and tired soldiers rioted, looted shops for food, and broke into property. Short of prosecuting vast numbers of citizens, there was little magistrates could do to enforce the order to billet. To everyone's relief the troops were eventually withdrawn, but the experience contributed to growing anger against the king and his advisers.

Anger in the country was reflected in Parliament. In the late 1620s Canterbury's other MP, sitting alongside Thomas Scott, was his kinsman John Finch. John's father, Henry, who had represented the city in the 1590s, was like Scott a radical Puritan, but his son followed a different path. In June 1625 he delivered a long and fulsome speech of welcome on behalf of the city to Charles I and his French wife: the royal couple spent their first night together in Canterbury after a proxy wedding in Paris. This address appears to have endeared Finch to the new queen: he received a knighthood and became an increasingly loyal supporter of the royal family. The king appointed him speaker of the House of Commons and on 10 March 1629 ordered him to adjourn an increasingly truculent Parliament.

IOHN FINCH LORD FINCH of FORDWICH.

Corn. Johnson pinx.

Facing Pla.19 Vol: P.75

When Finch attempted to obey the royal instructions, his fellow MPs held him down in the speaker's chair, determined to finish their business.

Once Parliament was finally adjourned, the king did not summon it again for eleven years. With no MPs to vote him supplies, he had to find other means of raising money. In the past, coastal communities had been required to provide the monarch with ships in times of national emergency. From 1634 Charles started to demand money in place of ships, even if there was no emergency. The mayor and sheriff of Canterbury handed over £415 9s. 6d. in March 1635

Engraving of John Finch. *Courtesy of the Chapter of Canterbury Cathedral.*

and £323 17s. 6d. the following February. In appropriately subservient language they told the Privy Council that they had 'willingly answered' the demand for money 'in respect of the general good of the kingdom'. They were concerned, however, that as city-dwellers they were being charged twice as much as people in rural Kent, and so they requested 'that for the future the lords will reduce their assessment'. The dulcet tone of their letter masked real grievance.

Another cause for concern was the fear that Charles might seek to restore Catholicism to England. The practice of the Catholic faith was still illegal, but when the Spanish ambassador visited Canterbury in 1623 Catholics had felt confident enough to demonstrate in the city. There was further outrage when a Catholic priest publicly ripped two pages out of the Bible in the cathedral. But what really shocked the people of Canterbury was the discovery in 1624 that Baron Wotton, the city's most eminent householder, had years before become a Roman Catholic. The secret came out when Wotton was summoned before the Maidstone assizes for not attending church. Catholic non-attenders ('recusants') normally faced fines or even confiscation of their property. Wotton escaped these penalties, probably because of his age (he was seventy-six), high standing, and long service, but he ceased to be a privy councillor. Meanwhile, fear that 'popery' was gaining ground was reinforced by the presence of a Catholic queen, for whom Mass was celebrated at court.

In 1633 Charles caused hackles to rise again when he appointed William Laud as the new archbishop of Canterbury. Laud was what later generations would call a High Church Anglican. He was determined to restore order, dignity, and respect to the church, but to many people the reforms which he and his supporters introduced smacked of Roman Catholicism. Richard Culmer, sometime curate of nearby Harbledown, criticised 'the Romishe dressing and bowing towards the High Altar' introduced into the cathedral. He particularly objected to a lavish gold and silver tapestry which hung behind the altar. This 'glory cloth' depicted glowing rays of light streaming down towards the altar and seemed to imply that God was especially present there. Culmer condemned it as both costly and 'idolatrous'. He was also scathing of clergy who on approaching the altar 'crouch and duck three times', 'ducking, ducking, ducking, like wilde-geese'.

Laud was concerned that 'the house of God' should be treated with proper respect. He was shocked to find newly built houses in the cathedral precincts, occupied not by clergy but by some thirty lay families. The dean and chapter received a missive from the king condemning 'this profanation'.

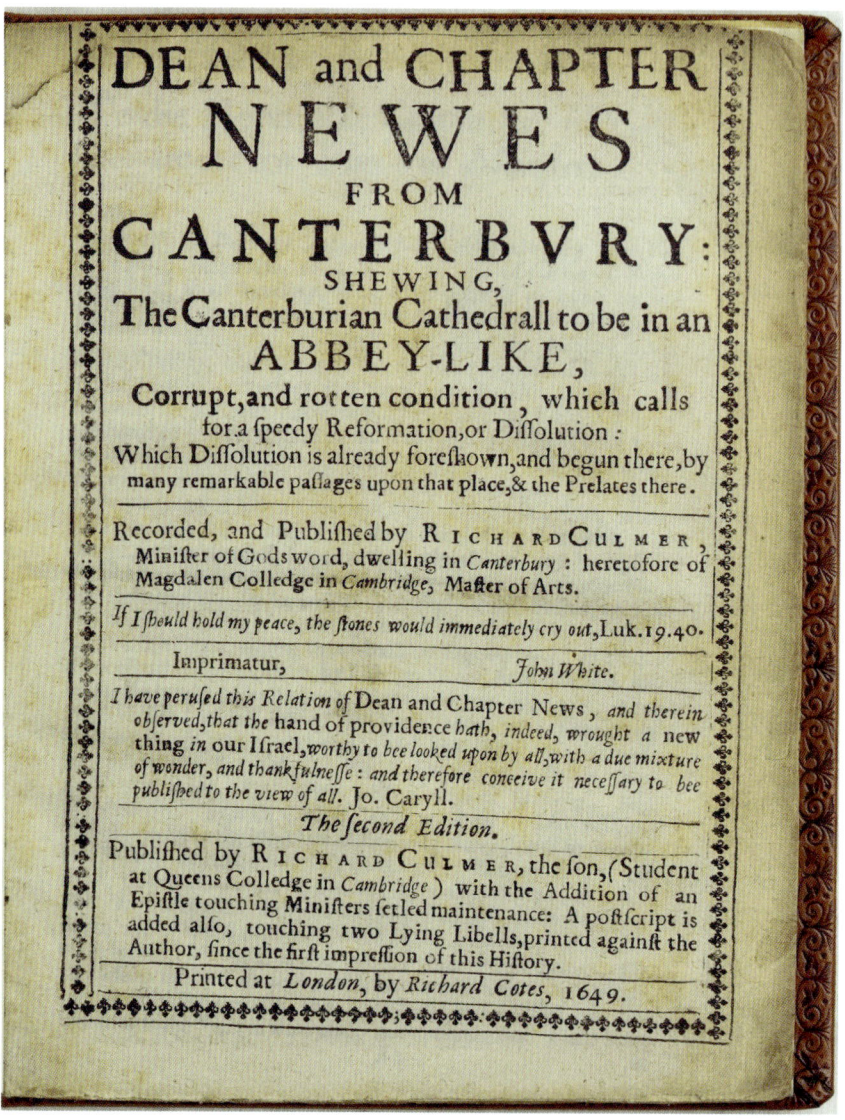

DEAN and CHAPTER NEWES FROM CANTERBVRY: SHEWING, The Canterburian Cathedrall to be in an ABBEY-LIKE, Corrupt, and rotten condition, which calls for a speedy Reformation, or Diſſolution: Which Diſſolution is already foreſhown, and begun there, by many remarkable paſſages upon that place, & the Prelates there.

Recorded, and Publiſhed by RICHARD CULMER, Miniſter of Gods word, dwelling in *Canterbury*: heretofore of Magdalen Colledge in *Cambridge*, Maſter of Arts.

If I ſhould hold my peace, the ſtones would immediately cry out, Luk. 19.40.

Imprimatur,   *John White.*

I have peruſed this Relation of Dean and Chapter News*, and therein obſerved, that the hand of providence hath, indeed, wrought a new thing in our* Iſrael*, worthy to bee looked upon by all, with a due mixture of wonder, and thankfulneſſe: and therefore conceive it neceſſary to bee publiſhed to the view of all.* Jo. Caryll.

The ſecond Edition.

Publiſhed by RICHARD CULMER, the ſon, (Student at Queens Colledge in *Cambridge*) with the Addition of an Epiſtle touching Miniſters ſetled maintenance: A poſtſcript is added alſo, touching two Lying Libells, printed againſt the Author, ſince the firſt impreſſion of this Hiſtory.

Printed at *London*, by *Richard Cotes*, 1649.

Pamphlet by Richard Culmer, castigating the cathedral. *Courtesy of the Chapter of Canterbury Cathedral.*

The letter stated that the leases should not be renewed and that when they expired the houses should be demolished. Many leases, however, were new, covering forty years, so little was done.

Parish churches, too, were subjected to the archbishop's reforming zeal. Laud ordered churchwardens to replace moveable communion tables with altars and to surround these with rails, to signify their holiness as places where people met with God. Puritans were not the only people who resented orders to spend money altering their churches in ways they deemed unnecessary. To make matters worse, they were expected to change their own religious practices. Laudian clergy insisted that parishioners knelt at the newly installed rails when receiving communion. An alderman's wife was among those who refused to do so. At St Mildred's in 1633 the churchwardens reported forty-seven people to the archbishop's officials for keeping their hats on in church.

To later generations these may seem trivial matters, but in the seventeenth century kneeling and removing headwear had important symbolic significance. Staunch Protestants could not bring themselves to make gestures which seemed to give honour to altars or church buildings. In the eyes of Puritans, these changes were part of a European-wide battle between the forces of good and evil, reformed religion and Roman Catholicism. Many citizens were delighted when the king endorsed the playing of games after church services, but Puritans maintained that keeping Sunday holy was the hallmark of a truly Protestant society. At Harbledown, Culmer reproved parishioners whom he deemed guilty of 'prophaning the Sabbath by Crikit playing'. They in turn threw stones at his sons and clamoured for his dismissal.

Some Puritans despaired so much of what was happening that they made the momentous decision to leave the country, joining what became known as the 'Great Migration' to New England. Around forty people from Canterbury were among those who boarded a ship from Sandwich in the summer of 1637. The journey alone, six weeks or more at sea, was a nerve-wracking undertaking, particularly for parents of young children. Whole families moved to the New World, headed by men who were already well established in their trades, a fact which suggests that their motivation was religious rather than economic. Edward Johnson, a joiner, travelled with his wife Susan, their seven children, and three other household members. The Johnsons lived in St George's, the parish in which Thomas Wilson had ministered, and probably reached their decision in consultation with fellow parishioners Joseph and Elizabeth Bachelor. The Bachelors had lost a son and twin daughters in recent years and had just one surviving child, a toddler, Mark. They were accompanied by other members of their extended family, maybe Joseph's brothers: John, like Joseph, was a Canterbury tailor while Henry was a brewer who had moved to Dover. He had recently married Martha Wilson, another resident of St George's. Now, with relatives and neighbours, the newly married couple were setting sail to start a new life on the other side of the Atlantic.

Meanwhile, refugees who had settled in Canterbury years before faced unpalatable changes. Archbishop Laud was deeply suspicious of foreign churches, which he regarded as 'nests and occasions of schism'. He conceded that there had been good reason to allow Strangers to worship in their own language when they first arrived in the 1570s, but many second and third generation church members had been born and bred in England. In 1635 Laud ordered that such people should attend their local parish churches like all other native inhabitants.

Laud's attack on foreign churches provoked consternation in Canterbury. Members of the Burghmote were only too aware of the problems they would face if the Strangers ceased to be treated as a separate entity responsible for the welfare needs of their own community. They petitioned the archbishop, pointing out that the Strangers currently maintained their own poor, at a cost of £153 a year. The city could not afford this additional burden on the poor rates. Nor could it afford to alienate the Strangers. Many of the refugees had retained close contact with friends and family abroad: Gilles Guerin's son Peter lived in Holland, while Michelle Nutient had a brother and two sisters in Flanders; Michael le Grand still owned property on the continent. If Canterbury became uncongenial, people such as these might decide to return to the lands their ancestors came from – to the detriment of their adopted city. Aldermen knew what an important contribution the immigrant community made to the local economy. In 1636 Strangers employed 150 spinners in the parish of Holy Cross alone. If they left Canterbury there was a real risk that some trades might fail, particularly those, in the corporation's words, 'of which no Englishman in their city has ever had any knowledge'. With the support of city dignitaries and the dean and chapter, the foreign church in Canterbury continued to function, although the smaller one in Maidstone collapsed. The long-term survival of the Canterbury community, one of the largest in the country, was helped by the fact that Laud ran out of time to enforce the full rigours of his policy. As one of the king's leading counsellors he was blamed for unpopular royal decisions and accused of misleading the monarch. In 1640 he was charged with high treason; his treatment of Strangers was one of the indictments against him.

By this time Charles was at war with his subjects in Scotland. Lords lieutenant of the English counties were ordered to send men north to quell the Scots, who had been incensed by the king's attempt to impose an

Engraving of William Laud.
*Courtesy of the Chapter of
Canterbury Cathedral.*

English prayer book on them. The demand for forces was not of itself novel: all able-bodied men between sixteen and sixty were liable to be called for military service, and each county had to ensure that a sufficient number of them were suitably trained and equipped. But citizen armies were not normally expected to travel so far afield. The mayor and corporation of Canterbury were particularly annoyed that the city was expected to provide eighty soldiers, far more than their fair share.

To pay for the war the king had to summon Parliament. In 1640, for the first time in years, electors had the opportunity of choosing representatives to speak for them. One of the candidates in Canterbury was Archbishop Laud's secretary, but the freemen of the city would not have him. According to Culmer they refused to allow the man to speak, hissed him down, and instead chose as their MPs two captains of militia companies which had been pressed into service against the Scots.

John Finch acted as the king's spokesman at the opening of Parliament, but neither he nor his royal master showed any recognition of the grievances which had accumulated during the last decade and a half. Finch was so closely associated with unpopular royal policies that it is not surprising that fellow MPs brought charges against him. Late in 1640, newly ennobled as Baron Finch of Fordwich, he wisely fled to the continent. He was allowed to return in 1653 but died seven years afterwards. Later generations, reacting against the traumas of civil war, commemorated Finch with a eulogistic memorial in St Martin's church.

Charles I's failure to respond to widespread frustration led to a flood of petitions demanding change. Some demands, however, were so extreme that they prompted counter-petitions, and a royalist party began to emerge.

Polemical sermons were preached, pamphlets circulated in unprecedented numbers, and there were fierce differences of opinion between communities throughout the land. In Canterbury 185 people, including the mayor and eleven aldermen, signed a pro-parliamentary petition – but sermons were preached in the cathedral about the sinfulness of armed resistance. Since the king would not compromise and MPs would not grant funds without concessions, the country dissolved into civil war. On 22 August 1642 Charles set up the royal standard on Castle Hill in Nottingham, effectively taking up arms against his own Parliament. A Canterbury gentleman, Thomas Belke, organised and trained a troop of volunteers in support of Parliament, one of the first such forces in the country. The *House of Commons Journal* for 14 September recorded: 'Whereas divers Volunteers of Canterbury, under the Command of Captain Belke, freely came to Dover, to defend the Castle there; the House doth well accept their Service, and doth return them Thanks for it.' But not everyone approved of such action. Canterbury, like so many other places, remained a conflicted community for years to come.

6

CIVIL WAR AND ITS AFTERMATH

30 August 1642

Thomas Paske, the sub-dean of Canterbury Cathedral, sits at his desk, shaking. He has just been into the cathedral. The altar rails have been smashed and the sacred altar overturned. He can't believe it. He picks up his pen and starts to write: the perpetrators, he records, 'giant-like began a fight with God himselfe'.

A few days after the king raised his standard in Nottingham, a group of soldiers burst into Canterbury Cathedral. Barely trained and ill-disciplined, they had been sent to Kent to disarm suspected royalists. They stormed the deanery to see whether the dean had any hidden weapons, but they far exceeded their brief when they proceeded to wreak havoc in the cathedral. Even people who shared their dislike of Laudian reforms were shocked by the damage they caused. Sir Michael Livesey, a senior commander and future regicide, confessed that he was 'ready to feint' when he saw what his troops had done, and he apologised on their behalf. The soldiers' behaviour showed that once the cork was out of the bottle, leaders could not always control their supporters.

The men who led the protest against the king had varied aims. Some simply wanted Charles to modify his behaviour and rule in conjunction with Parliament, as previous monarchs had done. Others looked for far more radical change. They believed that God was calling them to complete the religious reformation which had started a hundred years before, and they feared that they would incur his judgement if they failed to seize the opportunity he had given them. The scene was set for years of confusion, conflict, and unforeseen consequences.

In the first phase of civil war, between 1642 and 1646, most of the fighting took place in the midlands and the north. No town, however, could be confident it would escape unscathed, and in November 1642 the Canterbury Burghmote ordered that 'the city be speedily fortified and ordinance and ammunition provided'. Captain Belke, who had organised the volunteer force, and five others were charged to oversee the work, 'to digge Turfe and earth for the fortification where they shall find it most convenient'. These visible signs of a country at war were accompanied by demands for money which affected almost every family in the city. In 1641/2 Parliament levied a poll tax to which nearly 1,500 Canterbury households contributed a sum totalling £632 5s. The tax was graduated, with contributions ranging from sixpence to thirty pounds, but everyone over sixteen who was not in receipt of poor relief had to pay something. Once war actually broke out, the county of Kent came under parliamentary control, and local communities were required to provide men, horses, arms, and money for the parliamentary forces. The city accounts contain repeated references to the negotiation and collection of rates for this purpose. Civil war was expensive, and Parliament sought to cover the escalating costs by raising excise duties on tobacco, alcohol, and imported luxuries. From 1644 the levies extended to a wider range of items, including meat and salt. High levels of taxation had been a major cause of resentment against royal rule in the 1630s, so the constant rise in taxes in the 1640s contributed to an erosion of support for Parliament.

The king, for his part, depended on the generosity of royalist sympathisers. In 1643, to stop them replenishing the royal coffers, Parliament introduced a policy of sequestration, the confiscation of lands and property of known or suspected royalists. Catholics were obvious targets, and one of the people who suffered was Edward Wotton's widow, Margaret. An inventory was made of goods in her St Augustine's residence, most of which were then sold. The town crier walked round the city announcing the sale – and many women and local merchants flocked to get what they could.

Parliament was preoccupied not only with the demands of warfare but also with fostering the godly society for which its Puritan members had long yearned. These two concerns came together in the attempt to rid the

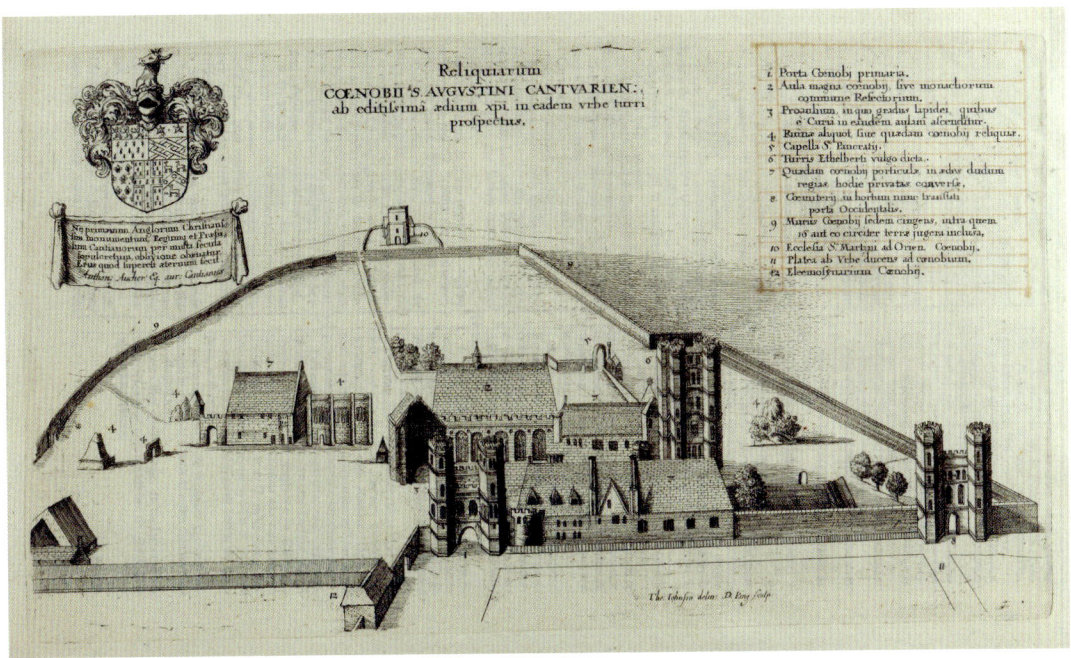

Lady Wotton's home, formerly a royal residence, on the site of St Augustine's Abbey, *Monasticon Anglicanum* (1655). *Courtesy of the Chapter of Canterbury Cathedral.*

country of 'scandalous, malignant priests'. 'Malignancy' denoted offences such as speaking against Parliament or sending financial aid to the king. Thus Daniel Bullen of St Mary Northgate was deprived of his living for deserting his parish and joining the royal army. Whether or not a minister was charged often depended on the attitudes of his parishioners, who could trigger a case by making accusations. Members of James Penney's St Dunstan's congregation complained that their vicar was a gambler; he was also accused of ignoring fasts and thanksgivings which Parliament had ordered. While some allegations may have lacked substance, there can be no doubt about those levelled against John Marston, rector of St Mary Magdalen and vicar of St Mary Bredin. In 1640 Marston had been accused of adultery, an offence he admitted and for which he served a three-month prison sentence. He then returned to his parishes, but in 1642 a group of parishioners signed a petition objecting to his 'scandalous course of life' and his antagonism to Parliament. Marston used his pulpit to read out a royal pamphlet 'without any order or warrant' and spoke disparagingly of a declaration which Parliament had sent to be read. But he had supporters as well as detractors among his parishioners. They organised a rival petition which maintained that Marston had paid for his sin: he had mended his ways and should be allowed to continue his duties. Civil war conflict extended right down to parish level.

As well as seeking to create a 'godly' ministry, Puritan MPs were also anxious to purge the country of statues and images which had survived the Reformation. In 1643 they ordered 'the utter demolishing, removing and taking away of all monuments of superstition or idolatry'. Included among these was a huge stained-glass image of Becket in Canterbury Cathedral, which sixteenth-century reformers had failed to reach. The cathedral clergy refused to engage in such destruction, and so the work was supervised by the mayor and three local ministers. In the absence of other volunteers, Richard Culmer climbed fifty-six steps up a ladder, pike in hand, to smash

Print of watercolour of Christ Church Gate by J.M.W.Turner, *c.* 1793, showing the central niche from which the statue of Christ was removed during the civil war. *Courtesy of the Chapter of Canterbury Cathedral.*

the north transept window, 'ratling down proud Beckets glassie bones'. He also helped pull down a statue of Christ, 'the meanes of much idolatry', from its niche in the Christ Church Gate. When all was done, he was escorted home by a troop of musketeers who had been keeping guard lest the populace protest. Some citizens did try to stop the demolition. Years later William Cooke, a cordwainer and 'most loyall subject' of the king, claimed compensation for 'most violent blowes' inflicted by Culmer's supporters, which had stopped him practising his trade.

Parliament's reforming zeal also affected the conduct of worship. In 1645 the *Book of Common Prayer*, which some Puritans had long disliked, was replaced by a new *Directory of Public Worship*. It is, of course, impossible to tell how far the guidelines it laid down for services were followed. Even if the old prayer books were removed, some incumbents may have continued to recite

Title page of the *Directory of Public Worship*.
Courtesy of the Chapter of Canterbury Cathedral.

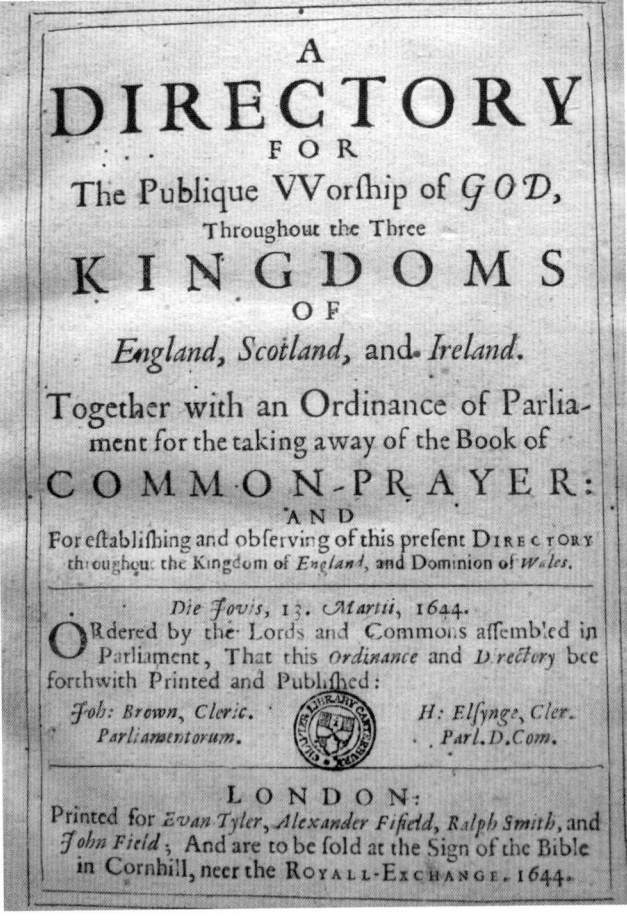

A

DIRECTORY

FOR

The Publique VVorſhip of *GOD,*

Throughout the Three

KINGDOMS

OF

England, Scotland, and *Ireland.*

Together with an Ordinance of Parliament for the taking away of the Book of

COMMON-PRAYER:

AND

For eſtabliſhing and obſerving of this preſent DIRECTORY throughout the Kingdom of *England,* and Dominion of *Wales.*

Die *Jovis,* 13. *Martii,* 1644.

ORdered by the Lords and Commons aſſembled in Parliament, That this *Ordinance* and *Directory* bee forthwith Printed and Publiſhed:

Joh: Brown, Cleric.   *H: Elſynge, Cler.*
Parliamentorum.   *Parl.D.Com.*

LONDON:

Printed for *Evan Tyler, Alexander Fifield, Ralph Smith,* and *John Field*; And are to be ſold at the Sign of the Bible in *Cornhill, neer the* ROYALL-EXCHANGE. 1644.

the familiar words of the liturgy from memory. Did clergy adhere to the new, stark orders to bury the dead 'without any ceremony'? And what happened at baptisms? The font in St Dunstan's church was severely damaged at the start of December 1645, so when George and Jone Martin took their daughter Margaret to be christened a few days later, she was baptised 'in a basin' because 'the Font was pull'd down'. But did the minister refrain as instructed from making the sign of the cross over the baby, an act which Puritans regarded as superstitious? Or did he perhaps maintain this traditional practice, which was popularly believed to protect children from harm?

One of the most controversial reforms was the *Directory*'s command that 'festival days, vulgarly called holy days, having no Warrant in the Word of God, are not to be continued'. In 1647 Parliament's attempt to ban all Christmas festivities gave rise to major riots in Canterbury. The mayor, William Bridges, ordered city tradesmen to treat Christmas Day, which fell on a Saturday, as a normal trading day. Few obeyed his instructions. Only a small number of stalls were erected for the usual Saturday market, and these were attacked by a gathering crowd which hurled their wares to the ground. The sheriff and mayor tried to intervene, but to no avail. Bridges was knocked down and chased back to his house by a jeering mob, which deposited a holly bush, a symbol of Christmas, outside his door. Sunday was calmer, but on Monday, violence mounted as people from surrounding villages flocked to the city. The captain of the guard, a local barber, provoked uproar by shooting a protester. A furious crowd dragged him out of the hayloft in which he was hiding, stormed the prison, and attacked the homes of officials. As angry men rushed around brandishing clubs, the sheriff's head was 'fearfully broke'. A chant echoed through Canterbury: 'For God, King Charles, and Kent.'

Within days of the 1647 riots a 'Declaration of Many Thousands of the City of Canterbury, or of the County of Kent' was published, articulating dissatisfaction with the changes introduced by Parliament. Puritans might dismiss Christmas festivities as popish and superstitious, but that was not how the people of Canterbury saw them. They merely 'desired to continue the celebration of the Feast of Christs Nativity 1500 years and upwards maintained in the Church'. The anonymous declaration suggested that popular disillusion extended far beyond the banning of Christmas which had triggered the riots:

> the common sort of people thought we should have had a golden Age ... they expected England to have become a second Paradise.

But ... the remedy of these pretenders to Reformation is worse than the disease ... We, the Inhabitants of the City of Canterbury and County of Kent, do protest against these exorbitant and wicked proceedings of the two Houses.

As parliamentary troops approached Canterbury to quell the rioting, a group of city dignitaries sought to negotiate a truce. Alderman Avery Sabine, Sir William Mann, and Francis Lovelace were anxious to avoid a damaging siege and thought that they could save the protesters from prosecution if they agreed to surrender their arms. The outcome was less favourable than they had anticipated. The parliamentary county committee gave orders that the city wall should be breached and the gates burnt down. Leading rioters were imprisoned – along with Sabine, Mann, and Lovelace, who had worked for a more equable settlement. A list of those arrested shows that people from a wide variety of trades had joined in the protests: labourers, bricklayers, joiners, carpenters, butchers, bakers, barbers, tapsters, brewers, pipe-makers, cordwainers, hemp dressers, a bookseller, a yeoman, and a gentleman. But the arrests did not help the parliamentary cause. In May 1648 two concurrent trials were held, one for inhabitants of the city in the Guildhall, the other for people subject to county jurisdiction in Canterbury Castle. To the fury of John Wilde, a leading parliamentary judge who presided at the Guildhall, the jury returned a verdict of 'ignoramus' ('we do not know'). In an atmosphere

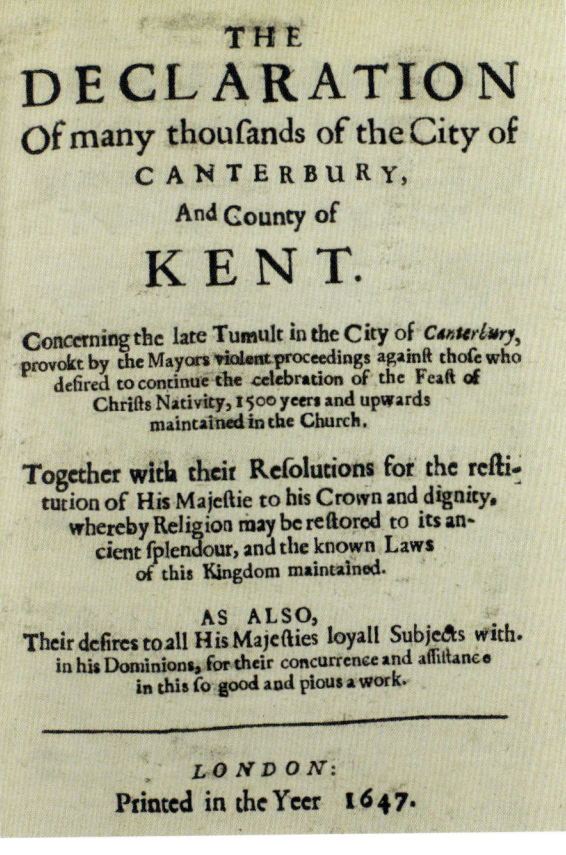

THE

DECLARATION

Of many thousands of the City of

CANTERBURY,

And County of

KENT.

Concerning the late Tumult in the City of *Canterbury*, provokt by the Mayors violent proceedings against those who desired to continue the celebration of the Feast of Chrifts Nativity, 1500 yeers and upwards maintained in the Church.

Together with their Refolutions for the refti-
tution of His Majeftie to his Crown and dignity, whereby Religion may be reftored to its ancient fplendour, and the known Laws of this Kingdom maintained.

AS ALSO,

Their defires to all His Majefties loyall Subjects with-
in his Dominions, for their concurrence and affiftance in this fo good and pious a work.

LONDON:
Printed in the Yeer **1647**.

The Declaration of Many Thousands... Courtesy of the Chapter of Canterbury Cathedral.

of heightened tension and feverish excitement, news of their decision was passed to the castle, whose jury followed suit, notwithstanding the intimidating presence of parliamentary cavalry. The following day, jury members started a new county-wide petition. They called for a settlement with the king (something which had been expected when Charles surrendered two years earlier) and government according to the 'established laws of this kingdom'. Parliamentary forces should be paid and disbanded, and innovatory taxes, especially the excise, should be ended.

Robert Bargrave met his cousin, John, on the continent where, as royalists, they sought safety during the civil war. John's beautifully illustrated 1645 travel diary is preserved in the cathedral archives. *Courtesy of the Chapter of Canterbury Cathedral.*

The events in Canterbury served as a catalyst for a second bout of civil warfare. County officials tried to suppress the petition, with the result that petitioners started to arm themselves. Some of the Canterbury men implicated in the Kentish rising of 1648 had originally supported Parliament's attempt to curtail royal power, but after six years they had become disillusioned with parliamentary rule. These local protesters were joined by committed royalists from elsewhere in England, but they were vastly outnumbered by the parliamentary forces. On 1 June they were roundly defeated in a bloody battle at Maidstone. Within days the parliamentary general, Sir Thomas Fairfax, was on the march towards Canterbury. With its gates burnt and its walls already breached, the city was in no state to resist him. On 8 June it agreed to surrender, and some three thousand weapons were laid down at the cathedral.

Seven months later, the unthinkable happened. King Charles I was tried by his own subjects and beheaded on 30 January 1649. Radical parliamentarians were incensed by his unwillingness to reach a settlement, as well as by his repeated double-dealing. Charles for his part believed that divinely appointed monarchs did not do deals with their subjects. William Bridges and some fellow aldermen were among the signatories of a petition calling for the king's trial and execution. Other Canterbury people, including loyal parliamentarians, were deeply shocked. Avery Sabine, who had served on the parliamentary county committee, drew up a new will shortly after the king's death, dating it, significantly, 'the 24th year of the reign of King Charles'. A royalist exile, Robert Bargrave, son of the former dean of Canterbury, was in Constantinople when he received news of 'the deplorable Tragedie of our King in England'. 'The Tide of our Joy,' he wrote, 'turnd into a Streame of Grief.'

***

Anyone returning to Canterbury in the early 1650s after a dozen or so years away would have noticed many changes. Old landmarks had disappeared, notably the market cross, which had stood for two hundred years in what is now the Buttermarket; it had been demolished in 1645 as part of the campaign against religious imagery. Gaping walls, burnt gates, and a scarred cathedral served as reminders of what the city had suffered. There was even a recommendation in 1652 that the cathedral be demolished, ostensibly to pay for war with the Dutch Republic, but nothing came of this. The cathedral survived, albeit part of a state church now theoretically Presbyterian, but with its personnel and ethos much changed, since the offices of bishop, dean, and chapter had all been abolished. The new regime regarded the cathedral, like all other places of worship, as a 'preaching house'. The Six Preachers, who delivered sermons there, were predominantly Puritan in outlook.

One of the changes that would have surprised a new arrival was the presence in the city of Independent congregations, established in the 1640s. Before this time, people who were dissatisfied with the Church of England had been prosecuted if they organised rival meetings for worship; as law and order collapsed, dissidents felt freer to act according to their own convictions. In 1645 William Kiffin, a travelling preacher who advocated baptism for adult believers (as opposed to for children), visited

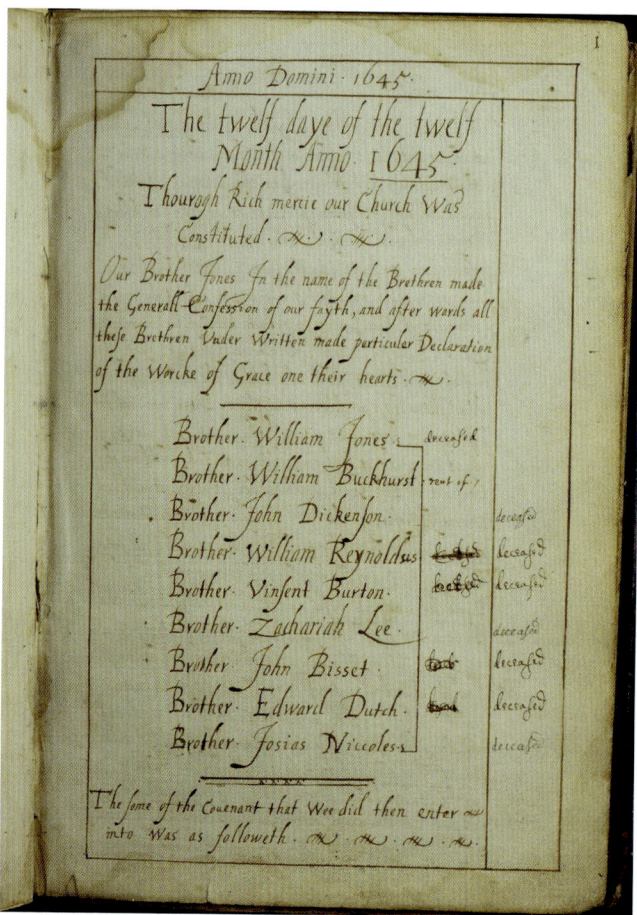

The first page (subsequently annotated) of the Independent congregation's 'church book' recorded the names of the nine founder members. *Courtesy of the Chapter of Canterbury Cathedral.*

Canterbury and held a service in the home of Anna Stevens, whom he 'dipped' (baptised by total immersion) along with three men, probably in the River Stour. On the 'twelf daye of the twelf month' of that year, another group of nine city residents decided to constitute themselves into an Independent church. By 1649 their numbers had risen to over seventy and they had appointed their own pastor, John Durant (a man often unfairly described by opponents as a 'washing-ball maker' because he had once been apprenticed to a London soap boiler). Groups such as this believed that each congregation should govern itself through a church meeting attended by all members. They exercised strict discipline, reprimanding or even expelling those who failed to maintain expected standards of faith and morals: in 1649 the meeting 'with one consent did excommunicate the sister Raye for that she did still persevere in her heresyes', while three years later Susan Godferyes was admonished for 'going unto witches to enquire about a husband'. It is a mark of how much had changed that, from 1650, this Independent congregation held its services in the cathedral Chapter House. Meanwhile, Durant, like a number of other Independent ministers, was invited to combine his pastorship with a role in the national church. He served as rector of St George's and as one of the Six Preachers. Oliver Cromwell, the dominant figure in government after the king's death, did not worry unduly about a minister's churchmanship, providing he was diligent and orthodox.

The ideological ferment of the age ensured that new sects continued to multiply in the 1650s. One of these was the Society of Friends of Truth, which repudiated the idea of a special clerical caste. Members of the society believed that there was an inner light within each human being and that God's Spirit could and did move through anyone. They were quickly nicknamed 'Quakers' because they sometimes quaked in ecstasy as they felt God prompting them to speak. Two 'travelling Friends', William Caton and John Stubbs, visited Canterbury in 1655 to 'declare the Truth'; following their visit a Quaker meeting was formed in the city. The Society of Friends was later to become renowned for its pacifism, but early Quakers were aggressive propagandists for their cause and did not hesitate to disrupt church services. Thomas Pollard was imprisoned for nine months for trying to interrupt John Durant as he preached in what Quakers disparagingly called 'the great Massehouse', Canterbury Cathedral. Quakers who were deemed to be disruptive and unorthodox were subject to persecution. By contrast Durant, who had once been suspected himself, was a pillar of the new establishment.

People of the time had no idea that the new regime would be short-lived. For them, welcome or not, it was the new reality, and they adapted accordingly. On 3 September 1650 the Burghmote resolved that: 'The arms of the Commonwealth are to be set up in the Town Hall on a frame'. When Oliver Cromwell visited the city in 1652, the cost of entertaining him and his trumpeters was noted in the same way as royal visits had been in the past. Meanwhile, although the government had changed, many daily routines continued much as before. Brewers, bakers, and butchers, tailors and shoemakers went on plying their trades, supplying food and drink, clothing, and footwear to fellow citizens. As always, some people behaved in anti-social ways. Andrew Smith, a labourer from St Paul's parish, was found guilty of stealing hens. John Gilbert, a baker, and Richard Whetland, a tailor, were charged with 'illegal fishing', taking fish from the river between Chartham and Canterbury with nets whose mesh was less than two and a half inches. Three Walloons were fined for 'casting soap suds into the common river'.

The Burghmote records show that, as in any age, much of the council's time was taken up with mundane matters. Members discussed who could sell what where and who should pay for street paving. One recurrent

The River Stour where people fished illegally and in which Baptists may have been baptised. *Author's photograph.*

concern, from the 1630s right the way through the Civil War and Protectorate, was the provision of water. There was repeated consideration whether to replace elm pipes with lead. Prices were set for the annual rent to be charged to anyone who wanted to run 'a small pipe' from the main pipeline to his or her own house. William Glover was warned on several occasions that his supply would be cut off if he failed to pay his arrears. The council engaged in lengthy negotiations with Mr Eborne for a new conduit head and cistern on the edge of his St Martin's Hill property 'for the use of this City for ever', only to discover after several years that they should have been dealing with Sir Henry Palmer. An obsequious letter entreated Sir Henry to grant the same rights which Mr Eborne had agreed. He was presented with a piece of plate in gratitude for his compliance. But problems over water continued. In order to improve the flow, it was decided to turn off public water cocks at certain times of day (and all day on Sundays) and to pay the person responsible for doing so forty shillings a year. People who tried to get more water than they should by filling 'any Tub or other greater Vessel' faced fines, as did those who 'shall wash or rinse any Cloaths' at the conduit or public water cocks. It was issues such as these that exercised the minds of local councillors during the Protectorate.

Significant events had always been marked by local festivity. In 1658 the proclamation of Richard Cromwell as 'Lord Protector' in succession to his father was commemorated by a banquet at the mayor's house and monetary gifts to the poor. But support for Richard quickly evaporated, and there was no agreement even among republicans how or by whom the country should be governed. After two years of dispute and prevarication, army coups, and increasing anarchy, a newly elected parliament made arrangements for the restoration of the monarchy. On Friday 25 May 1660 cheering crowds gathered at Dover to welcome Charles II to his kingdom. Fifteen miles away in Canterbury more crowds waited with eager anticipation: nothing like this had been seen for over twenty years. Proud and anxious, the mayor and aldermen, resplendently arrayed in scarlet robes, prepared to welcome the king to their city. Charles was to spend his first weekend back in England, as acknowledged monarch, in Canterbury.

7

Legacies of War

Friday 25 May 1660

William Somner waits apprehensively for Charles II to arrive. In his hand he clutches a copy of a book he has written: The Antiquities of Canterbury. There are loud fanfares of music and the crowd roars. People gaze in wonder at the towering figure of the new king. City officials move forward to present a golden tankard filled with gold pieces. Speeches are made. And now it is Somner's turn. 'On the bended knees of his body' he offers his book to the king. It is the proudest day of his life.

View of Canterbury from the 1703 edition of William Somner's *Antiquities of Canterbury. Courtesy of the Chapter of Canterbury Cathedral.*

William Somner was born in Canterbury, lived there all his life, and like his father before him served as cathedral registrar. Somner had no doubt where his loyalties lay. Shortly after Charles I's death, he described the king as the country's 'choicest treasure'. Somner had been appointed to his cathedral post by Archbishop Laud and in 1640 dedicated his *Antiquities of Canterbury* to him, an unfortunate choice given the archbishop's subsequent arrest and execution. The unbound copy of the *Antiquities*, which Somner presented to Charles II twenty years later, had a new title page.

It is unlikely that the king found time to peruse Somner's book during that first weekend in Canterbury. Four drummers and the waits, the city musicians, were paid to play during the three days of his stay, and men of status flocked to assure him of their loyalty. On Saturday 26th Charles appointed his first knights of the garter, assembled his council, and attended a service in the cathedral. According to one of his entourage, this was 'much dilapidated and out of repair, yet the people seemed glad to hear the common prayer again'. On Monday 28th the king set off along Watling Street, past the cheering crowds of Harbledown and Boughton-under-Blean, towards London.

Expectations of the new regime varied. People who had suffered in the royalist cause assumed that Charles would reward their loyalty to his father. Letters poured into the royal court from ordinary as well as eminent people, requesting appointments or alms. The daughter of a Canterbury cordwainer begged for relief on the grounds that her deceased father was 'of mean fortune, ran great risks, and was much impoverished in His Majesty's service'. Thomas Middleton, a local tailor, reported that he had received many wounds fighting for the late king. Francis Lovelace, the recorder of Canterbury, pointed out that he had suffered imprisonment, loss of office, and confiscation of lands. Some royalists wanted more than rewards for their own service. They also wanted revenge. The king, by contrast, was inclined to be conciliatory. He knew that a line had to be drawn under past hostilities if stability was to be secured, and he was aware that nothing would be gained by perpetuating division. Many men retained the posts they had held during the Interregnum. But the king needed to ensure that people in authority were loyal to his regime. In January 1661 five Canterbury aldermen, five councillors, and the 'common crier and bellman' were dismissed from office, 'deemed disaffected to his Majesty and his Government'. A new Corporation Act required all local officials to take oaths of allegiance and supremacy and to renounce previous loyalties. When this act was implemented in the summer of 1662, another three aldermen, several more councillors, the town clerk, and the keeper of the prison were removed from their positions.

Underlying such measures was fear that disaffected citizens would once again rise against the monarchy. No one could be sure that the regime would survive, and rumours of conspiracy, some well-founded, others fictitious, continued to circulate for decades to come. In 1663 a Captain Kingsley wrote to the secretary of state in a panic about supposed events in the Canterbury area: 'great conventicles', people carrying bundles 'supposed to be arms', and 250 lusty men with 'stout cudgels' at Reculver. 'Those who have shed their blood and suffered long imprisonment in the King's cause,' he explained, 'fear lest these desperate villains domineer once more, if care be not taken.' Francis Lovelace, whose royalist sympathies could not be doubted, questioned such alarmist reports, suggesting that there was 'little cause for Captain Kingsley's information'.

One of the legacies of the Civil War was distrust of members of radical sects who were suspected of fomenting revolution. Quakers were particularly mistrusted since they refused to take oaths. They maintained that one should always tell the truth, adhering literally to Christ's injunction 'Do not swear at all ... Let your word be *Yes, Yes*, or *No, No*' (Matthew 5:37). In a society which used oath-taking as a primary means of maintaining order, refusal to swear allegiance to the monarch seemed a clear sign of disloyalty. On 17 November 1660 two Canterbury Quakers, Henry Rogers and Thomas Pollard, 'being with other Friends publikely and peacably mett together', were brought before the mayor and required to take oaths of allegiance and supremacy. When they told him that 'for consiense sake' they could not, they were imprisoned and remained in gaol for 'nine weeks foure dayes'. Many Quakers spent time in prison – for refusing to pay dues to the established church, for declining to contribute to the city's armaments, and for holding meetings for worship, which the authorities deemed subversive. In 1665 a meeting in Henry Rogers' house was stormed by armed soldiers 'to ye affrightening of Children'. The significantly titled Quaker *Book of Sufferings* noted that on this occasion men were jailed for three months and some of the women for one.

Quakers received particularly harsh treatment, but they were not the only religious group to suffer. Although the king hoped to restore a broadly based national church, Parliament voted by a small majority to impose stricter controls on clergy than had ever existed before. Many men who might happily have remained in a less rigid church felt unable to swear 'unfeigned assent and consent' to the Book of Common Prayer. In 1662

Entry in the Kent Book of Sufferings for 1 August 1668 recording the prosecution and imprisonment of Ann Young, widow, and Elizabeth Polard, who refused to pay fines for absence from the parish church. *Society of Friends, East and West Kent Area Meetings.*

some two thousand of them were ejected from their posts. Among the Canterbury ministers who lost their jobs were Francis Taylor, the blind rector of St Mary Bredman, Thomas Ventris of St Margaret's, and Robert Beake of St Stephen's.

The ejected ministers retained the support of some sympathetic parishioners, which led to the emergence of new dissenting congregations. Gatherings of more than five people for worship outside the Church of England were banned, but Taylor and others ignored this ruling and held meetings in their homes. The city's Baptist congregation sought to evade detection by moving from house to house, meeting variously at 'Brother Tassell's', 'Brother Cooke's', and 'Sister Charringboul's'. The law was only spasmodically enforced. In 1669 Taylor and three fellow ministers were sent to prison, but a sympathetic gaoler let them out from time to time to preach. An episcopal survey that year reported that at least five hundred Independents met to worship in St Peter's and St Paul's parishes and that there were Presbyterian, Baptist, and Quaker congregations elsewhere in the city. Three years later the king issued a declaration which made dissenting worship legal. Thomas Ventris and Robert Beake were granted licences to preach in 'Mr Roper's Hall in the parish of St Dunstan's', while John Durant was allowed to hold services in the old almonry of St Augustine's Abbey. But this concession was short-lived. Parliament insisted that the king withdraw his statement, and holding services outside the established church was banned once again.

Another legacy of the previous twenty years was the dilapidated state of city buildings, not least the cathedral. With the re-establishment of deans, chapters, and bishops, Thomas Turner, who had been appointed dean of Canterbury in 1643, was at last able to take up his post. He made up for lost time with a vigorous restoration programme, ably assisted by William Somner, whose detailed knowledge proved invaluable to the newly appointed chapter. Years before, Somner had rescued pieces of the font which a mob had vandalised; this was now reconstructed. Medieval glass, which had been hidden during the Interregnum, was restored to the choir windows; pews were repaired, an organ installed, and new hangings, cushions, plate, and service books acquired. By the end of 1662 the chapter had spent over £5,000 restoring the cathedral. The new archbishop, William Juxon, gave money to repair the Christ Church Gate and extended his beneficence to the city. The doors of St George's Gate, Burgate, and West Gate had all been burnt down in 1648. Somner's brother, John, persuaded the archbishop to pay for replacements.

Engraving of William Somner.
Courtesy of the Chapter of Canterbury Cathedral.

John Somner, a well-to-do tailor, played his own part in the refurbishment of his native town. In 1665 he provided 'four hundred pounds and upwards' for a market house to be built on the site of the old market cross, which had been pulled down twenty years earlier. The new building, 'a piece of such Elegancy as much commends the Architect', had an open ground storey, two upstairs rooms which could be used for meetings, and a loft where grain could be stored to provide for the poor in times of hardship. Somner offered to lay in the initial stock of corn himself – but specified that it should be earmarked for six outlying

Archbishop Juxon's arms, carved on the doors of the Christ Church Gate contain four 'blackamoor' heads – probably reflecting family involvement in colonial and overseas trade. *Photograph by Sheila Sweetinburgh.*

parishes, along with St Alphege, 'because I was born there'. As the donor of the market house, Somner assumed that he could lay down rules about its use. He was annoyed when the Burghmote challenged his views about what should be sold there and jibbed at his request that he and his brother should have special rights to one of the upper rooms.

There were numerous quarrels within the city's ruling elite in the decades following the restoration of the monarchy: some personality conflicts, some reflecting tensions from the past, some a combination of the two. In 1675 an altercation between the mayor and Thomas Hardres, the city's recorder and one of its MPs, started over an apparently trivial matter. The mayor had ruled that St George's parish should support a woman with an illegitimate child, but Hardres issued a warrant for her to be taken to St Andrew's instead. The dispute escalated when Hardres asserted (wrongly) that the mayor had not sworn required oaths and refused to preside alongside him over the quarter sessions (even though they had officiated together three months earlier). The mayor's supporters retaliated by appointing Paul Barrett as recorder in Hardres' place. Hardres

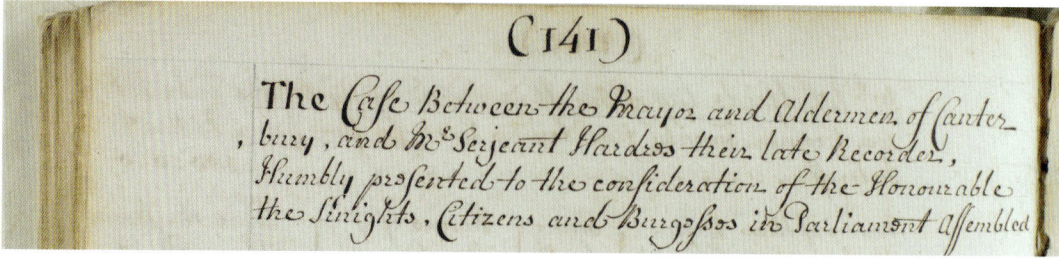

(141)

The Case Between the Mayor and Aldermen of Canterbury, and Mr Serjeant Hardres their late Recorder, Humbly presented to the consideration of the Honourable the Knights, Citizens and Burgesses in Parliament assembled

A copy of Thomas Hardres' appeal to Parliament from William Gray's eighteenth-century notebook. *Courtesy of the Chapter of Canterbury Cathedral.*

invoked his status as an MP and accused the council of breaching House of Commons privilege. Barrett, the mayor, and some aldermen were jailed for treating Parliament with contempt. They protested that as a result of this, 'the Government of the City is Neglected, and there is nobody to hold Sessions, or administer Justice'.

Clashes such as these show that Canterbury remained a conflicted community long after the Civil War had ended. The wrangling became particularly intense in the years after 1678, when Parliament made several unsuccessful attempts to exclude the king's Catholic brother, James, from the throne. The 'Exclusion Crisis' aroused fears that the country might once again be plunged into civil war, and suspicion mounted of any groups whose loyalty was doubted. Sir William Rooke, a Canterbury gentleman, bombarded government officials with letters complaining about 'fanatics' (his favourite word). To Rooke's horror, Jacob Wraight, the son-in-law of the Independent pastor John Durant (whom Rooke regarded as 'a leading rebel from his cradle'), was elected mayor in 1681. Rooke believed that Durant was guilty of regicide, even though (unlike some of his congregation) he had not petitioned for the king's execution. Now Rooke claimed: 'By the industry and cunning of the Nonconformist preachers and their party they have got themselves so into power in Canterbury, that the loyal inhabitants signify very little, being outvoted in all the elections'.

There is very little evidence to support Rooke's claims that 'the implacable dissenters' dominated the city council. Since 1661 civic office had been restricted to men who demonstrated their loyalty by receiving the Church of England sacrament. In the frenzied atmosphere of the early 1680s there were renewed attempts to enforce this requirement. Four members of the Canterbury council who refused to comply were dismissed, but others, including Jacob Wraight, eventually agreed to take Anglican communion. There is very little correlation between lists of councillors and those who were listed as members of Durant's church. Lidia Garlin, the wife of Wraight's predecessor, was a member of the church but her husband was described as 'not of us'. Jacob Wraight's name does not appear in the church's list of members. He may of course have attended dissenting services without becoming a member. But there is no reason to believe that he shared his father-in-law's views. On 3 June 1682 he assured the government that: 'The generality of this city are loyal, peaceable and obedient ... The magistrates dare vie in loyalty with the highest and hottest pretenders.' His letter reads as a deliberate riposte to men such as Rooke who 'pretended' that they alone were loyal. It seems likely that Rooke labelled anyone who had the slightest dissenting connection or was in any way sympathetic to dissent as a 'fanatic'. Other members of the Church of England viewed the situation very differently. The dean of Canterbury, John Tillotson, who was to become archbishop in 1691, wanted to include as many people as possible in a broad-based national church. Tillotson's open-mindedness extended even to Quakers, whom he regarded as 'mistaken, yet in the main ... very honest'. It is impossible to tell how much support there was in the city for Rooke's hard-line views and how much for Dean Tillotson's more conciliatory outlook.

What is clear is that government attitudes to dissenters hardened in the closing years of Charles' reign. The Independent Church Book contained no entries for over a decade after 1678, just one bald statement: 'then followed persecution and Mr Durant Our Pastor & some others went to Holland and some forsook the Church'. The local militia was instructed to stop dissenters meeting for worship. In June 1682 the archbishop was informed that 'there have been noe conventicles here for some months known publicly, except some desperate Quakers'. The Quakers were regularly hauled out of their meeting and warned that if they persisted in gathering to worship, soldiers would 'burne ye things in ye meeting rooms

Entry in the Kent Book of Sufferings for 16 August 1681 recording that Quakers returned to their meeting room, even before the threatening soldiers left. *Society of Friends, East and West Kent Area Meetings.*

and pull it downe'. The doors and windows of the hired house in which the congregation met were nailed up, but the Quakers gathered, undaunted, week after week in the street outside the building. One of the militia captains, Joseph Roberts, threatened that if he found them there again he would make them stand for three hours by the riverside 'if it were never so bitter wether'.

The renewed attack on dissenters was accompanied by measures designed to increase royal power over the composition of town councils. In 1684 Canterbury was one of many corporations required to surrender its charter in return for a new one – which cost the city £248 10s. 2d. Half of the aldermen who took up office under the terms of the new charter had not been members of the Burghmote before, among them Joseph Roberts, scourge of Quakers, and William Rooke, antagonist of dissenters of any kind. Rooke was made mayor and the following year received a knighthood.

Amidst all the acrimony and turmoil of the Restoration years, the council continued to carry out its normal responsibilities. The 'foulness of the river' was a recurrent cause of concern. In 1673 Burghmote members decided to provide carts, horses, and labourers at their own expense to clean the Stour, which was 'almost swollen up for want of cleansing'. The following year the chief inhabitants of the city were approached to see what they would donate for the same purpose. Another health hazard was the 'Black Dike' by the Dane John fields, which had 'always been used for laying of Dirt Filth and Sullage arising in the city'. The Burghmote decided that it should continue to serve this purpose but imposed heavy fines on anyone who tried to bury dead horses or carrion there. The most serious threat to health came, of course, from plague, but Canterbury seems to have fared far better in the epidemic of 1665/66 than coastal towns such as Deal, which was very badly hit. Restrictions were imposed on who could enter the city, a tax was levied to support victims and, as on previous occasions, isolation tents were erected on the Dane John fields. Fire was another persistent hazard: in 1677 a collection was made to cover the cost of two fire engines, and some fifteen years later the city acquired another machine, bequeathed by its inventor, Canterbury lawyer John Whitfield. As well as taking precautions against natural hazards such as these, the council also tried to protect citizens against anti-social behaviour. Was it a particular incident or a recurrent issue which prompted the 1685 ruling 'Every person who shall hereafter keep any Bull Dog or Masstiff Dog within the City shall keep such Dogs tied up or muzzled on pain of forfeiting to the Mayor and Commonalty 3s 4d daily for his Neglect'?

The second half of the 1680s brought major changes to Canterbury. In 1685 Louis XIV revoked the Edict of Nantes, which had granted French Protestants – Huguenots – protection for nearly a century. What had been a steady trickle of refugees became a flood as desperate people hurried to escape, some travelling with nothing but the clothes they were wearing. Canterbury was an obvious destination, in easy reach of the coast and with a flourishing French-speaking church. The Walloon congregation had a long tradition of aiding fellow exiles: its accounts listed gifts of money, food, clothing, medicine, and, sadly, shrouds, which it provided for 'les Français'. Some of the French exiles subsequently moved to London, but the Trouillard family, who fled from Guines, near Calais, were among those who made Canterbury their home. Pierre Trouillard served as pastor of the Canterbury church from 1686 to 1699. Five of his children had been baptised in Guines, but six more were born in Canterbury. Like their predecessors a hundred years before, the new refugees became a significant presence in the city. Canterbury had the largest foreign community in England outside London, maybe numbering as many as three thousand in the years after 1685.

The other pivotal event in 1685 was the death of Charles II and the accession of his brother James. Fears of Catholic 'tyranny' were still widespread, no doubt reinforced by the stories Huguenot refugees told of their sufferings in France. Such fears were soon to be realised, as James started to act autocratically in ways disturbingly reminiscent of Charles I. He overruled a law which banned Catholics from serving as army officers and prorogued Parliament when it objected – as his father had done in 1629. Edward Hales, a Catholic from Canterbury, became an officer and even featured in a court case which the king staged to prove that Catholics had the right to serve. James secured the result he wanted by removing six of twelve judges. He also ignored regulations which barred Catholics from civil office and replaced many existing officials with his co-religionists. Edward Hales became deputy lieutenant of Kent and a Justice of the Peace.

In 1687 the Canterbury Burghmote was one of many town councils which were required once again to surrender their charters. The king wanted to increase toleration for fellow Catholics and ordered the dismissal of hard-line Anglicans such as William Rooke, who had been appointed to the council only a few years earlier. John Kingsford, a member of Durant's congregation, became the new mayor of Canterbury. In the same year a royal Declaration of Indulgence granted freedom of worship for both Roman Catholics and dissenters. Canterbury Quakers promptly acquired

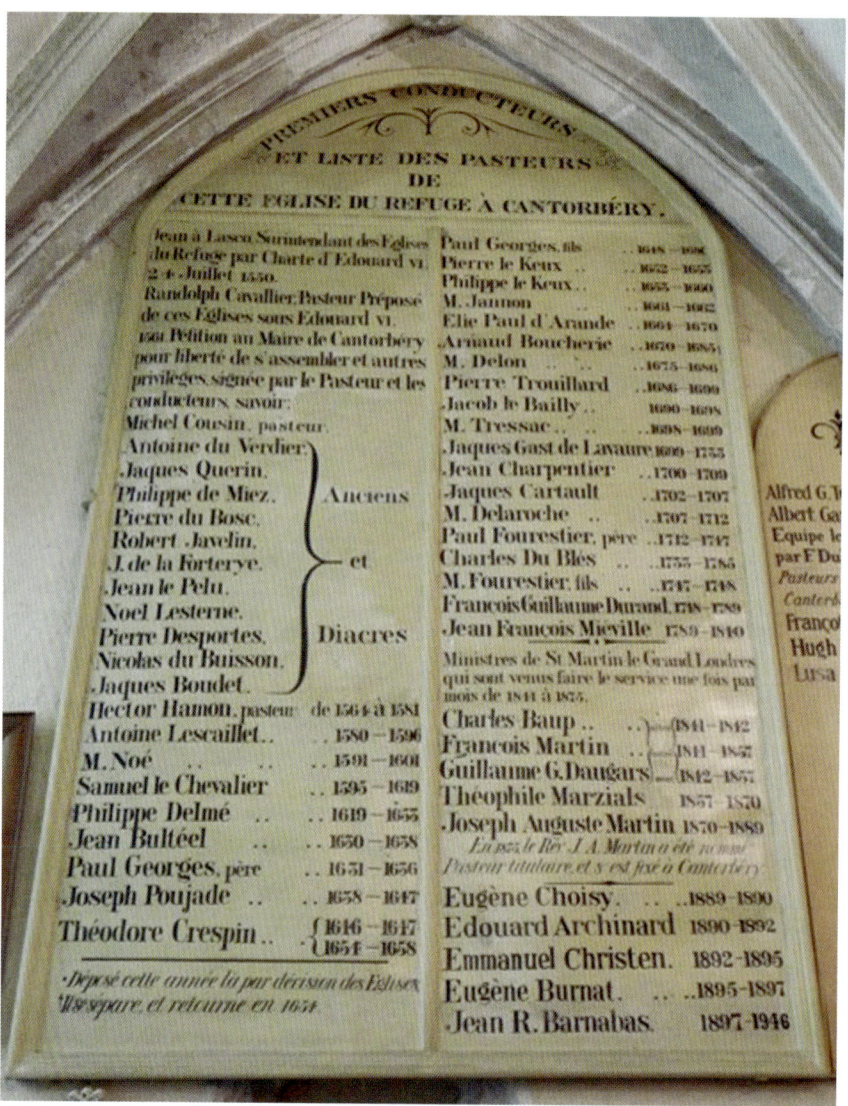

Pierre Trouillard, a recent refugee from Guines, features on the list of pastors displayed in the chapel of the French church in Canterbury cathedral crypt. *By permission of the Consistoire of the Église Protestante Wallonne et Huguenote de Canterbury.*

two cottages in Canterbury Lane and converted them into a meeting house. Dissenters benefited from these royal decisions, but many of them shared the unease of other citizens at the king's failure to work through or even consult Parliament.

Growing concern came to a head on 10 June 1688, when James' wife gave birth to a son. Had the baby not been born, the crown would have passed in due course to the king's Protestant daughter Mary, the wife of William of Orange. Now, however, it seemed that a Catholic dynasty would be perpetuated. The Canterbury Burghmote noted with a marked lack of enthusiasm: 'The Mayor is to cause a Bonfire to be made in Dungeon Hill and Wine is to be drank on Sunday next in the Evening it being a Day appointed for Thanksgiving on the Birth of the Prince.'

As national opinion turned against him, James made a last-ditch attempt to appease his disgruntled subjects by revoking some of his earlier orders. In Canterbury as elsewhere, aldermen and councillors who had lost their seats a few months before were restored to their places. John Kingsford ceased to be mayor. These belated reversals in policy were not enough to save James. As more and more eminent men turned to his son-in-law, William, he decided to abandon his country and his throne. In December 1688 Edward Hales escorted the king from London to Faversham, where another Canterbury man, William Rooke, was among those who waited on him. Royal hopes of sailing to France were thwarted when Hales was recognised. James was taken back to the capital but departed again a few days later with the glad connivance of William of Orange.

The accession of William and Mary enabled the country to move into a new era, less burdened by the legacy of civil war. Protestants who dissented from the national church were given the right to worship as they wished. In 1696 the Canterbury Independents erected a purpose-built meeting house on land donated by John Kingsford in Dancing School Yard (now a disabled car park behind the Beaney House of Art and Knowledge). John Durant, who had been their pastor since 1646, lived just long enough to see William and Mary become king and queen. William Rooke, whose hatred of dissenters dated back to the Civil War and the Protectorate, died two years later. As men who remembered the war passed away, a new generation of Canterbury citizens looked forward to the future. They celebrated the advent of a new reign in time-honoured fashion, with a sumptuous banquet at the Red Lion and the joyful clamour of cathedral bells.

8

An Eighteenth-
Century Town

1697

Celia Fiennes rides towards Canterbury, wondering what the city will be like. She has visited so many places. How will Canterbury compare with Bath, with Salisbury, or with Winchester? And will her lodgings be comfortable?

Celia Fiennes was an enthusiastic traveller. In the late seventeenth and early eighteenth centuries she journeyed to different parts of England, observing 'the pleasant prospects, good buildings, different produces and manufactures' of each place she visited. Her impressions of Canterbury, which she described as 'a noble Citty', were generally favourable. She noted its high gates, long streets, and handsome buildings ('very neat but not very lofty'), and admired its 'fine walks and seates and places for the musick'. But she was not impressed by its newest attraction, the mineral springs, which had been discovered just four years before she came. These were apparently praised by some visitors but others, like Celia herself, 'find it an ill water'. She only drank 'halfe a glass of it which I did not like'.

The late seventeenth and eighteenth centuries were a time of urban renaissance. Provincial towns became increasingly affluent and developed into recreational centres with enhanced facilities both for their own social elites and for prospective visitors. Canterbury shared in this renaissance, but it was never able to compete with fashionable spas such as Bath or with the other archiepiscopal seat, York, or even with its upstart neighbour Tunbridge Wells. Its mineral springs (on the site of today's Pound Lane car park) were open to the public during the summer season, but according to a late eighteenth-century chronicler, William Gostling, 'were never so much in fashion as to crowd the town with visitors'.

For centuries Canterbury's importance had rested on its ecclesiastical position. By the eighteenth century this was more nominal than real. Archbishops visited the city only occasionally and some did not even attend their own enthronements, being installed instead by proxy. The archbishop's palace had been badly damaged in the Civil War, and the site now contained carpenters' and masons' yards, along with several dwelling houses. If an archbishop needed to spend time in Canterbury for a diocesan visitation, he lodged either at the deanery or at an inn.

Engraving of Canterbury Cathedral, based on a drawing by Thomas Johnson *c.* 1656, showing the spire on the north-west tower which was damaged in the 'Great Storm' of 1703. *Courtesy of the Chapter of Canterbury Cathedral.*

The cathedral itself remained a real attraction. Celia Fiennes compared it with others she had seen and praised the windows in the choir as the 'most delicately painted as ever I saw'. When she visited in 1697 the north-west tower was still capped with a tall spire, but this was badly damaged in the 'Great Storm' of 1703 and had to be taken down. Even more powerful than the hurricane which devastated the south of the country in October 1987, the storm of 26–27 November caused a swathe of destruction across central and southern England. Queen Anne described it as 'a Calamity so Dreadful and Astonishing, that the like hath not been Seen or Felt, in the Memory of any Person Living in this Our Kingdom'. Daniel Defoe, the author of *Robinson Crusoe*, visited Canterbury in 1724. Like many other visitors before and since, he thought that the cathedral looked 'venerable and majestic at a distance, as well as when we come nearer to it'. Half a century later, William Gostling devoted a substantial part of his *Walk in and about the City of Canterbury* to a detailed description of the cathedral. His 1774 book was part of a growing genre of antiquarian and historical studies through which towns drew attention to their own distinctive identities.

One of the things that particularly struck Celia Fiennes about Canterbury was its industrial productivity. It was, she reported, a 'flourishing city' with 'good tradeing in the Weaving of Silks: I saw 20 Loomes in one house with severall fine flower'd silks'. The silk trade, which had benefited from the influx of Huguenot refugees, was at its height at the time she visited, but she would have been less sanguine had she come a few years later. By the second decade of the eighteenth century, English weavers were complaining that materials produced in India were 70 per cent cheaper than theirs, partly because Indian labourers were paid less than tuppence a day. To make matters worse, import restrictions were sabotaged by 'evil designing men', smugglers who evaded customs duties. As it became increasingly hard to sell home-produced cloth, weavers from Canterbury and other provincial cities moved to Spitalfields in London. In 1719 the Canterbury Silk-Weavers Company reported that twenty-five years earlier there had been around a thousand looms in the city, but that now there were only 334.

As silk-weaving declined, another industry was developing. Celia Fiennes observed 'great Hopyards on both sides of the Road' between Sittingbourne and Canterbury, and commented on the 'great quantetyes of that fruite' harvested in 1797. A quarter of a century later, Defoe was surprised how quickly and extensively hop-growing had spread into the area. Many inhabitants, he said, could remember when

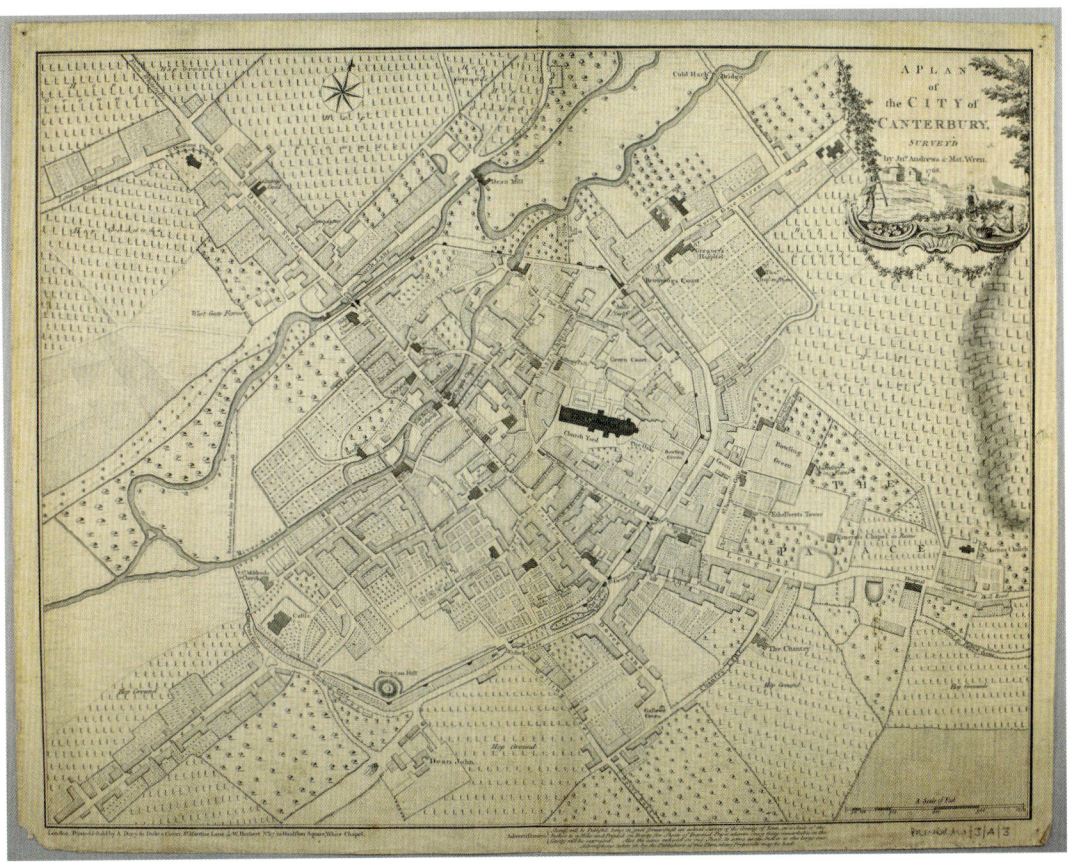

1768 plan of Canterbury by John Andrews and Matthew Wren, showing proximity of hop fields to city walls. *Courtesy of the Chapter of Canterbury Cathedral.*

there was not an acre of land planted with hops in the whole neighbourhood, or so few as not to be worth naming; whereas I was assured that there are at this time near six thousand acres of ground so planted within a very few miles of the city; I do not vouch the number, and I confess it seems incredible, but I deliver it as I receiv'd it.

Local tradesmen cultivated an acre or two of hops alongside their other jobs, and eighteenth-century maps show hop gardens right up to the city walls. In 1766 a new charter established a weekly hop market in the city, which made Canterbury the centre of the hop trade in east Kent. Neighbouring farmers came to buy and sell other products too. Gostling recorded that a live cattle market was held every Saturday, while Wednesday and Saturday markets in the Bullstake supplied the town 'with all articles of the poultry kind, as well as garden stuff, and the fruits of the season, from the country around us'.

Canterbury's role as regional centre for east Kent was reinforced in the eighteenth century by the publication of the city's first newspaper, the *Kentish Post or Canterbury News-letter*. The Licensing Act, which had restricted printing to London, Oxford, Cambridge, and York, had lapsed in 1695; thereafter printing presses were established in towns throughout the country. The *Kentish Post*, which appeared for the first time in 1717, was one of the early provincial papers. Most of these were produced weekly, but within four or five years of its foundation the *Kentish Post* was issued twice a week, the only one of some two dozen newspapers of the day to appear as often as this. Its printer, James Abree, was an enterprising man. In 1722 he tried to boost sales by serialising Defoe's latest novel, *Moll Flanders*. Abree was well aware that Canterbury was too small to support a newspaper by itself, and so he named his paper for the county as well as the city. His newsmen travelled around the region twice each week, selling the current edition and collecting advertisements for the next. It was hard to make

Kentish Post masthead. *Courtesy of the Chapter of Canterbury Cathedral.*

a living through printing alone, so Abree, like many other printers, also ran a stationery shop which supplied books and patent medicines which he obtained from London. His network of newsmen delivered a London monthly, the *Gentleman's Magazine*, medicines, and a variety of other products as well as the *Kentish Post* to inns and shops throughout east Kent.

Canterbury acted as a hub not only for the regional newspaper but also for transport. The *Kentish Post* carried regular advertisements for 'flying machines', stagecoaches which conveyed travellers from inns in Canterbury to London and back. Carriers emphasised the particular comforts they could offer, such as 'a new machine hung on six springs to carry 6 passengers'. Additional comfort was desirable since the journey took around eleven hours: in 1771 the *Gentleman's Magazine* noted that coaches which left London at 5 a.m. were scheduled to reach Canterbury around four in the afternoon. Prices varied depending on the number of seats, but people prepared to brave the elements and sit outside could travel half price, as could children on their parents' laps. Horses had to be changed several times, necessitating a good supply of animals, hence the postscript to one advertisement: 'Wanted about April or May in Canterbury a yard

Nineteenth-century painting of a stage coach (artist unknown). *Dover Museum and Bronze Age Boat Gallery.*

with stabling for 20 or 30 horses.' Other carriers offered transport within Kent, to places such as Elham, Faversham, and Maidstone. During the season, William Brett ran a daily service from Margate to Canterbury – and guaranteed to wait for the London coach before making the return journey. The creation of turnpike trusts did much to improve conditions of travel by levying tolls for the upgrading and maintenance of roads. Toll gates were erected on the main London route between Canterbury and Chatham in 1730 and on the Canterbury to Whitstable road in 1736. Subsequently tolls were introduced on journeys to Ashford (in 1762) and to Dover (in 1791). Canterbury's location on the main thoroughfare from London to France via Dover had always been one of its great assets, and eighteenth-century improvements in transport brought additional prosperity to the city.

Affluence was evident as early as 1697 when Celia Fiennes visited. Many of the city buildings, she noted, were made of brick. Less damp and draughty than older timber-frame structures, brick houses were increasingly favoured by more well-to-do citizens. Another sign of rising prosperity was the growth of luxury trades: by the 1770s Canterbury was well supplied with silver- and whitesmiths, clock- and watchmakers, glovers and mantua makers. The city also had eleven peruke makers. Such trades could only flourish where there was a large enough class of inhabitants with money to spend. According to Edward Hasted, the author of a late eighteenth-century survey of Kent, 'many gentlemen of fortune and genteel families' resided in Canterbury, 'and throughout the whole place there is a great deal of courtesy and hospitality'. Numerous privately run schools sprang up to educate the children of such people: Job Lawrence advertised that youths could be 'genteely boarded' at his school in Dancing School Yard, while Jane Gorsses offered young ladies boarding facilities, classes in French and English, and 'all manner of needlework'. Other opportunities to study French were provided for young gentlemen by the minister of the French church and for young ladies at John Chevallier's boarding house. In 1751 Chevallier was one of two London teachers who announced that they were opening dancing schools in Canterbury. He claimed that he had taught in the best schools in the capital for the last twelve years and was well qualified to teach dances practised both in London and at court.

Dancing was a desirable accomplishment since Canterbury was the recreational centre to which the leisured classes of east Kent gravitated to socialise with people of similar status. Country gentlemen brought their families to the city, maybe hoping that their daughters would attract desirable suitors. In 1718, soon after his arrival in Canterbury, James Abree printed *A Panegyrical Poem: on the fair and celebrated beauties in and about the city of Canterbury,* which opened with the words

> Canterbury!
> The Seat of Vertue, and of Love's Fair Birth;
> The Mansion of the Gods, when here on earth!
> I sing thy Beauties Praise.

The anonymous author then proceeded to celebrate – by name – over thirty girls, members of the city's social elite:

> No supercilious Frown fair MILLS does bear,
> But gentle Sweetness in each Charm shines clear …
> Take up the Glass and fill to HALES's charms;
> There's something in her Face that strangely warms!

'I bet the wenches must have been pleased to see themselves in print,' observed William Urry, the city archivist, centuries later.

The recreations such young ladies would have enjoyed are described in the letters of Elizabeth Carter, a future member of the Bluestocking Society and friend of Samuel Johnson. Elizabeth had lived in Canterbury for a year as a girl, and she returned periodically in the 1740s to visit friends in the city. Their style of life bore clear resemblance to that which Jane Austen was later to depict in her novels. Assemblies (which often did not finish until 2 or 3 a.m.) provided plenty of opportunity for conversation and flirting, for dancing and listening to music, for playing cards and drinking tea. On one occasion Elizabeth was 'well-entertained with talking for 6 hours', but on another 'heartily fatigued'. The assemblies she attended were probably held in an inn, but in 1750 Canterbury, like other aspiring social centres, acquired purpose-built assembly rooms. Gostling described these as 'perhaps the largest and most elegant assembly room built by a private owner in the kingdom', but his claim was probably a product of local pride rather than dispassionate judgement.

Another favoured leisure pursuit was watching plays. In the 1730s the upper storey of the market hall, which John Somner had built seventy years before, was converted into a theatre. The playhouse was tiny, but for over half a century it offered a variety of entertainment, ranging from Shakespeare to slapstick pantomime. In 1744 people in Canterbury had the opportunity to see Charles Macklin, one of the famous actors of the day, perform the role of Shylock, for which he was particularly celebrated.

1768 watercolour by Samuel Grimm depicting fashionable visitors in the cathedral precincts. *Courtesy of the Chapter of Canterbury Cathedral.*

It was common for two plays to be presented back to back, and so the last performance of *The Merchant of Venice* was followed immediately by 'a Farce, called *The Devil to Pay*: or *The Wives Metamorphos'd*'. Attendance at the theatre was not confined to the superior classes. They paid two shillings and sixpence to sit in boxes or on the stage, but artisans and shopkeepers could probably afford sixpence for seats just a few yards away.

As well as assembly rooms and theatres, any eighteenth-century town which catered for the growing leisured classes needed its own pleasure gardens, modelled on the famous Vauxhall and Ranelagh Gardens in London. In July 1752 the *Kentish Post* reported that 'Pursuant to an Advertisement inserted in this Paper, VAUX-HALL Garden near this City was Open'd on Thursday last, by the Gentlemen of the Musical Society of this Place, with a Concert of Vocal and Instrumental Musick.' The writer anticipated that 'with proper encouragement from the Nobility and Gentry and the further generous Assistance of the Musical Gentlemen of this City and Neighbourhood', the garden, with its 'elegant Improvements ... Walks and Plantations', might 'become in Time, if not equal to, yet deservedly as famous, and as favourite a Spot, as any of the kind in the Kingdom', a clear articulation of Canterbury's social aspirations.

The main event in the city's recreational calendar was the annual race meeting, which was held a few miles away on Barham Downs every summer from the 1730s onwards. So many racecourses were established at this time that in 1740 legislation was introduced to reduce their number: it specified that in future all prizes must be worth at least £50. Many courses disappeared, but the Canterbury races survived. Hasted recorded that they were

> attended by most of the Kentish gentry and a great number of people from the neighbouring parts; and this city being their usual rendezvous, it brings a vast concourse of them to it for the time when there are plays, and other entertainments, during the whole time of the race week.

'The Canterbury Races' by Thomas Rowlandson (1757–1827). ©*Canterbury Museums and Galleries.*

Among the visitors from further afield at the 1765 races were the Mozart family. The *Kentish Post* advertised a concert in the town hall at 11 a.m. on Thursday 25 July featuring 'Master Mozart, the celebrated German Boy aged eight years and his Sister who have exhibited with universal Applause to the Nobility and Gentry in London'. It appears, however, that the young Mozart caught a cold and the concert never took place.

Assemblies, plays, and races were not the only recreations on offer. Bourne Park, the mansion at which the Mozarts stayed, a few miles outside the city, was a popular venue for cricket matches. The *Post*'s first reference to a match in Canterbury itself came in 1762, when the gentlemen of the city challenged those of Dover to a game at St Stephen's fields. By Gostling's day there was a skittle ground, a fives court, and a bowling green in the once sacred premises of St Augustine's Abbey – and even a cockpit in the 'great room over the gate'. Cockfighting was a popular pastime, and fights were regularly advertised in the *Kentish Post*, often between the 'Gentlemen of Canterbury' and those of neighbouring towns. Many took place in inns, which had always been focal points of community life: business was transacted, news disseminated, meetings held, and celebratory feasts consumed. The *Post* carried frequent advertisements from the various inns for 'Auricula Feasts', competitions between keen polyanthus growers which were invariably accompanied by a meal. Travelling showmen (such as a puppeteer who put on plays with over fifty 'Lilliputian figures') performed at inns, and there were also travelling exhibitions. A 'collection of curious wild creatures', including a camel and two ostriches, was displayed at the Golden Fleece in 1750, and waxworks representing the royal family the following year. Every Wednesday evening from October to May a 'Catch Club' met at the Prince of Orange tavern to sing 'catches' or 'glees' and to listen to an orchestra led by the landlord, John Goodban. Gentlemen's clubs of this kind were increasingly popular in the second half of the eighteenth century, but in its early days the Canterbury club, which Goodban founded in 1779, appears to have embraced a wider range of members than others. John Marsh, a lawyer turned country gentleman, recorded in his journal that members paid sixpence for each evening's entertainment (whether or not they attended), which entitled them to 'an unlimited quantity of pipes & tobacco & beer ... in consequence of which many of the members, amongst the lower kinds of tradesmen ... go at 6 and smoke away till 11 or 12'. The strong smell of smoke permeated other members' clothes, so much so that 'Mr Knowler used to keep an old drab coat to put on those occasions w'ch he used to call his Catch Club coat'.

Lithograph commissioned to celebrate Canterbury Catch Club, 1826. ©*Canterbury Museums and Galleries.*

John Marsh's journals provide a vignette of life in Canterbury in the mid-1780s. He and other keen musicians met regularly in each other's homes to play ensembles, and he also took over the organisation of fortnightly subscription concerts which were held throughout the winter months. (Half of these were for gentlemen only but the others – scheduled for moonlit nights – were also open to ladies.) Marsh was a composer as well as an instrumentalist, and some of his recorded work is still available today, as are pieces for the viola written by a Canterbury bookseller, William Flackton. Visiting musicians from London were sometimes invited to perform at the concerts, but most of the city's music-making, like that of other provincial towns, depended on local talent. Marsh was not always complimentary about his colleagues: he noted that Mr Philpot, the dancing master, Mr Williamson, a surgeon, and Mr Goodban, the publican, were all competent string players, but Mr Burnby, a mercer, played neither in time nor in tune, while Mr Sharpe was a rather timid cellist. He was even more critical of the city's supposedly genteel society:

> the style of living being for gentlemen to dine together and meet at whist or smoking clubs almost every evening at different inns ... only joining the ladies at immense routs where, owing to the largeness of the circle at Canterbury, the rooms were generally much crowded and the spirit of card-playing ... carried to excess.

After a few years Marsh sold the estate in Kent which he had inherited and relocated to Chichester, where he lived for the rest of his life.

The social round, despised by John Marsh, was only one aspect of Canterbury life. There was also provision for people who enjoyed more bookish pursuits. In 1769 John Callaway, a master silk-weaver (who boosted the ailing industry by devising 'Canterbury muslin'), helped found a 'Society for the Cultivation of Useful Knowledge'. Members agreed 'to read such books, make such experiments and debate such matters ... as shall be thought best for our instruction, pleasure or amusement'. They met each Monday evening to hear readings on any subject 'serviceable to mankind'. The society developed its own library, and there were also several circulating libraries in the city, run by bookseller-stationers such as the viola-playing William Flackton. James Simmons' library alone contained around 3,500 volumes. Simmons and some of the other booksellers were also printers. William Gostling's *Walk in and about the City of Canterbury* and Edward Hasted's multi-volume *History and Topographical Survey of the County of Kent* were two of many works published in the city.

Notwithstanding its active social, cultural, and recreational life, its flourishing hop industry, and its position as a staging post for coaches, Canterbury was a far less significant place in the late eighteenth century than it had been in earlier times. In 1500 it had been one of the ten most populous provincial towns. In 1700 it was still within the top twenty, but by the end of the century it was surpassed by at least thirty other towns, some of which were many times its size. Estimates suggest that Canterbury's population in the late seventeenth century was something in excess of seven thousand. A hundred years later, some 11,500 people lived in the city and its immediate suburbs, but by then Manchester and Liverpool each had more than 75,000 inhabitants. The city's decline in ranking was paralleled in other market towns throughout the south of England. But Canterbury's position was changing even within its own county. Maidstone, which had been only half Canterbury's size at the start of the century, was fast catching up. Well placed to meet growing demands for food from the capital, it had, according to Defoe, 'the best market in the county, not Rochester, no not Canterbury excepted'. The most fashionable place of recreation in Kent was the purpose-built resort of Tunbridge Wells. In 1735 Beau Nash, who had transformed the fortunes of Bath, became Master of Ceremonies at 'The Wells'. The following year more persons of quality flocked there for its summer season than ever before, dukes and duchesses, earls and barons among them. Canterbury was never in this class. Like many other cathedral cities and regional centres, however, it played a significant role as the social capital of its own area. With its new facilities – assembly rooms, a theatre, pleasure gardens, a racecourse – it catered well for its own genteel residents and for those of its hinterland, providing a range of recreational activity through the winter as well as the summer months. During race week, in particular, it attracted visitors from all over the county. Spending by the leisured classes and by stagecoach travellers enhanced its economy, as did the week-by-week trading of local producers at city markets. Eighteenth-century Canterbury did not enjoy national eminence, but it was a lively and busy market town, the unchallenged commercial, social, and cultural hub of east Kent.

9

GOVERNING THE CITY

1 August 1748

William Gray waits uneasily in his home. The mayor and aldermen are meeting at the Guildhall to elect a successor to Alderman Botting. Gray doesn't want to be an alderman – at least not yet – but is fearful that he may be chosen. A knock at the door confirms his fears.

William Gray was a city grocer who kept a notebook in which he commented on contemporary events. He had become a common councillor in 1724 and nearly a quarter of a century later was elected to the upper, aldermanic, tier of the council. He recorded his feelings on this unwelcome promotion in his notebook: 'On the "unlucky first of August"', he wrote, 'Jn Watts esq then Mayor thought fit to name me for an Alderman which was unanimously voted … to my very great concern'.

Gray had good reason to be worried. Holding civic office was regarded as a public duty, and in Canterbury, as elsewhere, men who declined to serve as councillors or aldermen had to pay hefty fines. If he had said no, Gray would have been charged £30, the equivalent of around £2,500 today. In the light of this, he noted, 'I was advised to accept'. He knew that the job he was taking on would be onerous. Each alderman had responsibilities towards one of the city's six wards and could be fined if he failed to attend Burghmote meetings. Only aldermen could serve as mayor and many held this office more than once. Being mayor absorbed at least half the holder's working week, leaving many out of pocket. Ex-mayors continued to serve as city magistrates. The governing elite exercised great power, but they also carried a heavy workload.

Councillors and aldermen were appointed for life. William Gray was a member of the Burghmote for nearly sixty years and only relinquished office shortly before he died, at the age of eighty-nine, in 1784. Men who sought to resign prematurely faced fines, although occasionally members were released because of 'great age'. In 1723 Alderman Bridger was discharged from office without penalty on a plea of ill health, but the Burghmote minutes stressed that this was not to be regarded as a precedent. Some men relinquished their responsibilities because they had moved outside the city boundaries and were no longer eligible to serve. The suburb of St Dunstan's fell under county, not city, jurisdiction so men who moved there had to be discharged from office, as were those who went further afield. This meant that there was some turnover of membership, but Gray was not alone in holding office for a long time.

In Gray's day Canterbury was still governed by a self-perpetuating oligarchy. The names of the same families recur on lists of councillors, generation after generation: William Gray's father had been an alderman before him. When a vacancy arose, either in the common council or on the aldermanic bench, existing members decided who should be approached to fill it. It would be wrong, however, to assume that the Burghmote was a closed shop, excluding other citizens who longed for office. On the contrary, some men preferred to pay the required fine rather than accept nomination. Most councillors were tradesmen: some men who refused to serve may have feared that the demands of office would interfere too much with the needs of their businesses.

While the Burghmote determined its own membership, it had to submit its choice of mayor to the electorate. Each year the aldermen put forward the names of two of their number and invited the city's freemen to choose between them. It was common practice for candidates to 'treat' the electors, who sometimes sought to prolong the period of voting to keep the free drink flowing. In 1780 Gray noted that, on the second day of polling, the freemen were 'slow in voting as they was Yesterday in order to keep it open'. In the eighteenth century, treating was not regarded as corrupt: the vote was a form of property which, like other properties, carried certain rights – such as the provision of free drink. The first time Gray served as mayor, he recorded that the election 'occasion'd me a large Expence'. Elections were generally entertaining affairs, accompanied by parades, music, and drumming, and a good time was had by all – except perhaps the hapless candidates who had to pay for the drink.

Ironically, citizens had more influence over the choice of national than local representatives. By the standards of the time Canterbury had a large electorate, since all freemen were entitled to vote. There were some 1,300 voters in the middle of the century and around 1,700 by 1800. In many constituencies electors rarely, if ever, had the opportunity to cast their votes, as over half the country's MPs were elected unopposed. This was not the case in Canterbury, where every parliamentary election between 1715 and the end of century was contested. Its substantial electorate and a tradition of contested elections ensured that no single interest could control Canterbury. On several occasions sitting MPs lost their seats.

One of the most contentious elections took place in 1734. Sir Thomas Hales, who had served as one of the city's two MPs since 1715, had gone against the advice of city councillors and supported an unpopular government bill to impose excise duty on wine and tobacco. This may have contributed to his defeat in 1734, but Hales had a different explanation. In the eighteenth century there was still no fixed time at which polls closed. In his *Walk in and about the City of Canterbury*, William Gostling explained that voters went to the Guildhall, climbed the staircase on one side of the gallery, announced who they were voting for, and then descended by a staircase on the opposite side. The sheriff, as returning officer, decided when everyone entitled to vote had done so. His choice of when to close the poll could determine the result of the election. On this occasion, Hales claimed that 159 voters who had said they would support him had been unable to get through obstructive crowds to cast their votes. A petition was sent to Parliament, which overturned the result, and Hales was reinstated as one of the city's MPs. This was not the only time that the Canterbury result was challenged. In 1796 the two defeated candidates complained of bribery and intimidation, and the election was declared void.

Nearly all the men who became MPs for Canterbury had local connections. Many were country landowners with estates near the city. When an outsider from the north, William Mayne, stood in 1761, he was defeated. Excited supporters had stressed that his links to the court would benefit the city, but a critic claimed that he was luring voters with unfulfillable promises. As was common at the time he also issued threats, warning that Mr Loftie's lieutenant son would never gain promotion if Loftie voted against him. Mayne was successful when he stood again in 1774 but lost his seat six years later. One of the victorious candidates on that occasion was Alderman George Gipps, who had started life as an apothecary. His election – and that of a prosperous paper-maker as MP for Maidstone – gave rise to a mocking verse, which Gray copied into his notebook:

> When the Freemen of Canterbury made G Gipps their choice
> Those of Maidstone, as free, gave Squire Taylor their voice
> And each Voter avowed he took this Resolution
> As the best way to Save England's Sick Constitution
>   For Gipps he may purge her from all Ills that betide
>   And Taylor find paper to wipe her Backside.

Citizens did not necessarily treat their elected representatives with respect.

The names of people entitled to vote in general elections were recorded in poll books, which show that nearly 40 per cent of electors did not live in Canterbury. Some had homes in suburbs just outside the city boundaries, such as St Dunstan's or Hackington; others had moved to towns and villages elsewhere in Kent, but around 11 per cent of the electorate were residents of London. Many of these men returned to Canterbury for elections, enjoying a free holiday at the expense of candidates who paid for their travel in return for their votes. (Travel expenses, like free drink, were seen as a perquisite of the franchise.) The poll books show that the city's freemen were not confined to the more affluent classes. Quite a few were labourers, maybe men who had acquired their freedom by birth but whose families had gone down in the world. There were some 'gentlemen' and a few surgeons, but the majority of freemen were craftsmen or traders: weavers, tailors, cabinetmakers, tanners, shoemakers, upholsterers, drapers, hairdressers, hatters, bricklayers, millers, brewers, publicans, victuallers, butchers, bakers, or grocers like Gray.

Freemen had trading rights as well as voting rights, but these came at a price, as a doughty cabinetmaker, Thomas Roch, discovered. Roch moved to Canterbury from Ireland and became a freeman in 1745 on payment of a £20 fee. To his dismay, he was also required to pay £4 for membership of the Company of Builders and Carpenters. Guilds of this sort had traditionally protected the trading interests of their members, but by the eighteenth century their role was more recreational than economic. Roch believed that they did little for their members, many of whom could ill afford the annual dues. Most of the money seemed to be spent on feasting and drinking, and after a few years Roch refused to pay. Neither threats nor promises persuaded him to succumb, and a long legal battle ensued. The leaders of several guilds, including the

No.	NAME.	Street or Place.	County.	Profession or Trade.	G	H	B	S
1078	William Bartlett	Waltham	Kent	Yeoman	—		—	
1079	Ralph Tench	Wincheap P.	Canty.	Cordwainer	—		—	
1080	Richard Redwood	Ickham	Kent	Labourer	—	—		
1081	John Williamson	St. Alphage	Canty.	Surgeon	—		—	
1082	Nicholas Blogg	Hawkhurst	Kent	Coach-painter				
1083	John Upton	All Saints	Canty.	Victualler				
1084	Richard Tadman	Northfleet	Kent	Grazier	—			
1085	Thomas Spratt	St. George	Canty.	Labourer				
1086	William Poole	Northgate	ditto	Cordwainer			—	
1087	Thomas F. Lepine	Private in the	East	Kent militia				
1088	William Cooper	Private in the	Somerset	militia				
1089	George Barber	St. George	Canty.	Yeoman	—		—	
1090	William Flackton	St. Alphage	ditto	Stationer	—		—	
1091	William Crosoer	Barham	Kent	Gent.				
1092	John Lucas	Rosemary-lane	Lond.	Cordwainer				
1093	Henry Thornton	St. Mildred	Canty.	Baker	—		—	
1094	Charles Tape	Private in the	Somerset	militia				
1095	Valentine Friend	Southwark	Surry	Tallow-chand.			—	
1096	Richard Hadmans	All Saints	Canty.	Hair-dresser	—			
1097	William Elgar	St. Andrew	ditto	Cordwainer	—			
1098	James Homersham	Westgate	ditto	Carpenter	—			
1099	James Hadmans	Northgate	ditto	Basket-maker	—			
1100	James Olive	St. Dunstan	Kent	Cordwainer	—			
1101	Thomas Burgess	Burgate	Canty.	Labourer				
1102	R. C. G. Skinner	St. Andrew	ditto	Hatter			—	
1103	Edw. Parker, jun.	St. Peter	ditto	Lamp-lighter			—	—
1104	Edward Duthoit	St. Margaret	ditto	Brazier			—	—
1105	Geo. W. Le Grand	Fish-street-hill	Lond.	Linen-draper	—	—		
1106	James Pillow	St. M. Bredm	Canty.	Sadler				
1107	Stephen Chalk	St. George	ditto	Surgeon	—			
1108	Richard Boghurst	Frindsbury	Kent	Grazier	—			
1109	Thomas Goulden	Westgate	ditto	Upholsterer	—			
1110	John Briggs	St. Andrew	Canty.	Linen-draper	—			
1111	Thomas Knell	Bishopsgate	Lond.	Weaver				
1112	Charles Knell	Spitalfields	ditto	ditto				
1113	John Penfold	Dover-lane	Canty.	Labourer			—	—
1114	Henry Irons	Butchery-lane	ditto	Butcher	—		—	
1115	William Porter	Curtain-road	Lond.	Cordwainer	—		—	
1116	Richard Dixon	St. M. Bredm.	Canty.	Baker	—		—	
1117	Edward Hobbs	St. George	ditto	Grocer	—		—	
1118	Paul Stokes	St. George's F.	Lond.	Fruiterer	—		—	
1119	George Kingsford	Portsmouth	Hants	Hatter	—		—	—
					26	24	18	16

E 3

Page from 1796 pollbook. *Courtesy of the Chapter of Canterbury Cathedral.*

master of the builders' company, sat on the city council, which ordered Roch to pay his dues. Roch complained that the council did not give him a chance to make his case and hit out against 'corporation tyranny' in a pamphlet entitled *Proceedings of the Corporation of Canterbury: Shewing the Abuse of Corporation Government*. Roch's belligerence and dogged determination, articulated in long, tedious diatribes, probably won him few friends, but eventually the case against him was dropped. In Canterbury, as elsewhere, men ceased to join trading companies, whose influence steadily declined.

Whether or not Burghmote members deserved Roch's criticism, it is clear that they expended much time and effort on public service. One of the most industrious was Cyprian Rondeau Bunce, who served as mayor in 1789 but whose contribution to the city extended well beyond his own times. Bunce took upon himself the monumental task of collating the city

Cyprian Rondeau Bunce. *Courtesy of the Chapter of Canterbury Cathedral.*

records. He abridged 250 years' worth of Burghmote minutes and, to the immense benefit of later historians, arranged them thematically. His work demonstrates the range of Burghmote activity. Councillors discussed mundane matters such as the time city gates should be opened for dung carts (not 'before 4 in the morning in summer and 6 in the winter'), as well as issues of greater moment such as the construction of a new cut 'cross Wincheap Mead from the River ... of great Service for conveying of the Water to the City Mills'. The minutes recorded decisions relating to the management of the river, the provision and maintenance of conduits and water pipes, and the upkeep of bridges and streets. There were responses to individual requests, such as Lawrence Bridger's application to put up pales in front of his Castle Street house (approved on payment of an annual fee of one shilling providing they were no more than a foot from the building). Other householders who had surreptitiously allowed their properties to encroach into the streets were ordered to cut them back. Sir William Boys was told 'to take away the Frame and Window by him made in the City Wall against the Cattle Market and to work up the Hole'. Records such as these, painstakingly transcribed by Bunce, provide a vignette of life in eighteenth-century Canterbury.

One of the Burghmote's responsibilities was the control of markets and commerce. As in centuries past, it tried to uphold the trading rights of freemen, warning Abraham Gold in 1705 that unless he purchased his freedom within a month he would be prosecuted for selling beer without a licence. Its success in controlling illicit trade of this kind appears to have been limited. Both Thomas Roch and James Abree, who produced the *Kentish Post*, traded for some five years in the city before eventually paying their fees to become freemen. Occasionally the Burghmote authorised people who had not been given the freedom of the city to trade. In 1700 it permitted Michael Crawford to work as a 'soap-boyler' for a year 'to see if he can get a livelihood thereby'; if he could, he would then be required to purchase his freedom. Single women were banned from keeping shop since 'such tolerations are very prejudicial to the Freemen', but from time to time widows were permitted to do so (as long as they remained widows). Some under-age boys were allowed to go on running their dead fathers' businesses until they were old enough to become freemen in their own right. The council was also concerned to ensure that traders did not cheat their customers, hence the purchase of a 'metal Winchester Bushell properly sized & compared with the Standard in the Exchequer ... for all Persons who may wish to ascertain their Measures thereby'. A further way in which the Burghmote controlled trading was by regulating where products could be sold – in the terminology of the day, where people could 'utter and sell their Goods'. In 1739 the council paid for the erection of a new herb market in St Andrew's parish, on the site of the old Salutation Inn. It ruled that the stalls should 'be let to such Fruiterers Gardeners Hucksters and Sellers of Tripe there as shall take or hire the same at 8d a week'. No fruit, herbs, or tripe were to be sold anywhere else.

Another council responsibility was the appointment – and payment – of numerous officials. It appears that menial jobs were often kept within the same family. Hannah Stone, a widow, was appointed market sweeper in 1732, followed by John Stone in 1735, and Elizabeth Stone in 1746. For over fifty years the position of common crier was held by three successive

The West Gate was used as the city gaol. The building to the left of the towers was erected in 1829 to provide extra cells. The West Gate now houses a museum. © ONE POUND LANE (onepoundlane.co.uk).

members of the Hawker family. But the Burghmote was also capable of creative innovation when it combined some posts with other diverse responsibilities. In 1707 the council decided that 'the Prisoners Basket Carrier', who had the job of collecting food for poor prisoners in the West Gate gaol, was also to be 'the Driver of Swine and other Cattle taken in the Streets to the Common'. James Ardon, who was appointed prisoners' basket carrier some forty years later, was charged 'to keep clean the Sewer at King's Bridge'. Like other outdoor workers, he was given 'a new great coat at the city's expense'. New outfits were also regularly ordered for men who held ceremonial responsibilities:

> The Sword Bearer, Mace Bearer, and four Sergeants at the Mace are to have new Hats with dark blue Coats and a narrow gold lace round the Collars and Cuffs with a yellow button bearing the City Arms and a blue Waistcoat with the like buttons. They are to be desired to provide themselves with a neat pair of black Breeches to wear therewith when on Duty.

When not fulfilling such duties these officials, too, performed other functions. In 1792 John Smith was appointed not only mace-bearer but also keeper of the hall, inspector of the water, 'and to take care of the pens in the cattle market'. At the same time, Philip Penn, a sergeant at mace, was charged to act as corn inspector and 'to make the Return of the Prices of Corn and Meal'.

One of the heaviest responsibilities carried by senior Burghmote officials was the exercise of justice. The city had its own quarter sessions as well as several lesser courts. Its county borough status gave it the right to deal with offences as serious as murder which might otherwise have been heard in county courts. One of the mayor's many responsibilities was to preside over all these courts, a task which occupied him at least once a week. Much court time was taken up with relatively trivial matters for which the penalty was often a fine. Thus in 1790, two people were fined five shillings for failing to sweep the pavement in front of their houses. People who did not pay their fines, such as a victualler who cheated his customers by using false measures, were imprisoned until they did pay. Prison sentences as such were rarely imposed and, when they were, tended to be short. A widow who stole a silver spoon was imprisoned for just a fortnight. Other offenders were subjected to corporal punishment: Elizabeth Priest was burnt on the hand for stealing a petticoat. Elizabeth Cook, who was convicted of petty larceny, was sentenced 'to be stripped naked from the

Record of sentence passed on Alice Dawkins, Canterbury Quarter Sessions, 10 January 1791. *Courtesy of the Chapter of Canterbury Cathedral.*

waste upwards and privately whipt' in the gaol. Female modesty was not always preserved since many whippings took place in public, both as a deterrent and as added humiliation. Mary Butt, who was found guilty of theft in 1742, was condemned to be whipped publicly 'until her back be bloodied'. While some whippings took place in busy places such as the corn market, Jane Calman, 'an idle and disorderly person', was whipped 'at the cart's tail' the whole length of the main street from West Gate to St George's Gate. This harsher punishment was also inflicted on a number of small-scale thieves such as William Page, who had stolen a tea kettle.

Occasionally there were hangings in the city. In 1703 the Burghmote accounts recorded the costs of setting up gallows to hang John Busher for stabbing Robert Amsden, while nineteen-year-old Margaret Mantle was put to death in 1754 for murdering her bastard child. Two years earlier Parliament had given courts the right to decide what happened to the bodies of people executed for murder. Margaret's body was handed over to surgeons for dissection 'in a room across the Watter at the Workhouse'. A few people, such as a thirty-nine-year-old soldier, Thomas Stokes, were put to death for robbery, a sentence carried out, like most eighteenth-century hangings in the city, on gallows at Oaten Hill. But death sentences were rare and, even if passed, were often commuted to transportation. In the last two thirds of the eighteenth century just eight people suffered the death penalty in Canterbury.

Much court time was taken up with matters relating to bastardy and settlement: who should support people unable to provide for themselves? In earlier times, each parish had been responsible for its own poor, an arrangement which did not work well as the parishes with least resources were invariably those with the largest number of needy dependants. In 1727 Canterbury took advantage of new legislation which enabled groups of parishes to work together. An act of Parliament was obtained 'for erecting a workhouse in the City of Canterbury for employing and maintaining the Poor there', and the old Poor Priests Hospital was converted into a workhouse for all fourteen parishes in the city. (The act also authorised 'setting up lamps in the most proper places of the same city to burn in the dark nights between Michaelmas and Lady Day'.) A new statutory authority, a Board of Guardians, was established for the administration of poor relief. This was made up of the mayor (yet again), the city recorder, and Justices of the Peace, along with two representatives of each parish, 'to be chosen out of the Ablest and discreetest Inhabitants'. The guardians were independent of the Burghmote (although there was considerable overlap in membership) and controlled their own very substantial income: the poor rate which they levied on city inhabitants amounted to £1,000 or more a

The medieval Poor Priests Hospital which was used as a workhouse. *Ymblanter, Wikimedia Commons.*

year. The guardians had discretion to give relief outside the workhouse to the sick and to others unable to work, but from 1730 they required such recipients to wear 'a Badge on the right sleeve of their upper Garment' bearing the letter P. Workhouse inhabitants, as the name suggested, were expected to work. Contracts were issued to city traders, who employed some of them in tasks such as hop-picking and making hop bags. The workhouse, however, also housed people who were too old, young, or sick to labour. The rules specified that inmates should be fed bread, cheese, and milk, with meat once a week; if they smoked, they should receive a weekly supply of two ounces of tobacco. Alderman Gray, who served as president of the Board of Guardians on numerous occasions, noted that in the year 1751/1752 there were on average two hundred residents a week.

The poor rate was only one way in which eighteenth-century Canterbury provided for its poor. It had long been common for better-off citizens to leave legacies to help the needy, and this practice continued. A bequest by Mrs Bridger made possible the building of six small tenements 'without Newingate' as almshouses for six unmarried women, while James Hiett left funds for ten woollen coats a year for 'aged and infirm' men over fifty. Many of these legacies were entrusted to the mayor and corporation, who had not only to administer them but also to ensure that the funds were appropriately invested. In 1566 a London merchant, Sir Thomas White, had established a trust to help young men in a number of towns set up in business. Once every twenty-four years Canterbury was allocated £104 from this trust, and councillors had to choose four worthy candidates to receive interest-free loans of £25 each. (The remaining £4 was allocated to administrative costs.) After ten years the council reclaimed the capital and lent it out again to another four recipients. Several other legacies operated in a similar fashion. Looking after these charitable bequests took up a considerable amount of council time.

Well-to-do residents not only left money in their wills but also made provision for the public good during their lifetime. Notable among them was Sir John Hales, who in 1733 significantly improved the city's water supply by running pipes from a spring head on his Old Park estate – a gift which was welcomed 'with ringing of bells and much festivity'. The Burghmote offered Sir John the freedom of the city, 'to be presented in a silvergilt box'. This offer was declined, perhaps not surprisingly, as Sir John was becoming a recluse (his body was not discovered in his Hales Place home until some time after his death), but in response to the proposed compliment he sent the corporation a buck from his park. MPs too sometimes made gifts to their constituency, acknowledging the privilege of election while also seeking to elicit future votes. Soon after he was elected, Thomas May, who served from 1734 to 1741, contributed £100 towards the rebuilding of the city's corn market. Gray observed in his notebook that it was customary for each MP to supply the various trade companies with wine for their annual feasts, at a total cost of £38 8s. a year.

Feasting was one of the perquisites of civic office. There were banquets to entertain distinguished visitors and celebrations on significant national occasions such as the king's birthday. In June 1764 George III's twenty-sixth birthday was observed in Canterbury with what the *Kentish Post* called 'the usual rejoicings': three volleys were fired at noon, and in the evening the mayor and corporation drank his majesty's health at the Red Lion with the 'principal inhabitants' of the city. Sometimes the festivities got out of hand. When the archbishop paid a rare visit in 1782 Gray noted that 'Some of the Company Not to their Credit took possession of the Table and Scrambled for the fruit and other good things there provided, like so many hungary Animals, that many persons who had a Claim for a part, was obliged to go without'. He described another contretemps the following year, which arose when a newly elected mayor invited town and country gentlemen to dine with him, but 'omitted the Traders and Freemen of the City which was resented'. In response some 'Spirited freemen' arranged to dine together at the Red Lion tavern where, Gray claimed, they 'Enjoyed themselves in great Harmony'.

Some occasions of national significance were marked by civic processions. Gray recorded:

> War declared with Spain In this City between the hours of Eleven and One Octtober the Twenty Seventh 1739, first at the Guildhall, second at the Bullstake or Butter Market, third at St Andrew's Church, Fourthly and lastly at Iron Cross or the Three Tuns Corner and then we adjourned to the Fountains Tavern and refreshed ourselves after so great fatigue.

Declarations of peace at the same four locations provided opportunity for lavish celebration. When the end of the war was proclaimed on 9 February 1748, Burghmote members and other civic officials, appropriately arrayed in their ceremonial gowns, processed round the city accompanied by a troop of soldiers, the city drummers, a large band of musicians on horseback, and by a 'numerous assembly on foot'. 'The whole City,' Gray wrote, 'was like a Grove with Green Holly and adorned with Costly Garlands.' There was a grand firework display in front of the West Gate, ending with the launch of twenty-four sky rockets – after which Gray and his colleagues adjourned to the King's Head tavern.

Civic festivity sometimes had to be curtailed when money was scarce, a problem afflicting many borough corporations in the eighteenth century. By the early 1740s Canterbury was 'greatly in debt' due to capital outlay on the new herb market, wage costs, and the expense of maintaining highways and buildings. It was proposed that expenditure should be capped at £5 when the king's health was drunk on 'public rejoicing nights' and that 'no Coffee or Tea be allow'd the Mayor and Aldermen as had been for some time usual on a Sunday morning in the back roome before going to Church'. Forty years later, when money was again tight, a Burghmote party the night before the king's birthday was 'discontinued by reason of the Expence'. A more significant way of saving money was to delay paying the mayor's salary. The £100 fee which the mayor was supposed to receive each year probably fell short of the expenses of office, and an incumbent often did not receive it till years later. In 1772 the city owed its ex-mayors £900.

Being an alderman, as Gray realised in 1748, was a mixed blessing. Membership of the Burghmote gave status and power: aldermen and councillors often held multiple posts of authority, serving as churchwardens, as officials of trade companies, and as guardians of the poor. Administering city charities and appointing people to jobs gave them considerable powers of patronage. They could dictate what happened in the city. At the same time, being an alderman made real demands on a person's time and could involve financial loss. Nevertheless, both Gray's notebook and Cyprian Bunce's transcription of civic records make abundantly clear the fascination which the task of local government held for these two men who, with their colleagues, devoted so much of their lives to running the city.

10

JAMES SIMMONS AND THE REMODELLING OF CANTERBURY

December 1789

Alderman James Simmons admires the silver bowl on the table before him, a gift from colleagues on the city council. He starts to draft a letter of thanks: 'To deserve well of my fellow citizens,' he writes, 'is the chief pride of my life.'

When the composer John Marsh left Canterbury in March 1787, he described the city as 'a very dirty old fashion'd ill paved place'. Had he waited only a little longer he might have judged differently. His departure coincided with the passing of a parliamentary 'Improvement Act' for the 'Better Paving, Cleansing, Lighting and Watching' of the city. Many eighteenth-century towns applied for such acts, which enabled them to undertake major public works. By the end of 1789 the improvements which the act authorised had been effected. According to the *Kentish Traveller's Companion*, Canterbury, which had been one of the 'worst paved' cities in the kingdom, had become one of the best. The guidebook paid particular tribute to James Simmons, 'by whose persevering and disinterested zeal, and unwearied efforts ... these public improvements originated, were carried on, and completed'. The inscribed silver bowl was presented in recognition of all that Simmons had done to transform the appearance of the city.

The son of a peruke (wig) maker, James Simmons was born in Canterbury in 1741 and educated at the King's School. He was apprenticed to a stationer in London but subsequently returned to Canterbury, where he lived and worked for the rest of his life. As the son of a freeman, he was granted the freedom of the city in 1767 and set up a stationery and printing business. The timing was opportune as James Abree, the proprietor of the *Kentish Post*, announced his retirement at the start of May 1768. Simmons proposed to Abree's successor, George Kirkby, that they should go into partnership, but Kirkby declined. Simmons immediately established a rival paper, the *Kentish Gazette*, and produced the first issue on 26 May. Kirkby soon changed his mind: in July he and Simmons declared themselves joint directors of the *Kentish Gazette or Canterbury Chronicle*. The decision to use the name of the newly established paper, rather than that which had been in production for over fifty years, suggests that Simmons was the dominant partner. Like other booksellers/printers, Kirkby and Simmons published books as well as newspapers. They also sold patent medicines and ran a lending library. Simmons, who has been described as 'Canterbury's Great Tycoon', had other business interests too. In 1788 he joined forces with members of the Gipps family to found the city's first bank, and in the following decade he and Alderman Joseph Royle built a six-storey mill on the site of the old Abbot's Mill, generating a profitable trade in corn. When Simmons died in 1807 he was worth over £66,000, more than £2,000,000 in today's money.

Simmons was elected to the Burghmote in 1769 and served twice as mayor, in 1776–77 and 1788–89. His second period of office came at a particularly busy time. As well as establishing a new bank, he was also treasurer of the Pavement Commission, which had been established as a result of the Improvement Act. Being treasurer was a major responsibility since the commissioners were empowered to raise their own funds, independently of the city council. The commission met for the first time on 9 April 1787. Within three weeks it had instructed the gatekeepers on turnpike roads to collect money for improvements by levying duties on carriages and horses which entered the city and also on imports of coal. New toll gates were erected on roads which had no existing collectors. Galvanised by Simmons, the commission continued to work at breakneck speed: each area of the city was surveyed and paved in turn and the whole task was completed in just over two and a half years. Paving was of necessity preceded by the removal of protruding doorsteps and other obstructions. Although the Burghmote had sometimes tried to stop

Canterbury High Street, repaved 1787–89, depicted by Sidney Cooper, 1832.
©*Canterbury Museums and Galleries.*

individual householders extending their properties into the street, over the years many such encroachments had occurred. In his first fortnight as a commissioner, Simmons drew up guidelines which, he hoped, would replace medieval disorder with cleaner, more elegant street lines: walls of buildings were to be kept flush with their foundations; projecting windows would be permitted only in wider roads and even there would be limited to around nine inches; proper guttering and drainpipes had to be installed, down the side not the front of houses. Orders were issued for what were sometimes drastic alterations: seven owners of High Street properties had to remove their front windows, while another thirty-three had to cut theirs back to the required size.

The success of the exercise may have owed something to the size of the commission. Over 250 people, Canterbury's most prominent citizens, were appointed to it, although a quorum of nine members sufficed for many decisions. Property owners, who were most likely to be affected, felt some sense of ownership of the project and voted in favour of many resolutions by large majorities: plans for the ancient Mercery Lane, one of the narrowest streets in the city, were approved by 140 to 21. There were of course individual protests. John Callaway managed to save his Palace Street shopfront by 17 votes to 3. But overall the changes appear to have been welcomed. In the early 1790s over two thirds of the residents of Westgate, North Lane, and Northgate, areas not covered by the Improvement Act, signed petitions asking the commissioners to pave, watch, and light their streets too.

The changes authorised by the Pavement Commission were only part of the transformation which Canterbury experienced in the late eighteenth and early nineteenth centuries. Medieval city gates were not well designed for modern stagecoach travel and over time all but one were demolished. The process started in 1770 when local residents petitioned for the removal of the narrow, dilapidated Wincheap Gate on the grounds that it endangered pedestrians. The construction of the New Dover Road in

1776 engraving of St George's Gate which was demolished in 1801. *Courtesy of the Chapter of Canterbury Cathedral.*

1790 increased congestion around St George's Gate and it was taken down, albeit 'not without due consideration or deep regret'. The substantial cost of demolishing this gate (and of transferring water cisterns from its towers to a nearby bastion in the city walls) may explain why the great West Gate was spared, even though it too had been scheduled for demolition. It alone survived after the North Gate (which was surmounted with a church) was taken down in 1830. The removal of gates did not altogether obviate the difficulties faced by stagecoach drivers: to reach the main street, coaches entering from the north had to negotiate a circuitous route through narrow medieval lanes. In 1803 the council decided to facilitate access by building a new road. Like so many other projects, this owed much to financial assistance from James Simmons, but he died before New Street (now Guildhall Street) was completed.

Simmons' most striking expenditure on behalf of the city was his transformation of a patch of rough pasture land within the walls into landscaped gardens for public use. In March 1790 he leased the Dane John fields at a peppercorn rent, promising that he would spend at least £450 of

Engraving of Dane John Gardens from a drawing by L.L.Razé (1805–73).
©*Canterbury Museums and Galleries.*

his own money improving the terrain and laying out walks. In the event the project cost him over £1,500. Given the amount he had spent for the city's benefit, Simmons was understandably angry to be summoned by the guardians of the poor for failing to pay poor rate on the land. He resigned the lease in 1795, leaving the council to take over responsibility for the new gardens. Eight years later Alderman Bunce persuaded his colleagues to add a new feature, a monument erected by public subscription to commemorate Simmons' generosity in creating the gardens and his many other 'public services'.

Simmons was Canterbury's most notable late eighteenth-century benefactor, but he was not the only one. In August 1790 various gentlemen, who were attending the Canterbury races, decided that 'the establishment of a COUNTY HOSPITAL near the City of Canterbury would be of great public Utility'. A public subscription was raised and in a remarkably short period of time, just three years later, the Kent and Canterbury Hospital was opened on the site of the old St Augustine's Abbey. The inclusion of 'Kent' in its name reflected its purpose: to provide for 'the sick and lame

The Kent and Canterbury Hospital, Canterbury. Line engraving by Lester, 1810, after R. Dighton. *Wellcome Collection. Public Domain Mark.*

THE KENT AND CANTERBURY HOSPITAL.

(from the South East)

Published by Rouse, Kirkby, & Lawrence, Canterbury, June 1810.

poor from any part of the County'. Canterbury was probably chosen for the county hospital because it was well provided with medical personnel, some sixteen physicians and surgeons. Doctors made their money by attending people in their own homes but gave their services to the hospital free. This was not purely altruistic, since election as an honorary surgeon or physician enhanced a practitioner's status. Treatment at the hospital was restricted to people who could not afford to pay a doctor to visit them and whose eligibility was confirmed by a letter of recommendation from a subscriber, a practice which continued into the twentieth century. Some people, however, were excluded: vagrants and anyone who begged for alms, pregnant women, and children under seven. As a voluntary hospital dependent on public subscriptions, the Kent and Canterbury operated on very limited funds. There was no way it could meet every need, and it had to take precautions against the spread of germs and vermin which could have harmed other patients. 'No person disordered in their senses' could be admitted, nor anyone 'suspected to have the small pox, itch, or infectious distemper, or who are not free and clean from vermin – nor any who are apprehended to be in a consumptive or dying condition, or who are suspected to have the venereal disease'. A heartening clause added that exceptions could be made 'in cases of accidents, or other extraordinary emergencies'. One accident victim, admitted fourteen months after the hospital opened, was a sixteen-year-old boy who had climbed a ruined tower in St Augustine's Abbey looking for birds' nests. He must have been relieved that treatment was available nearby when he broke his thighbones in a thirty-foot fall. He was conveyed 'in great agonies' to the Kent and Canterbury Hospital.

While major building works were underway in Canterbury, dramatic events were taking place across the Channel in Paris. At first people in England assumed that when the French freed themselves from autocratic rule they were belatedly following the example which the English had set in 1688. This appears to have been the tenor of a play performed in Canterbury in February 1790, 'an entire new and splendid Entertainment, founded on the subject of the French Revolution, called THE TRIUMPH OF LIBERTY or The Destruction of THE BASTILE'. The performance took place in the city's New Theatre in Orange Street. This had been erected by an enterprising Kent actress, Mrs Sarah Baker, after the Pavement Commissioners ordered the demolition of the market hall in the Buttermarket, which had housed the old theatre. The French Revolution play took full advantage of the greater space of the new theatre. An advertisement promised:

A view of the Outside of
THE BASTILE AND DRAW BRIDGE
A picturesque view of THE INSIDE OF THE BASTILE
With the various Instruments of Torture, the different Gratings,
Dungeons and Cells, from which the several miserable Objects
made their Emancipation
The scenery entirely new and painted expressly for the occasion.
The whole to conclude with
A TRIUMPHAL PROCESSION and CHORUS.

The performance appears to have pleased the city's theatregoers since it was repeated a month later, 'by particular desire'. As the crisis in France escalated, however, English feelings changed from approval to disgust. Residents of Canterbury were among the first in England to receive the news that Louis XVI had been executed on 21 January 1793. 'Our exertions to keep pace with the Public expectation at this interesting period, are unremitting,' wrote a *Kentish Gazette* correspondent. 'In our detail of the melancholy circumstances which attended the execution of the King of France, we anticipated the London papers one day.'

A month after Louis was guillotined, war was declared between England and France. Like many other places, Canterbury expressed its patriotism by responding to a call for volunteer forces. The first Canterbury company was formed in May 1794, with James Simmons as its captain, and two more followed over the next couple of months. The volunteers do not appear to have seen action, but in 1798 all three companies expressed their willingness to go beyond the bounds of their own county in the event of invasion. People in Canterbury were well aware, however, of those who did fight: in November 1793, £73 7s. was raised at the King's Arms to supply British troops in Flanders with flannel waistcoats.

The city's proximity to France meant that soldiers were a familiar sight on its streets. Over the centuries troops had often been billeted in Canterbury, but never on the scale of the 1790s. As part of a nationwide programme to counter the French threat, the government ordered the erection of new permanent barracks in strategic locations. Canterbury was one of these. Cavalry barracks were constructed in 1794, followed by barracks for infantry in 1798 and for artillery a few years later. The huge military complex extended half a mile down the Northgate Road towards Margate. A War Office return of 1809 recorded that the barracks had stabling for over a thousand horses and currently contained 3,750 officers

View of Canterbury by Thomas Ashenden *c.* 1856 depicting troops in the grounds of the barracks. ©*Canterbury Museums and Galleries.*

and men. The resident population of Canterbury and its suburbs at the time was around 12,000.

Relations between the troops and the city appear to have been cordial. The Sussex militia, which was billeted in Canterbury in 1793, behaved in such an 'orderly and soldier-like' manner that citizens raised nearly £40 to provide a Christmas dinner for some nine hundred men. Inevitably there were some problems, as when three soldiers ('mischievous offenders') damaged trees and plantations in the new Dane John Gardens, but in many respects the city benefited from the presence of the military. In 1795 farmers were told that they could apply to commanding officers, who would supply troops to help with the harvest. The barracks provided employment for builders and craftsmen, cooks, cleaners, and washerwomen, and even for boys who were paid to remove quantities of horse dung. As a large-scale miller, it is likely that James Simmons was one of many traders whose businesses profited from the barracks – as did publicans and prostitutes.

When times were hard the presence of so many soldiers put extra pressure on scarce resources. 1795 was a particularly difficult year. The *Kentish Register*, a monthly magazine printed by Simmons and his partners, recorded that on Sunday 4 January the temperature was only 10 degrees Fahrenheit and three weeks later it fell to -2 (-19 degrees Celsius). On the north Kent coast the sea froze from Margate to Sheppey. A 'sudden thawing of the snow' on 28 January caused serious flooding: 'many houses in the lower parts of the city were immersed in water, so that the inhabitants betook them to their chambers, and others quitted their dwellings'. Five days later Daniel Sandom's wife fell into the River Stour as she tried to fill her tea kettle: she was swept away and drowned. Wheat and flour prices were high, since the previous harvest had been poor, and in time-honoured fashion the mayor appealed to better-off citizens to help needy neighbours. A subscription fund, launched on 20 January, raised over £500 in four days. For the next month some 2,500 poverty-stricken people received weekly assistance in the form of tickets for bread and flour. But prices continued to rise over the months that followed. To increase the availability of bread, privy councillors announced in July that they would personally forego fine flour loaves, which wasted a lot of grain, and eat only standard wheaten bread. A week later a meeting of prominent citizens in Canterbury agreed to follow their example. City officials ordered bakers to produce and sell only standard loaves. At the same time, collections were made in every parish for another subscription fund to subsidise bread for the poor.

Five years later wheat prices rocketed again. In March 1800 the cathedral and council joined forces to raise money for a soup kitchen, which issued seventy thousand pints of soup over the next nine weeks, sustaining around a thousand people a day at a token charge of a farthing a pint. The soup kitchen was revived at the end of the year with the added provision of the sale of subsidised potatoes. Individual businessmen also helped, notably James Simmons, who set his prices as low 'as the cost of wheat and the labour of the mill' would permit. He charged only 1*s*. 6*d*. rather than 2*s*. 2*d*. for a gallon of meal. A Burghmote resolution of 1801 thanked him for his 'munificence and unremitting exertions during the late alarming scarcity, for his liberality in supplying numerous poor of the city with good and wholesome flour from Abbot's Mill under Market Prices'.

In October 1806 Alderman James Simmons was elected unopposed as one of Canterbury's MPs, a tribute to all he had done for the place of his birth. Sadly, he died less than three months later, on 22 January 1807. Characteristically, he continued to plan new improvements right to the

end. A portrait painted shortly before his death depicted him holding plans for a canal to link Canterbury to the sea. Simmons had mooted this project twenty years earlier, but it was difficult to enlist support for such a capital-intensive scheme in wartime. He would have been delighted that an act enabling work to go forward was eventually passed in 1811, but saddened that practical problems precluded the realisation of his dream. More than most men, however, he had succeeded in implementing his visions, fundamentally transforming the city over which he held such sway. Its streets, now thronging with soldiers, were well paved and unimpeded. At night, Hasted reported, they were 'lighted with upwards of 240 lamps'. When Jane Austen visited with her brother, who lived nearby, she might well have wandered along the gravelled walks of the Dane John Gardens, admiring the flowering shrubs and pausing to rest on one of the 'commodious seats'. The improvements which Simmons had masterminded served as a catalyst for further developments. According to the *Kentish Traveller's Companion*, there was 'such a spirit of emulation for improvement' among the residents of Canterbury that many had reconstructed their old houses 'in modern style'. Most of the shops, Hasted claimed, 'were fitted up in a handsome style, in imitation of those in London'. As Canterbury emerged from the hardships of the 1790s, its inhabitants could take pride in the elegance of their refurbished city.

11

INTO THE VICTORIAN ERA

3 May 1830

Perched high on his father's shoulder, a child stares over a sea of heads. Important-looking men wearing white rosettes are getting out of a train carriage. A band of musicians puff and scrape their instruments. Church bells are ringing and everyone is clapping, clapping, clapping … A cannon fires. 'You'll remember this day for the rest of your life', his father says.

When the future Queen Victoria was born in 1819, people travelled, if at all, by stagecoach, on horseback, or on foot. By the time she was thirty-one in 1850, the country was criss-crossed by over six thousand miles of railway lines, most of them laid in the previous ten years. The people of Canterbury were among the first to have the opportunity to travel by train. The problems which had beset attempts to link the city to the coast by canal prompted investors to explore a newer mode of transport. A railway between Canterbury and Whitstable was mooted as early as 1823, and opened in May 1830. A specially commissioned engine, the *Invicta*, was built by George Stephenson's company and was transported by sea from Newcastle to Whitstable. Spectators who watched the opening of the railway in Canterbury, however, did not see the *Invicta*. Two static engines situated high in the woods hauled the unroofed carriages out of the city by means of ropes supported on small iron drums. The company directors,

Opening Day of the Canterbury-Whitstable Railway. ©*Canterbury Museums and Galleries.*

civic dignitaries, and ladies who undertook the first nerve-wracking journey were towed through the claustrophobic darkness of an 828-yard tunnel. They were dragged up steep gradients and then clung to their seats as the train speeded downhill under its own momentum, steadied only by the unwinding rope and the skill of the brakesmen. Not until these challenges were passed were the carriages attached to the 'loco-motive', or moving engine, which pulled them the last two miles into Whitstable. A few hours later, after an 'excellent lunch' at the Cumberland Arms, the passengers made the return journey to Canterbury, where their safe arrival was celebrated by cheering crowds.

The Canterbury–Whitstable railway was opened four and a half months before the more famous Liverpool–Manchester line, hence the claim that it provided the first steam-drawn passenger service. A few years later its proprietors launched the world's first season ticket, for use during the sea-bathing season between 25 March and 1 November. The railway's primary purpose, however, was not to transport passengers but freight, particularly coal. In 1832 Thomas Telford, the pioneer of civil engineering, built a new harbour at Whitstable, which enabled vessels to dock at any time whatever the tide. A regular stream of hoys (sailing barges) brought groceries and other goods from London, which were then conveyed to Canterbury by rail. But the railway company did not prosper. The cost of building the line had far exceeded original estimates, leaving a debt which absorbed any potential profits. The *Invicta* proved incapable of dragging loads up the one-in-fifty gradient from Whitstable, and it was temporarily replaced by horses while a third stationary winding engine was installed. From 1832 the locomotive chugged backwards and forwards over just one mile of level ground. The Canterbury–Whitstable railway suffered from being one of the first to be built, and engineers learnt from its problems: future lines were laid through newly hewn cuttings and along embankments rather than

The *Invicta* can be seen in the Whitstable Community Museum.
Whitstable Museum.

up and down inclines. In 1844 the Canterbury and Whitstable Company leased its line to a larger corporation, the South Eastern Railway, which two years later opened a new railway linking Canterbury to Ashford.

Railways might have been a symbol of a new industrial age but agriculture remained fundamental to Canterbury's economy. When St George's Gate was demolished in 1801, its stones were used to repave an enlarged cattle market just outside the city walls. With the help of a public subscription, a magnificent Corn Exchange was erected in 1824 to house corn and hop markets and to provide rooms where farmers could do business. But the men who gathered behind its elegant neo-classical facade had little to celebrate. A few months after the opening of the new railway, farmers were confronted with a major outbreak of machine-breaking and arson. What became known as the Swing Riots spread across the whole of southern England, but the attacks on farm machinery started very near Canterbury, at Barham, on 24 August 1830. Over the weeks that followed, labourers ventured onto many east Kent farms, under cover of darkness, to destroy threshing machines and set fire to barns. Years later an alderman's

Early twentieth-century photograph of the Cattle Market and St George's Terrace (built 1822-26). *University of Kent Special Collections and Archives, Fisk-Moore Studio, Paul Crampton Photographic Collection.*

son, who was thirteen at the time, recalled climbing the mound in the Dane John Gardens after dark and seeing 'three and four, and sometimes five, farms blazing away at one time, in different directions'. Night after night, messengers rode into the city 'at full speed to summon the assistance of the fire-engines, which were kept in constant readiness, manned and horsed'.

It was widely accepted, even by the conservative *Kentish Gazette*, that the primary cause of the riots was 'dire distress'. Agriculture had faced problems ever since the end of the Napoleonic wars in 1815, and farmers had sought to reduce their losses by laying off labourers. The introduction of threshing machines threatened to throw even more of them out of work. Long-term problems were exacerbated by a run of bad harvests. A severe winter in 1829/30 was followed by a wet summer and yet more crop failures. Farmers suffered as well as their labourers: according to the *Gazette* they had 'no corn to bring to market'. Like other householders they had to pay poor rates to support labourers who were unable to find employment. Small tenant farmers seem to have been both sympathetic to the plight of labourers and terrified by those who swarmed onto their land at night with blackened faces, brandishing hammers, saws, and axes to smash the machines which deprived them of work. The first offenders were brought to court in Canterbury on 22 October 1830, but the presiding magistrate, Sir Edward Knatchbull, passed an unexpectedly lenient sentence – a few days' imprisonment for an offence which could have been punished by transportation. As protests continued, however, the authorities reacted more repressively. At the end of November Knatchbull sentenced six men to transportation, and in December two brothers suffered the death penalty for setting fire to a barn in Blean, near Canterbury. Order was not easily or quickly restored. Special constables were enrolled to enforce the law, but many Kentish farmers refused to serve – possibly out of sympathy for the labourers, possibly because they feared retaliation.

The Swing Riots contributed to a growing sense that the usual means of maintaining law and order no longer worked. For decades Liberals and Radicals had called for parliamentary reform, but now they gained unexpected allies. On 30 October the Earl of Winchilsea, an Ultra-Tory, attended a meeting at Canterbury's Corn Exchange to discuss how to 'secure tranquillity among the labouring classes' and prevent the destruction of property. A few days later he stood up in the House of Lords and called not only for an inquiry into the condition of agricultural labourers but also for a moderate measure of parliamentary reform 'to win back the respect and confidence of the people'. His change of heart contributed to the fall of the

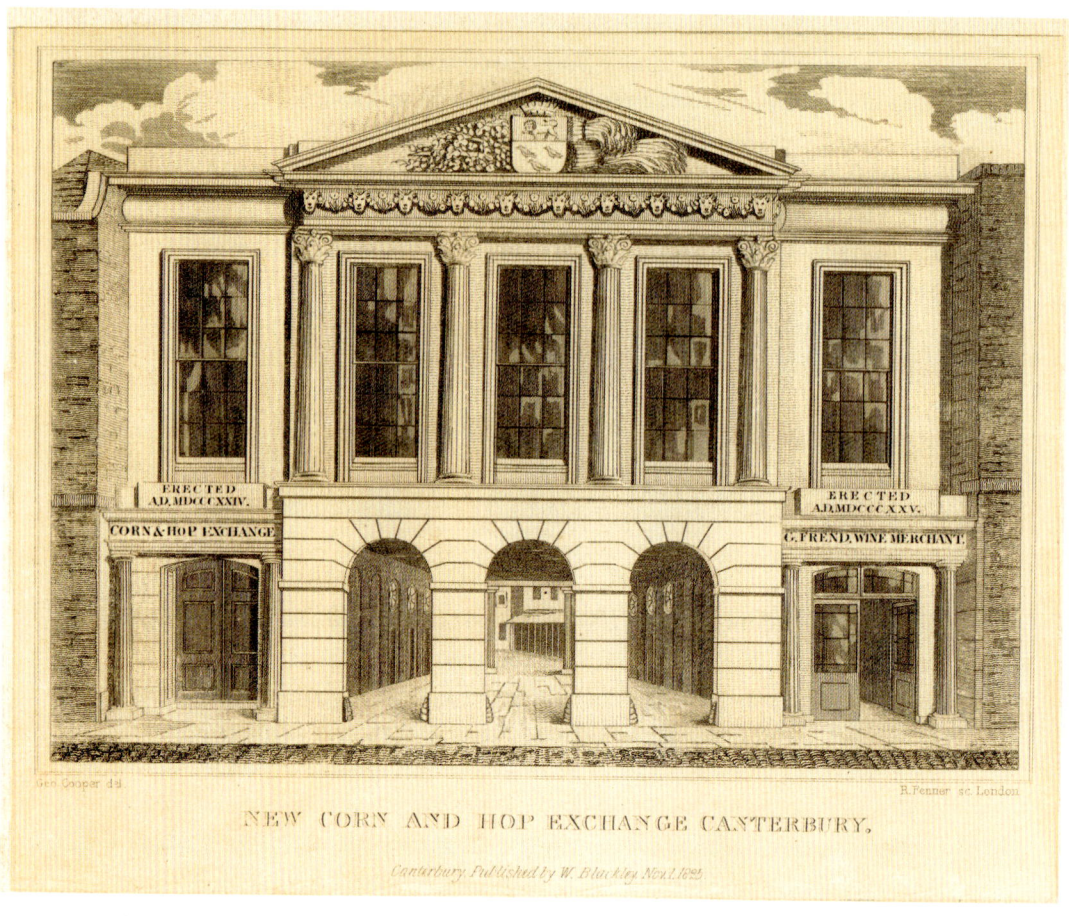

The Corn and Hop Exchange. ©*Canterbury Museums and Galleries.*

Tory government and opened the way for a new Whig administration to introduce a reform bill on 1 March 1831. In Canterbury as elsewhere, this received much popular support. On 8 March the mayor chaired a hastily summoned meeting in the Guildhall, which agreed to petition Parliament in favour of the measure. The city's two MPs were sympathetic to reform, and in the general election which was held the next month they were returned unopposed.

The reform crisis stirred and divided the country in a way few, if any, parliamentary measures ever had before. The bill was more sweeping than many had anticipated, and Lord Winchilsea, among others, soon backtracked. The *Kentish Gazette* described the measure as a 'Bedlam scheme' which realised 'the worst anticipations of our fears'. Equally bitter feelings were evoked on the other side when the House of Lords rejected the bill. The liberal *Kentish Chronicle* described the Lords' vote as a 'calamitous event'; its issue of 11 October appeared with black borders around every column of print. The mayor chaired another public meeting which the *Kent Herald* described as the 'the most numerous assembly we ever saw collected in this hall'. The *Herald* was the most radical of the three city papers. Its editor, who was one of the speakers at the meeting, told his hearers:

> Gentlemen, it is for you to decide whether this miserable junta of 199 individuals shall dictate to and domineer over millions! Will you – I know you *will not*, consent to endure this disgraceful usurpation? (Loud applause and a burst of exclamations – of No! No! We will not!) I anticipated your answer! You will unite with thousands of your countrymen who are now rising throughout the nation to vindicate their just and natural rights. (Cheers). But you will unite to support the King, the Government, and the glorious cause of Reform (We will!)

The furore over parliamentary reform was only resolved when a royal threat to create new peers induced the House of Lords reluctantly to pass the bill in June 1832. Feeling, however, remained high. When Archbishop William Howley, who had opposed reform, visited Canterbury in August he was greeted with 'groans and hisses'. Missiles, variously described as 'hats, caps, pieces of brickbat, cabbage stalks' and 'mud, rotten eggs, and stones', were flung at his carriage, falling 'as thick as blackberries'. The visit descended into farce as the coachman took a wrong turning, enabling the protesters to continue their assaults until the archbishop was finally delivered to the safety of the deanery. A month later, on 4 September 1832, the city celebrated the passing of the Reform Act. The *Kentish Chronicle* described the 'beautiful and imposing scene': blue and pink banners were paraded past houses decked with oak and laurel. Elegantly dressed ladies waved handkerchiefs from their windows. The orderly conduct of 'our operative citizens' was praised not only by the *Chronicle* but also by the *Gazette*. Tables were erected in a field near the Dane John Gardens and a meal was served to between three and four thousand working people, who feasted on roast and boiled beef, mutton, vegetables, and plum pudding, and, the *Chronicle* eulogised, displayed 'not a symptom of greediness'. The city's retiring mayor, John Brent, hailed the Act as 'the new Magna Carta of our Liberties'. A fire-balloon of coloured silk, bearing the words

'Canterbury Reform Festival', 'unfortunately ignited', but this appears to have been the only mishap. The festivities were brought to a fitting end with a firework display.

Notwithstanding all this euphoria, the 'Great Reform Act' made little difference to Canterbury. Elsewhere it had a major impact. Mushrooming urban areas such as Manchester, which was ten times the size of Canterbury, gained representation in Parliament for the first time. A number of boroughs lost one or both of their MPs, but Canterbury retained its two members. The electorate in some towns which had previously had a very restricted franchise was significantly increased, but in Canterbury all freemen already had the right to vote. The act replaced the old diversity of practice with a standardised system for all boroughs, enfranchising male householders who occupied properties worth at least £10 a year. Existing voters who did not meet this qualification retained their voting rights – but only if they lived within seven miles. This requirement did impact on Canterbury, many of whose freemen voters were non-resident. Three hundred householders who did not hold the freedom of the city acquired the vote for the first time, but the disenfranchisement of men who did not live locally led to an overall reduction in the size of the Canterbury electorate.

The passage of the act was followed in December 1832 by a general election in which the two sitting Canterbury MPs were again returned to represent the city. Viscount Fordwich and the Honourable Richard Watson both came from established moneyed families: anyone standing for Parliament had to be able to finance themselves, since MPs did not receive a salary until the twentieth century. Both men supported the Whigs (Liberals). They would have been elected unopposed had not aggrieved Tories given them the expense of a contest by persuading a maverick Cornishman, John Tom, to stand against them. Tom was a charismatic, mentally unstable demagogue. On arrival in the city a few weeks before, he had claimed to be Count Moses Rothschild, but he soon changed his alias to Sir William Courtenay, Knight of Malta. A striking figure, six feet tall, exotically dressed in crimson velvet trimmed with gold, and wearing silk stockings and Turkish slippers, he even carried a sabre. He promised his entranced listeners the typical fare of populist oratory: reduced taxes, abolition of tithes, roast beef, plum pudding, and nut-brown ale. He managed to persuade 375 people to vote for him.

One of the aims of the parliamentary reformers had been to end electoral corruption, but in this respect the act was only partially successful. It certainly did not stop bribery in Canterbury. Decades later, in 1853,

William Courtenay campaigning in the Guildhall, 1832. *By kind permission of the Williamson Family.*

a royal commission 'into the Existence of Corrupt Practices in the City of Canterbury' reported that the custom of handing out coloured tickets which voters could exchange for cash 'prevailed at all elections in the city as far back as we could trace'. One witness told the commissioners that in the 1841 by-election some £11,000 was spent on bribery. Both parties regularly gave money to agents, who paid electors to vote for their candidate. Voters clearly regarded such payments as a customary part of electoral procedure

– and even met in public houses to determine the price they would set on their votes. No one, a Liberal alderman John Brent lamented, 'would vote unless he had some inducement for it'. But he and fellow civic leaders 'whose position in life should have taught them better' were themselves criticised in the report: Brent had tried 'to keep back ... the real facts', while Conservative Party dignitaries had even gone so far as to destroy the accounts in which bribes were recorded. The commissioners concluded that bribing and other forms of corruption regularly determined election results in the city. Following their report, the two Conservative MPs elected in 1852 were discharged from their seats. Canterbury was to remain one of the more corrupt parliamentary boroughs for decades to come.

While practice in general elections continued largely unchanged in Canterbury, the operation of local government underwent major alteration.

The medieval Guildhall, in which the council met, was given a new frontage in the early nineteenth century. The building was demolished in the 1950s. *University of Kent Special Collections and Archives, Fisk-Moore Studio, Paul Crampton Photographic Collection.*

It was clearly ridiculous to reform the franchise for national but not for local elections, and so in 1835 Parliament passed a Municipal Corporations Act. This gave all male ratepayers the right to vote, ending the practice whereby aldermen and councillors were chosen by existing Burghmote members. In the elections that followed, six members of the old council who stood for re-election were defeated. Eight others successfully retained their seats, but two thirds of the members of the new council had not served before. Continuity was provided by John Nutt, who had held the crucial role of town clerk since 1820 and remained in post until 1861, but the complexion of the city's governing body was changing. Tories had been in a minority on the old council but had exercised considerable influence. This was now much reduced, since the new chamber was strongly liberal/radical in its sympathies. Nevertheless, Conservatives retained a significant presence on two other statutory bodies which survived alongside the council, the Board of Poor Law Guardians and the Pavement Commission. The continued existence of these parallel authorities, each with fundraising powers, was to be a potent cause of conflict in the decades ahead.

One major responsibility, transferred from the Pavement Commissioners to the new city council, was that of 'watching' the city. The 1835 act authorised borough corporations to establish a full-time police force, in place of the old watch which operated only at night. Some boroughs simply reappointed the old watchmen, but Canterbury dismissed them with ten shillings compensation. They were also allowed to keep the thick coats which had been purchased for them. In their place the council employed fifteen constables. Other councils delayed equipping the new policemen, but Canterbury supplied them straight away with uniforms, boots, truncheons, and lanterns. Two inspectors and a superintendent were appointed, partly to deter constables from patronising public houses. Sick pay of one shilling and sixpence a day was authorised. The council's willingness to incur these expenses is all the more remarkable as it had inherited a debt of over £15,000 from the old corporation. The *Kentish Gazette*, which had little time for the new Liberal administration, was scathing. It described the new force as an 'unnecessary institution', 'a dead weight upon the purses of the ratepayers'.

While these changes were taking place, Canterbury's unsuccessful parliamentary candidate, John Tom alias William Courtenay, was languishing in the county lunatic asylum. In July 1833 he had been found guilty of perjury and sentenced to transportation, but this was never carried out since he was certified insane. His behaviour in the asylum

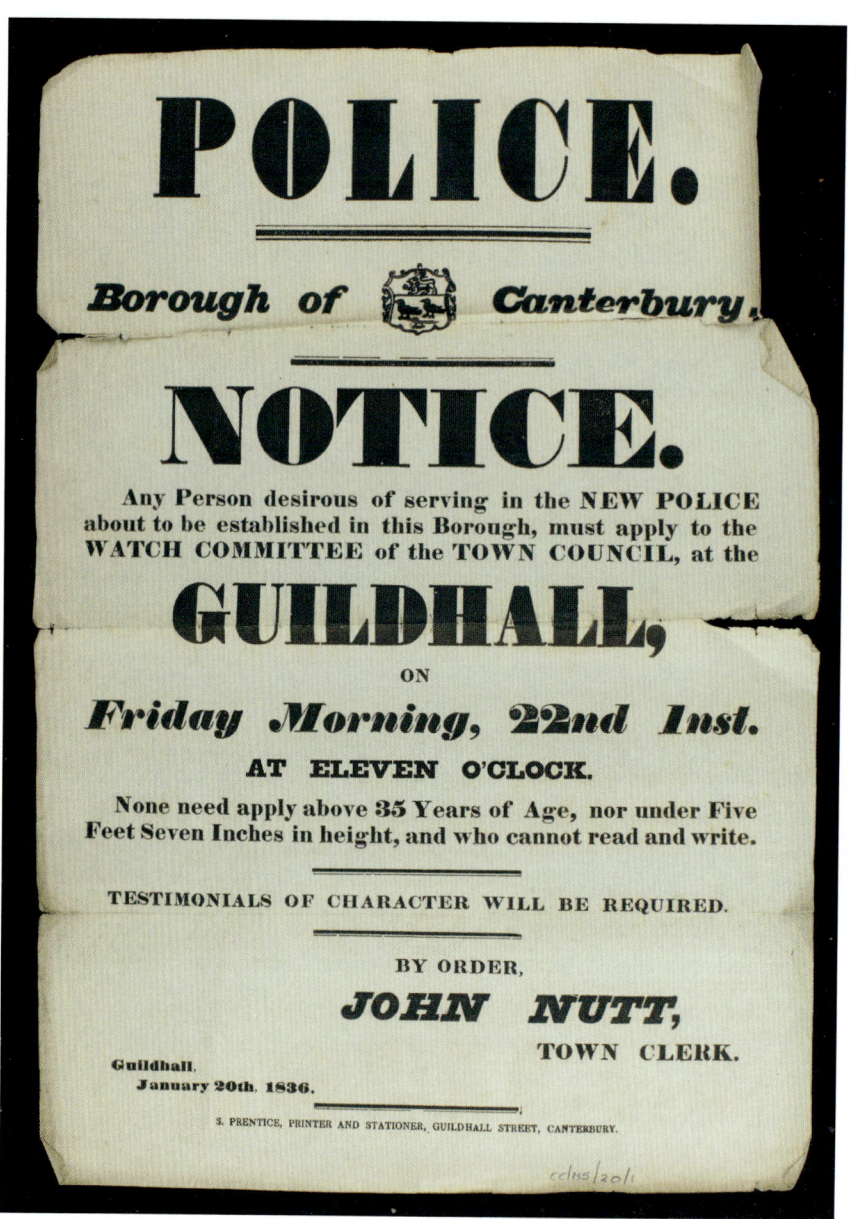

1836 advertisement for policemen. *Courtesy of the Chapter of Canterbury Cathedral.*

helped convince well-wishers of his sanity, and after four years his family managed to secure his release through a royal pardon. Tom was supposed to return to Cornwall, but he remained in Kent, where he captured the imagination of poverty-stricken inhabitants of villages between Canterbury and Faversham. In 1837/38 agricultural labourers and small farmers were suffering from yet another bad harvest followed by a harsh winter. Their plight was exacerbated by a new poor law introduced in 1834, which aimed to restrict poor relief to the workhouse. In practice, out-relief, in the form of food and money, continued to be given, but often at reduced rates. Families who relied on doles to feed dependent children were particularly hard hit. In such circumstances, as so often in the past, biblical images of a coming millennium when all wrongs would be put right spoke to their need and provided hope for the future. A messianic figure, Courtenay proclaimed that there was 'great oppression in the land' but promised that he would 'lead them on to glory'. 'You could not always understand what he said,' one follower explained, 'but when you did it was beautiful, and wonderful,

A depiction of the battle of Bosenden Wood at which Courtenay was killed from *The Life and Extraordinary Adventures of Sir William Courtenay* (1838). *University of Kent Special Collections and Archives.*

and powerful, just like his eyes.' On 29 and 30 May 1838, a small band of some thirty to fifty men marched with Courtenay through villages and hamlets, holding aloft a traditional sign of popular protest, a loaf of bread on a pole. They anticipated that others would join them, but their hopes were not realised. The fate of the rising was sealed when infantrymen were dispatched from Canterbury a few miles away. Courtenay confronted one of the advancing soldiers, and in the shooting that followed they both died, along with seven of his followers. The 'Battle of Bosenden Wood' has been described as the last battle on English soil.

Courtenay was a short-lived celebrity. Less than a month after his death Canterbury was once again in festive mood, celebrating the coronation of a new young queen. There had been disagreements how best, if at all, to mark the occasion. The *Gazette*, always quick to criticise the new Liberal council, suggested that until the last minute it appeared that nothing would happen. In the event, notwithstanding dank and wet weather, even its reporter had to admit that people enjoyed themselves. At midday, poor women were invited to gather in a field

Image of Victoria from the Chapter House east window. *By kind permission of the Chapter, Canterbury Cathedral.*

near the Dane John Gardens to draw lots for fifty legs and shoulders of mutton. Hundreds attended (although, the *Gazette* peevishly protested, hundreds more were unaware of the event, since it had not been properly publicised). Members of the city's new police force, stationed around the field, ensured that everything proceeded peaceably. In the evening public houses 'in the extreme quarters of the city' distributed free beer, providing 'a rare jollification'. Roast beef, plum pudding, and ale were even served to inhabitants of the workhouse and the prison. Meanwhile, around a hundred members of the city's elite attended a public dinner in the Guildhall where, for a short time, political differences were forgotten as 'partisans on each side bandied compliments with each other'. The most notable feature of the celebrations was the gas illumination. Gas lighting had been introduced to Canterbury in the 1820s, and on the evening of the coronation private houses and public buildings were ablaze with light. There were shop window displays featuring musical instruments suspended from floral arches in Wellard's Musical Repository. The proprietors of two taverns, the Crown and the Castle, opted for stars and the initials VR, which the latter kept alight the following evening when Sunday school children were entertained in the orchard. The most novel illumination, the *Chronicle* suggested, was at the Fountain Hotel, where a crown and the word 'Victoria', both brightly lit with gas, were encircled with boughs. As the people of Canterbury thronged the streets, despite the rain, to admire such decorations, few would have guessed that the new monarch would outlive the century and give her name to the intervening decades.

12

WORK AND RECREATION

November 1836

William Biggleston gazes, entranced, at his new-born son and wonders what life holds for him. Maybe one day the firm of Drury & Biggleston will become Drury, Biggleston & Sons. He blushes as he catches his wife's eye. It is too soon to think of such things. Henry Moss Biggleston is only a few days old.

In 1835, the year before his son was born, William Biggleston and his new partner, John Drury, announced that they were 'commencing business as Iron and Brass Founders and Smiths in general'. The iron foundry which they acquired in Crown Yard, just off the main street, was to continue in operation for over 125 years. Its presence in the heart of the city serves as a reminder that manufacturing was not confined to the heavily industrialised north but took place even in small southern market towns such as Canterbury. The firm's success lay in the partners' readiness to seize new opportunities

Biggleston and Drury swan-necked lamppost. *Author's photograph.*

provided by technological progress. They supplied girders for railway bridges and constructed gasworks in neighbouring villages. Some of their distinctive swan-necked lampposts survive in the city to this day, along with the clock face they made for the tower of St George's church. In due course Henry followed his father into the business, as did John Drury's son, George. Later generations of the Drury family, however, moved in other directions, and in 1906 Drury & Biggleston became H. M. Biggleston & Sons. Henry Moss Biggleston died in 1913, having worked energetically for the family firm for over sixty years.

Biggleston's was not the only industrial dynasty in Canterbury. In 1816 John Holman set up business as a millwright and wheelwright. The firm's original function was the building and upkeep of mills in east Kent, but in 1857 John's son, Thomas, ventured further afield. At the behest of Sir Moses Montefiore, a leading Jewish financier and benefactor, Holman's constructed a

Biggleston and Drury clock on St George's church tower. *Author's photograph.*

windmill in Jerusalem, a landmark which subsequently featured on Israeli postage stamps and banknotes. Like John Drury and William Biggleston, the Holman family succeeded because they were quick to diversify in response to new opportunities. By the 1850s both firms included the word 'engineers' in their trade descriptions. Realising that steam power could transform farming, Holman's developed a new line of business, hiring out and maintaining traction engines. At the same time the firm continued to service wind- and watermills and to accept small commissions, such as the repair of a perambulator or the construction of a 'new strong coal cart on springs' for a local merchant. An 1877 sales ledger recorded that ironwork was supplied 'for supporting tree at Cricket Ground', presumably the famous lime, which was supposedly well established when the ground was opened in 1847. Holman's, like Biggleston's, survived well into the

THE FIRST WINDMILL AT JERUSALEM.

The Jerusalem windmill, constructed 'under the personal superintendence of Mr T.R.Holman'. *Illustrated London News, 18 December 1858, University of Kent Special Collections and Archives.*

next century: the business did not close down until the founder's great-grandson retired in 1975.

Much of the industry in Victorian Canterbury took place within the city walls. George Neame's soap and candle manufactory was situated within yards of Drury & Biggleston's foundry. Nearby, carts and drays which served one of Canterbury's many breweries queued in the appropriately named Beer Cart Lane. There was a tannery a short walk away in Stour Street and, beyond that, the gasworks. According to advertisements in the *Gazette*, another Stour Street business, Mrs Beasley's 'Steam Dyeing Establishment', raised the pile of velvets 'in a superior style by the aid of gas'. Prospective customers were also assured that black clothes for mourning could be dyed by a new process 'warranted not to rub off'. Many people who worked in or near Stour Street also lived there: they had little escape from the noise and noxious smells which permeated the area.

In comparison with other towns, including several in Kent, Canterbury's industry was small-scale. Indeed, most people continued to earn their livings in traditional ways. There were some professional men, such as lawyers and surgeons, but a substantial part of the labour force was made up of craftsmen and small tradesmen who, like generations before them, provided a multiplicity of goods and services. An 1847 directory listed eighty-eight shoemakers and sixty-six bakers. These figures may seem remarkably high but shoes and bread, like many other products, were still made locally. The 1841 census recorded that 181 men who lived in the town were employed as agricultural labourers, a figure which had increased to 338 thirty years later. Hop fields, on which the breweries depended, still bordered the city walls, and local children regularly helped with hop-picking. The Wesleyan day school started its 1871 autumn term a week late 'owing to hopping being still unfinished'. The largest civilian male occupation was unskilled labour. Employed women were predominantly domestic servants.

A Victorian Baker photographed in studios in Canterbury. *Derek Butler Collection.*

Assessing how many people lived and worked in Canterbury is not easy. Population figures vary according to which sources are used and where boundaries are deemed to fall. The census returns for Canterbury did not include areas such as St Dunstan's, Holy Cross, St Gregory's, and Staplegate, which are now regarded as part of the city, since they were in a different registration district. A further complication was the presence of soldiers, whose numbers varied from year to year: there were 1,248 soldiers in the city in 1841 but only 337 in 1851. What is clear, however, is that Canterbury was growing at a much slower rate than many other places. The population of England as a whole doubled in the first half of the century and nearly doubled again in the second half. By contrast, the number of people living in Canterbury increased from around eleven or twelve thousand in 1801 to between twenty-two and twenty-four thousand in 1901. But while growth was much slower than that of many towns, the presence of increasing numbers of people created a demand for more homes and led to a boom in the building trades. Canterbury had five times as many bricklayers in 1901 as in 1841. The result of their labours can still be seen in rows of small terraced houses near the West Gate, in taller, more elegant, town houses around the old St Augustine's Abbey, and in stately mansions up the New Dover Road.

One of the factors which influenced the speed with which nineteenth-century towns grew was the coming of the railways. For centuries all the main London to Dover traffic had passed through Canterbury, and many travellers had broken their journey in the city. According to evidence given to a parliamentary committee in 1836, coaches made ninety-one journeys to and from Canterbury each week, carrying some eight hundred passengers. In 1842, however, a railway line was opened from London to Ashford and extended to Dover the following year. While the population of Ashford increased fourfold during the next six decades, Canterbury was bypassed. Fear of isolation led the city council to welcome proposals for a branch line, which was completed in 1846. There was some concern how the new Ashford to Canterbury track should cross St Dunstan's Street. The mayor, soap manufacturer George Neame, told a parliamentary committee that local people feared a bridge would spoil the handsome street. The level crossing which they wanted was created. (The *Gazette* warned that this might prove a 'great inconvenience' to traffic, a sentiment often repeated since.)

Initially the railway seemed to bring few benefits to Canterbury. As the coach trade collapsed, hoteliers and innkeepers complained of loss of

To the Directors of the

SOUTH EASTERN RAILWAY,

This Print representing the Station at Canterbury.
Is respectfully dedicated by
The Publisher

Canterbury Station (now Canterbury West) 1846, from a drawing by L.L.Razé.
©*Canterbury Museums and Galleries.*

trade. There were protests about the new postal service which replaced the old mail coaches. In 1850 the South Eastern Railway Company changed its timetables, with the result that postbags were delayed at Ashford and did not reach Canterbury until after dark. Steep fare increases were a further cause of annoyance and helped mobilise support for an alternative north Kent line, which would run from the Medway towns to Dover via Canterbury. The South Eastern Company fought hard to maintain its monopoly on east Kent services, but parliamentary approval was eventually given for what became the London–Chatham–Dover line. A second Canterbury station was opened on the other side of the city in July 1860. To the disappointment of local residents, who wanted a level crossing, this crossed Wincheap Street by means of a bridge, which they regarded as unsightly and likely to devalue property.

The coming of the railways led to the decline of some traditional occupations and the expansion of others. The importing of goods by train lessened the need for local production. In Canterbury as elsewhere there was a marked reduction in the number of shoemakers, notwithstanding the growth in population: 234 men worked for shoemaking firms in 1841, but only 99 in 1901. Tailoring was another decreasing occupation: while the number of men in the trade went up slightly from 125 to 134 over the same sixty-year period, they constituted a far smaller proportion of the total population. But the decline in local crafts should not be overemphasised. There were nearly twice as many female milliners and dressmakers in the

Late 1880s advertisment for Frederick Finn's department store from *A Map of Environs of Canterbury. Derek Butler Collection.*

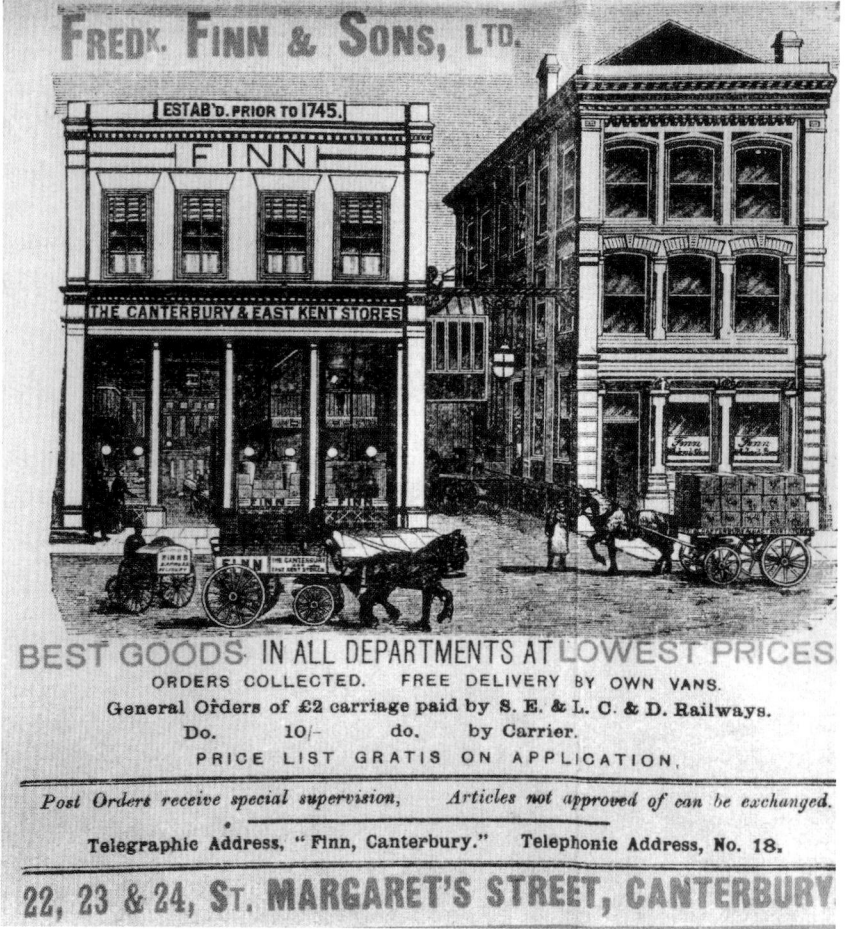

city in 1901 as there had been in 1841. Trade directories confirm that many other products were still made locally, ranging from brushes, baskets, and bricks to corsets, straw hats, and umbrellas. There were clock- and watchmakers, cabinetmakers, cork makers, gunsmiths, and picture-frame makers. At the same time, however, a new type of trading developed which took advantage of speedy deliveries from London. In 1885 the *Kentish Gazette* praised Frederick Finn for buying the 'best goods at cheapest market rates'. It even claimed that his substantial department store in St Margaret's Street was 'one of the largest and most complete trading establishments of the kind in the whole of England'. Finn was not the only retailer to bring together a variety of wares previously sold in small specialist shops. Canterbury-born William Lefevre, a descendant of Huguenot immigrants, took control of businesses run by other members of his family to create a multiple store, which stocked goods ranging from clothing and millinery to baby linen, curtains, and furnishings. The merchandise which Finn and Lefevre ordered from London arrived by train, but it was delivered to their shops by horse and cart. Indeed, the coming of the railways boosted horse-drawn transport of all kinds. Carrier firms proliferated, conveying goods and passengers from the stations to towns and villages which were not on a railway line. By the 1880s carriers from Canterbury served forty-three different destinations. The number of people working in other horse-related occupations also increased: there were around 30 saddlers and tanners in the city in 1841, but 204 by 1901.

Early fears that the railways would harm Canterbury's tourist trade soon disappeared. Guidebooks stressed how easily the city could be reached from London: 'by the omnipotent agency of steam, the journey may be made cheaply and expeditiously, both by land and sea'. Another advantage was proximity to Kent's increasingly popular seaside resorts: 'During the summer cheap return tickets are issued by the Railway Companies ... enabling those who are staying at the seaside to visit Canterbury very easily and inexpensively, while those who prefer to stay in Canterbury find it a most convenient centre from which to visit various towns on the coast.' The advent of the railways enabled local people as well as tourists to enjoy 'cheap pleasure excursions'. Day trips were advertised 'allowing a stay of seven hours at Brighton' or nine hours in London. Special offers were often scheduled for traditional holidays such as Good Friday or Whit Monday and Tuesday, when people were most likely to be off work. But such excursions, even in uncomfortable third-class carriages, were beyond the means of many poor citizens and were rare treats for others.

Most employees – shopworkers, craftsmen, domestic servants, unskilled labourers – worked long, hard hours. Inevitably most recreational activity took place close to home.

For men the most popular place of recreation was, as it always had been, the pub. By 1882 there were 165 'licensed houses' in the city, around one for every 130 inhabitants, often several in a single street. Among their customers were soldiers from the barracks, whose presence was reflected in the names which proprietors gave their establishments: the Military Tavern, the Royal Dragoon, the Three Grenadiers, and the Gallant Hussar. Pubs supplied soldiers with other services as well as drink. In April 1859 a policeman informed magistrates that, in one day, he had found twenty-five prostitutes operating in eleven city pubs. Over half of these were near the barracks, but other parts of the city were affected too. Residents of Westgate Grove complained about the way the Cock public house was run, 'there being Prostitutes kept in the House and frequent disturbances with them and soldiers who use this House'. 'Frequent disturbances' were also reported by people living near a 'Common Brothel' in Turnagain Lane. Soldiers were not the only offenders. The police superintendent noted that Saturday night dances at the Kentish Arms in 1849 brought together 'a disorderly lot of prostitutes and a great number of young lads'.

Canterbury was well-supplied with breweries as well as pubs. The huge Northgate Brewery, depicted here in the 1880s, was one of seven listed in trade directories of the time. *Derek Butler Collection.*

Another problem associated with pubs was drunkenness, a cause of much concern in Victorian England: a family could easily fall into penury if the main breadwinner took to drink. A vigorous temperance movement developed to prevent this. This campaign gained widespread popularity in the closing decades of the century, but the *Gazette* described an 'Annual Temperance Festival' in Canterbury as early as 1850. On Whit Tuesday people from neighbouring towns and villages processed through the city, accompanied by music and flags. They enjoyed a tea party ('the utmost hilarity prevailing') and listened to talks full of 'interesting anecdotes' and 'important statistical facts'. Children who 'signed the pledge' had a society

Baker's Temperance Hotel. *University of Kent Special Collections and Archives, Paul Crampton Photographic Collection.*

of their own, the Band of Hope. Among the attractions on offer for youngsters who attended the Canterbury branch was a fife and drum band, which contributed to quarterly concerts. In 1867 bands from Canterbury and Whitstable enjoyed a special treat when they travelled to London on a cheap excursion train to take part in a national temperance fête at the Crystal Palace. Temperance societies thus generated their own forms of recreational activity. It is a mark of the movement's strength that by the end of the century there were three temperance hotels in Canterbury – but these were, of course, vastly outnumbered by all the pubs.

Public houses might cause problems but they also served as venues for eminently respectable activities. Mutual insurance societies were invariably based in pubs. A 'Burial Society', which was formed at the Cross Keys in 1840, enrolled 220 members in its first four months, an indication of the popularity of such organisations. In return for regular contributions burial societies paid out a fixed sum in the event of a member's death. There were '£10' societies at the Sign of the Cock and the City of Canterbury, '£20'

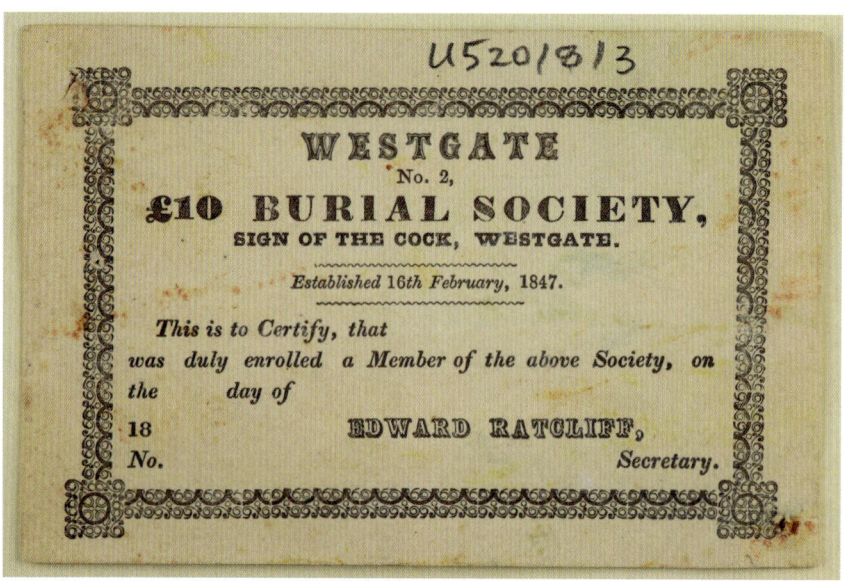

Burial Society card. *Courtesy of the Chapter of Canterbury Cathedral.*

societies at the Blue Anchor and the Black Dog, and a '£50' burial society at the Shakespeare Arms. 'Friendly Societies' offered insurance against a wider range of ills. Members paid an initiation fee and a small weekly or monthly subscription so that they – or their widows – could apply for relief in times of sickness, injury, or distress, as well as death. Certain conditions, however, had to be met: members of the Number One Wellington Lodge of Oddfellows had to belong for twelve months before they could ask for assistance, and the amount they received was reduced if they had attended fewer than twenty meetings the previous year. The Wellington Oddfellows met at the City Arms at 8.30 p.m. every Tuesday. A member who arrived improperly dressed or drunk was liable to a fine, as was anyone who sang a bawdy song or gave an indecent toast. Friendly societies were a lower-class variant of freemasonry and, like every other town in the land, Canterbury was well supplied with them: the Order of Prussian Hermits, based at the Crown and Sceptre; the Independent Order of Ancient Druids at the Seven Stars; the Kent and Sussex Labourers' Union at the Black Dog; and many more. They provided not only a safety net for the future but also a weekly respite from the demands of work. These societies were for men. There was far less organisational provision for women, but towards the end of the century some churches set up Mothers' Meetings. Members of the meeting established at the Wesleyan chapel in 1881 saved money through weekly payments and received bonuses on their savings towards the cost of clothing and household linen. There were regular sewing meetings and occasional teas, entertainments, and excursions.

Pubs and churches were not the only places where the people of Canterbury could pass their leisure hours. In 1825 the city's Philosophical Society (a descendant of the earlier Society for the Cultivation of Useful Knowledge) launched a public subscription for a Literary and Philosophical Institution, which contained a lecture room, a library of more than two thousand books, and a museum of curious objects. In 1847 this was taken over by the council, and eleven years later it became one of the first free public libraries in the country. Other 'Mutual Improvement Associations' were formed, inspired by the self-help ethic of the day. These offered lectures and demonstrations on every conceivable topic, some serious, some light-hearted: Sir Walter Raleigh, current politics, ventriloquism, and (a talk designed specifically for ladies) the use of chafing dishes. Many of their meetings took place in recently erected halls, which were also used for events such as flower shows and exhibitions, balls and banquets, concerts and song recitals. Singing appears to have been particularly popular, appearing on programme after programme. On 11 February 1867 Drury & Biggleston held their annual dinner at the Music Hall in St Margaret's Street, with entertainment provided by two visiting vocalists: Mr E. W. Mackney, 'the Inimitable Delineator of Negro Song and Dance', and Mr W. T. Critchfield, a 'Celebrated Comic Singer'. From time to time, officers of the garrison rented St George's Hall for amateur theatricals in aid of the Kent and Canterbury Hospital, while the mayor hired the Foresters' Friendly Society Hall to provide 'Christmas entertainments for the working classes'. In 1882 these took the form of five concerts, staged with the help of three local choirs. The *Gazette* reported that each performance was attended by an audience numbering between six and eight hundred people.

Much of Canterbury's recreational provision was home-grown, but the city also enjoyed visits by national and even international stars. In August 1861 the 'celebrated and original' Christy's Minstrels, a singing and dancing troupe distinguished by their blackened faces, performed at St George's Hall. That month also marked the opening of the Theatre Royal, a replacement for the old Orange Street Theatre. It was here, a few weeks later, that Charles Dickens gave a reading of *David Copperfield*, a novel partly set in Canterbury. Dickens attracted a full house, some eight hundred people

whom he complimented as 'the most delicate audience I have seen in any provincial place'. A much larger crowd gathered on 12 October 1871 when the renowned tightrope walker Blondin visited Canterbury. Around five thousand people packed the infantry barracks to see him perform a variety of feats. He walked along the rope with the trusting superintendent of the garrison gymnasium on his back, and even bicycled along it. Two days later he gave an abbreviated repeat performance. The railway companies, quick to identify opportunities for profit, ran special reduced-rate trains.

As the nineteenth century progressed, facilities for leisure multiplied. Many towns opened skating rinks and swimming pools: Canterbury acquired both in 1876. In one week its open-air pool in Whitehall Road

Canterbury's open-air swimming pool was situated in what is now Toddlers' Cove. It remained in use until the second world war and subsequent fear of polio led to its closure. *Derek Butler Collection.*

Members of one of the city's cycling clubs in the early twentieth century. By this time women were admitted as well as men. *Derek Butler Collection.*

attracted as many as 998 bathers. A swimming fête the following year, organised by a newly formed swimming club, featured serious events such as 'high diving' along with competitions such as 'eating, drinking, and writing on a slate under water'. A bicycle club started at much the same time, and by the end of the century bicycle races had become a regular feature of annual Whit Tuesday sports at the County Athletic Grounds in Wincheap. Churches, the barracks, and businesses such as Finn's set up football and cricket teams which competed against each other in local leagues.

The main sporting event in Canterbury was the annual 'Cricket Week' at the start of August. This attracted large numbers of visitors, who booked accommodation in hotels and lodging rooms. The *Illustrated London News* reported that on 'Ladies Day' in 1881 between eight and nine thousand people watched a Kentish twelve beat an All-England twelve. Cricket Week had long supplanted the Barham races as the fashionable highlight of the year. There were balls and banquets as well as performances at the Theatre Royal by the 'Old Stagers', now believed to be the world's oldest surviving amateur dramatic society. Fashionable visitors patronised city shops, and may also have availed themselves of the opportunity to wander round William Masters' 'Exotic Nursery' (on the site of today's Pound Lane car park), where they could see rare tropical plants in full bloom. The opening of a third Canterbury railway station in 1889, conveniently close to the St Lawrence Cricket Ground, enabled more people to reach the city by means of the new Elham Valley line.

Cricket Week was for the well-to-do. The recreational highlight of the year for the poorer classes was probably the Michaelmas Fair, which in 1814 had relocated from the cathedral precincts to the cattle market. Most of the old medieval fairs had died out by Victoria's reign: the Wincheap Fair was suppressed in 1859 in response to a petition from residents of St Mildred's, but the Michaelmas Fair survived, attracting people from both town and countryside. There was recurrent criticism that with its dancing and drinking booths it encouraged gambling and drunkenness, immorality and pickpocketing, but some city dignitaries defended it. Alderman William Linom, a linen and woollen draper, stressed that local tradesmen benefited from increased custom. According to the *Gazette*, he agreed that 'grosser vices and disorders' should be curtailed but told fellow councillors that he 'did not see why the country people and the labouring class generally should be deprived of the pleasures which they always seemed to enjoy at the fair ... He would not curtail the few enjoyments of the poorer classes.'

Elephants of Barnum and Bailey's circus by the West Gate in the 1890s.
Saunders postcard.

Anyone, however poor, could enjoy street spectacles. The arrival and departure of different regiments clad in distinctive, sometimes striking, uniforms, brought colour to the main thoroughfares, while the cheerful sound of military bands reverberated round the Dane John Gardens. An even greater treat was offered by visiting circuses, which came to town nearly every year. People who could not afford sixpence or a shilling for one of the performances could nevertheless watch the 'great and gorgeous' processions which preceded them. Advertisements promised performing dogs, 'laughter-loving clowns', and 'a horde of Bedouin Arabs'. As they jostled with the crowds and peered over shoulders, spectators could see horses 'unequalled for beauty of spirit and action' and even perhaps catch a glimpse of lumbering elephants. Such events could provide a welcome interlude in the lives of even the poorest citizens in nineteenth-century Canterbury, men, women, and children who crammed into squalid, unhygienic dwellings, and who faced the constant threat of disease or destitution.

13

DRAINS, DISEASE, AND DESTITUTION

1847

Dr George Rigden sits at his desk in the Canterbury Dispensary thinking about the patients he has just visited. 'In St Gregory's Square,' he writes, 'there are 39 adult persons and 43 children residing in 26 rooms; it is not drained, nor has it but one pump, and one privy for the use of all its inhabitants.'

George Rigden, who grew up in a village near Canterbury, was one of the first doctors to qualify at University College Hospital. In 1837, at the age of just twenty-one, he was appointed to the new Canterbury Dispensary. This aimed to provide free medicine and home visits to people who were not eligible for treatment at the Kent and Canterbury Hospital, such as children with infectious diseases, the aged, and the bedridden. Dispensaries for the 'sick poor' had proved popular in other towns, and when one was proposed for Canterbury donations poured in: the dispensary, like the hospital and many other welfare organisations in Victorian England, depended on voluntary subscriptions. Rigden devoted his life to it, serving as house surgeon for over sixty years. When he eventually retired at the age of eighty-four, he was awarded an annuity in appreciation of his long service but, characteristically, donated a quarter of the money he received to the dispensary.

Rigden was a compulsive collector of statistics and published the information he collated long before this became official practice. One of several tables which he included in a *British Medical Journal* article showed that 185 of the 448 people who died in Canterbury in the year 1861 were children under the age of ten. Childhood was by far the most dangerous time of life in Victorian England. While the number of deaths in mid-life was high by modern standards, Rigden's figures demonstrated that over a quarter of Canterbury's inhabitants lived to a good age. Of the people who died in 1861, 125 were over sixty, 34 of them over eighty. But Rigden did not treat the city as a single entity. He contrasted death rates of 13 and 15 per 1,000 in the elevated, well-drained parishes of St Dunstan's and St George's with those of poor, low-lying wards close to the smelly, polluted river. The densely populated St Alphege and St Gregory's had rates of 30 and 27 per 1,000. Rigden, who visited patients in these places, was only too aware of the conditions in which they lived. His 1847 report on the 'Sanitary Condition of Canterbury' contained detailed, graphic descriptions. He noted that the families of labouring men were generally 'properly covered with good warm clothing', but they did not have adequate footwear and often could not afford bedding: 'a very large proportion have but one bedstead where the man and wife sleep with some of the children, while the remainder sleep upon the floor; they have little other clothing for their beds than what they themselves have worn in the day.' When clothes were washed, they often had to be dried in the same single room in which the poorest families lived. With inadequate ventilation and no drainage, houses were 'constantly damp and extremely unhealthy'. Another source of ill health which Rigden highlighted in his report was 'defective drainage'. Many of the city's drains were only just below the surface of the road, 'at every few yards depositing their heavier contents into innumerable cess-pools, or mud-collectors, of which several hundreds are distributed about the town in different parts, emitting their offensive smells, and … poisonous exhalations'.

The nation's health became a matter of major concern the year after Rigden wrote his report, when England suffered a serious cholera epidemic. In comparison with many places Canterbury was not badly hit. There were just forty-three deaths from the disease, but the impact nationally was such that Parliament decided to pass a Public Health Act. For government to intervene in such matters went against widespread assumptions about the proper role of the state: deep antagonism to anything which smacked of dictation from Westminster and a firm conviction that public expenditure should be kept to a minimum. The act was, therefore, permissive rather than mandatory, and councils in many towns, including Canterbury, declined to set up the local boards of health it proposed. The city councillors did, however, agree to appoint a 'Nuisance Inspector'. His report books contain numerous references to foul privies, full cesspools, choked drains, 'filth', and 'offensive manure'. Pigs, 'some very dirty', were kept in backyards throughout the city, as many as twenty-four in sties in a Pound Lane yard and fifteen at a property in Burgate Lane. Individual householders were instructed to deal with these problems, but some councillors, as well as doctors, were aware that much more needed to be done.

The opportunity to make improvements came at the end of 1864, when the city suffered adverse publicity about a scarlet fever epidemic. The reformist mayor, Peter Marten, took advantage of this to suggest that it was 'false economy to allow things to remain in their present state if … an improved system of drainage … could check the ravages of disease'. A majority of councillors, both Liberal and Tory, supported him, but he faced fierce opposition from some colleagues, who resented suggestions that their city was dirty and unhealthy. They also issued dire warnings that rates would rise if the mayor's proposals were accepted. Drainage was actually the responsibility of the Pavement Commission, not the council, but after bitter debate and much personal recrimination councillors approved a major change. They implemented an 1858 parliamentary measure whereby all matters relating to sanitation were referred to a Board of Health under the auspices of the council. The Pavement Commission, which had operated alongside the council for nearly eighty years, was at last discontinued. In 1866 the city engaged a drainage engineer, James Pilbrow, to design a new sewage system.

The next few years were fraught with controversy. Pilbrow, who had produced schemes for other towns, reported that Canterbury was 'in a most deplorable state as regards both Drainage and Water Supply; probably a worse state for so distinguished and wealthy a City scarcely can exist'. Forty-five houses between St Mildred's and Abbot's Mill emptied their privies directly into the River Stour. Most other properties made use of cesspools, situated perilously close to the wells from which householders drew their drinking water. Pilbrow's report was welcomed by the *Kentish Gazette*, which commented: 'We have good society, a splendid ecclesiastical establishment, a fine natural position, but – we are not clean!' Its enthusiasm for change was not universally shared. A new drainage system for the whole city was expensive. When Pilbrow produced his plans, shocked councillors asked him to revise them and reduce his estimate. There were lengthy debates about whether money could be saved by using different pipes (which did not meet the engineer's specifications).

Sidney Cooper, View of the River Stour, from which householders drew water.
©*Canterbury Museums and Galleries.*

It is understandable that questions about alternative schemes were raised, since construction of sewage systems was in its infancy: it was only a few years since Joseph Bazalgette had started his monumental work on the sewers of London. But a few councillors who had opposed new drainage in the first place were persistently obstructive. They cast doubt on Pilbrow's competence and occasionally managed to rescind earlier decisions. James Pilbrow had reason to feel riled over incessant amateur interference.

Given all the altercation it is remarkable how quickly construction proceeded. Roads all over the city were dug up, and by May 1868 thirteen miles of sewers had been laid. But there were many teething problems, and controversy continued. In order to keep expenditure down the council had left the supply of a new water system to the Canterbury Gas and Water Company – but a year after the sewers were completed there was still no water to flush them. The huge new waterworks which the company erected in Wincheap did not come into use until 1870. Meanwhile, the newly laid sewers turned out not to be watertight, and sewage was still discharged into the river. There was nothing unusual about this: Dartford, Maidstone, Ashford, and Broadstairs all suffered from defective new sewers. Conflict between councillors, sewage engineers, and water companies was common too: Pilbrow and Canterbury Council disagreed over what it owed him. James Pilbrow was clearly not an easy colleague, but his legacy to the city extended beyond the much-needed sewage system. Fascinated by the recent development of photography, he took pictures of the Roman remains which were revealed when trenches were dug for sewers. He made careful measurements of what he found, and in 1871 published an article in an archaeological journal describing the discoveries unearthed during the excavations. His report is still consulted by local archaeologists a century and a half later.

The construction of new sewers did not resolve all the problems of drainage and water supply. Pilbrow's sewage works, which had been constructed a mile or so outside the city at Broad Oak, proved unfit for purpose. They had to be supplemented by an additional complex on the Sturry Road, which in turn was soon extended. Complaints that the river was polluted by sewage were still being made at the end of the nineteenth century. Matters were made worse when heavy rainfall caused the Stour to overflow its banks. Southern England suffered from particularly bad floods in the autumn of 1882. The *Illustrated London News* reported that 'pasture land and gardens extending over several miles, both above and below Canterbury, were covered to a considerable depth'. Its pictures of boats gliding along inundated streets and of a postman delivering letters through upper storey windows (by means of a long pole) publicised the city's plight but did so in a rather prettified fashion. The reality – flood water intermingled with sewage – would have been grimmer. Some citizens still drew their water from wells and this was often polluted, even when there were no floods. During a few months in 1884 the city sanitary inspector analysed ninety-eight samples of well water, eighty-one of which were contaminated. Householders who drank water from condemned wells were told that they should connect their properties to the mains supply, but some challenged this ruling. In December 1884 Mr Fairbrass of North Lane informed magistrates that he and his eighty-six-year-old mother had used the same water for the past half-century, 'and no illness had as yet taken place and he did not think any illness would take place ... The laying on of the company's water would cost him an additional £1 10s a year and this would no doubt go into interested persons' pockets.' Twenty years after the opening of the waterworks a fifth of the city's houses were still unconnected.

Picture of the 1882 floods. *Illustrated London News, 11 November 1882, Mary Evans Picture Library.*

Drainage and sewage were not the only health hazards in Victorian towns. Another common problem, identified by Rigden in his 1847 report, was a marked shortage of burial space. In 1840 a *Kent Herald* correspondent had complained of the 'mass of human remains by which we are surrounded. In almost every street walled in by dwellings are small graveyards absolutely filled with corrupted remains.' At St Mary Northgate it was 'almost impossible to find room to open a grave without exposing yet undecayed bodies'. In some burial grounds corpses were buried three deep. Population growth was putting pressure on parish graveyards throughout the country, and in the 1850s the government passed a series of burial acts to facilitate increased provision. In 1856 George Rigden's father-in-law, Alderman William Masters, proposed that the council should acquire land 'within reasonable distance' of Canterbury for a cemetery. Other councillors, however, argued that this was not yet needed, and a hundred ratepayers signed a petition to postpone any action. New burial grounds were opened in Folkestone, Deal, and Margate in 1856, but Canterbury delayed another twenty-one years before a municipal cemetery was established on the northern outskirts of the city.

In 1878, the year after the cemetery was opened, a twenty-six-year-old doctor, Frank Wacher, became the medical officer of health for Canterbury. He remained in post for the next fifty years and like Rigden spent the whole of his career campaigning to improve conditions in the city. His fortnightly reports drew attention to practices conducive to disease, such as the keeping of pigs and the emptying of waste from private slaughterhouses into choked drains. He attributed typhoid to impure water and urged that wells used by victims be analysed. Wacher was well aware that the young were particularly vulnerable to epidemic disease: he reported that 129 of the 421 people who died in the city in 1888 were children under five, thirty-four of them succumbing to measles and four to whooping cough. He was keen for Canterbury to have an isolation hospital, which would help stem the spread of infection, but it took him nearly two decades to persuade the city authorities to build one. He also shared Rigden's concern over poor living conditions, complaining repeatedly that tenements in passages off Stour Street were 'unfit for habitation'. On 24 September 1895 the city's General Purposes Committee proposed that the council should purchase the properties and pull them down, but the following week this suggestion was repudiated in full council. Two years later a government body stressed that the council could and should do something about the crowded passages, but a councillor objected that if the inspectors had their way, 'they might pull down half Canterbury'. He maintained that the council was doing all it could. Nearly half a century after George Rigden produced his report into the sanitary condition of the city, some residents still lived in insalubrious slums. Fortune's Passage in Stour Street, which Wacher had condemned, was not demolished until 1915.

Another all-too-common problem faced by the poorer classes in Victorian England was how to feed their families. Seasonal unemployment, as well as illness or death, could easily bring households to the breadline. According to the 1834 Poor Law, the only way such people could obtain relief was by entering a workhouse, but workhouses were designed to be so uncongenial that only the most desperate would seek admission, an

Fortune's Passage *c.* 1910. ©*Robin Edmonds.*

arrangement intended to deter scroungers. The act as originally passed failed to recognise that many of the poor, including the old, the young, and the sick, were victims of misfortune or adverse circumstances, and it was never implemented in its full rigour. In 1849 a new, purpose-built workhouse, capable of accommodating four hundred paupers, was opened in south Canterbury, but it was never more than half full. Poor Law guardians in Canterbury as elsewhere continued to give money and food to petitioners in their own homes. An inspector who visited in 1872 criticised the city because its poor rates exceeded others in Kent. Pedalling the official government line, he stressed that out-relief encouraged dependency and hoped that on his next visit he would find fewer paupers outside the workhouse and more within. Some heed was paid to his exhortations, and over the next few months the number of 'outdoor poor' in receipt of help declined. When Jane Ferrett, an abandoned wife, applied for relief, it was noted that nearly every union in Kent refused aid in such cases. Jane's request was rejected. On the other hand, the Poor Law guardians agreed to support William Stephens, a forty-five-year-old farm labourer whose 'afflicted daughter' needed constant attention. The *Gazette* reported

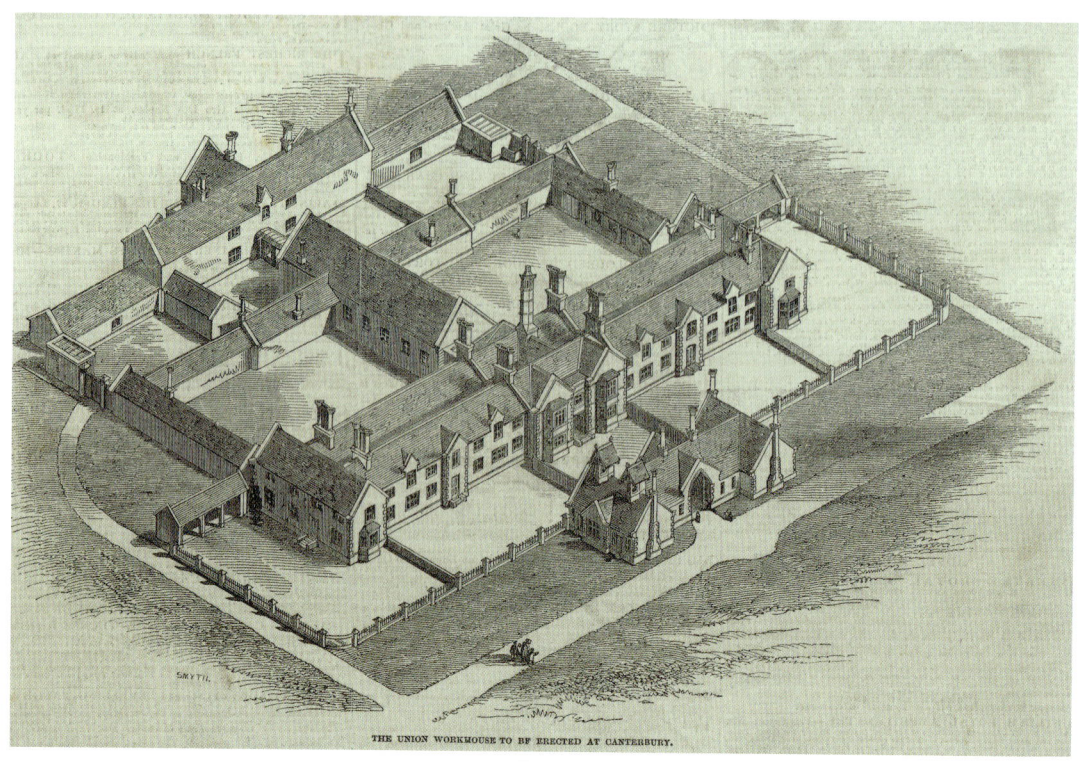

Preliminary design for the Canterbury workhouse. *Illustrated London News, 7 November 1846, University of Kent Special Collections and Archives.*

that, unlike their counterparts in Chelmsford who turned down a similar application, they awarded Stephens two shillings and a loaf each week. There was also some sympathy for the elderly: one guardian said that he thought there should be some provision outside the workhouse 'for those who had worked honestly through life and found themselves in distressed circumstances in their declining years'. In the mid-1890s the Canterbury guardians still paid a couple of shillings each week to between two and three hundred people. By contrast the number of local residents (as opposed to wandering vagrants) in the workhouse hovered between about 130 and 170. Far from being the indolent scroungers envisaged by hard-line proponents of the 1834 Act, many of these people were old, sick, or very young, and therefore not in a position to help themselves. Recognising this, the guardians sought to ameliorate their harsh conditions with occasional treats: on New Year's Day 1873 about a hundred 'aged inmates and children' sat down to tea, followed by an entertainment of songs and readings, and gifts of oranges. But the act had succeeded in stigmatising workhouses. Some elderly people categorically refused to enter them, however dire their circumstances. Barely 2 per cent of the city's resident population were in receipt of poor relief either within or outside the workhouse.

Some needy citizens received assistance from city charities. The council still administered a number of legacies which had been left, centuries before, to provide for particular needs: an 1887 schedule listed twenty-four such charities. Many bequests aided people in city almshouses; others provided clothing or other forms of assistance. In 1870 money left by John Aucher, who had died in 1701, was used to build six 'Gothic villas' near St Dunstan's church for clergy widows. Ann Smith's charity, which dated back to the seventeenth century, regularly paid for poor children from St Paul's parish to be apprenticed. Support of this kind was a lifeline for some, but many poverty-stricken residents had no option but to fend for themselves.

The idea of self-help, articulated in a best-selling volume from 1859, was firmly rooted in the Victorian psyche. Samuel Smiles' *Self-Help* was designed to demonstrate that those who struggled doggedly in the face of adversity could get on in the world. Inevitably, many of Canterbury's poor struggled doggedly without their circumstances improving, but a fortunate few demonstrated, in true Smilesian fashion, the possibility of rising from rags to riches. One of these was Sidney Cooper, who became one of the leading artists of the day. His father deserted the family when Sidney was five, and as a child he had to draw on a slate, since he had neither paper nor pencils until a 'kind gentleman' gave him some. Sarah Cooper supported her five children by working as a dressmaker or an upholsterer. She managed to apprentice her older son, William, to an apothecary, but Sidney, who persisted with what his mother called his 'stupid drawing', refused to be apprenticed. Instead he took a job painting coaches, progressed to theatrical scenery, and then in his mid-twenties decided to try his luck in Europe. He paid his way by painting well-received portraits and, on his return to England, consolidated the name he was beginning to make for himself by concentrating on pictures of animals. With the help of a patron he became a leading exponent of the genre, commissioned to paint the queen's favourite cow and exhibiting 266 works at the Royal Academy. He purchased land for a house on the edge of Canterbury (which he named 'Vernon Holme' after his patron) and, like other successful Victorian men, used some of his wealth for community benefit. He funded the new theatre, which opened in 1861, and, after the death of his mother, established an art school and gallery at

Sidney Cooper, Sketch of Queen Victoria's Jersey Cow. ©*Canterbury Museums and Galleries*.

Students at Sidney Cooper's School of Art in St Peter's Street. *The Ancient City of Canterbury, 1905*.

Drains, Disease, and Destitution

the site of his childhood home. His aim, he said, was to honour her and provide others with 'facilities I had been denied in my youth'.

The generosity of the well-to-do such as Cooper played a crucial role in ameliorating the conditions and extending the opportunities of the underprivileged. The Kent and Canterbury Hospital for the 'sick and lame poor' depended on annual subscriptions, legacies, and constant fundraising to cover its running costs. There are records of the charity sermons that were preached and the donations that were received. Other instances of beneficence, however, remained unrecorded. Sidney Cooper's older brother, William, must surely have received some help from sympathetic sponsors to study and qualify as a licentiate of the Society of Apothecaries. William Cooper subsequently worked as an apothecary-surgeon in Canterbury, was elected to the council, and in 1852 and 1868 served as the city's mayor. Another bright lad who may have been helped by philanthropic patrons was James Beaney. The son of a labourer who died when he was two, Beaney was born in 1828, a quarter-century after the Cooper brothers. He worked as an errand boy for George Rigden, who was struck by his intelligence and by his voracious reading of the surgical and medical books which surrounded him. Did Rigden perhaps pay for the boy to be apprenticed to William Cooper or did Cooper take him on at minimal charge? After serving his apprenticeship, Beaney studied medicine at Edinburgh. But it was not easy for a young man without means or family connections to acquire a medical practice in England, which may explain why Beaney eventually moved to Australia. Here he acquired fame and infamy: he built up a socially prestigious practice, published on sexual diseases, was accused – and acquitted – of murdering a patient, and made a great deal of money. Ostentatious and self-promoting, he was nicknamed 'Diamond Jim'. Fellow doctors in Australia envied and disliked him, but on visits to his native town James Beaney was treated as an honoured guest. When he died in 1891, he left £100 to the Canterbury Dispensary, where he had worked with George Rigden, £200 to the Kent and Canterbury Hospital, £1,000 to the cathedral, and £10,000 'to buy a piece of land and erect thereon a Free Library & Reading Room for the Working Classes (the Building when erected to be called "The Beaney Institute for the Education of Working Men")'. These legacies ensured that Beaney would not be forgotten in the place of his birth. Two years after his death, a grandiose memorial was unveiled on the south side of the cathedral nave (a condition of his bequest to the dean and chapter). This was followed in 1899 by the Beaney Institute, a flamboyant Tudor-Gothic building which still dominates the High Street.

THE HONORABLE JAMES GEORGE BEANEY, M.P. M.D. F.R.C.S.E.
SURGEON & TEACHER OF PRACTICAL SURGERY AT THE
MELBOURNE HOSPITAL.
MEMBER OF THE SENATE OF THE UNIVERSITY OF MELBOURNE
FELLOW OF THE ACADEMY OF MEDICINE IN IRELAND.

James Beaney by P. Bionda, 1886. *©Canterbury Museums and Galleries.*

Diamond Jim's generosity did not extend to his pauper sister. A doctor and a clergyman who knew her circumstances wrote to the *Gazette*, pointing out that this 'most respectable' seventy-year-old woman and her late husband had for years been in receipt of parish relief. She was now completely deaf and unable to help herself. Meanwhile, Beaney's nephew, 'a man of weak mind', was a workhouse inmate. Correspondents to the paper hoped that some who had benefited from Beaney's largesse might do something to help his poor relations. In response to such pleas the Australian executors sent £17 14s., while £2 5s. was raised in Canterbury. These sums may have provided a little belated relief but, like so many people who lived with the constant fear of destitution, James Beaney's sister died in unremembered obscurity.

14

COMMUNITIES OF FAITH

Spring 1851

William Lyall, the dean of Canterbury, studies an official form: 'Estimated Number of Persons attending Divine Service on Sunday, March 30, 1851'. How can he tell? He enters '500' for the morning service and '700' for the afternoon. He adds a note: 'The congregation at the cathedral is not a fixed congregation and cannot be exactly averaged.' He signs the form, but does not bother to date it or to add his address. Officialdom knows where he lives.

Canterbury Cathedral was the mother church of the Church of England, but many of the people who attended Sunday services in the city chose to worship elsewhere. In 1851 the first – and last – national, government-sponsored religious census confirmed that there were fourteen parish churches and nine nonconformist congregations in Canterbury. Some of these were admittedly very small: just nine Quakers met in silence in Canterbury Lane, while the French church had a mere twenty-one worshippers at its service in the cathedral crypt. But overall attendances at nonconformist services equalled those of the Church of England. Independents who worshipped in Dancing School Yard recorded congregations of four hundred in the morning, one hundred in the afternoon, and six hundred in the evening (surely rounded figures). The best-attended service on census day was not at the cathedral but at the Wesleyan chapel. According to the minister who signed the return, 828 people worshipped there on the evening of 30 March.

The expansion of nonconformity dated back to a revivalist movement of the previous century. When John Wesley, an indefatigable travelling preacher, paid the first of forty annual visits to Canterbury in January 1750, people turned out to hear him preach at five o'clock in the morning before they went to work. Wesley's followers were nicknamed 'Methodists' because their founder was so methodical. As their numbers increased they built first, in 1764, an octagonal preaching-house in King Street known as the 'Round House' or 'Pepper-Box', and then in 1811 a 'new, large, and commodious chapel', which still stands in St Peter's Street. Here the choirmaster for many years was a local bootmaker, Thomas Clark, who published popular volumes of psalm and

The octagonal Pepper Box chapel, originally Methodist, subsequently Baptist. *Canterbury Methodist Church.*

St Peter's Street Wesleyan chapel before 1828 when the poplars were felled to make way for a graveyard. *Canterbury Methodist Church.*

The interior of Zoar Chapel in 2015, little changed from the Victorian period. The chapel has now been sold. *Author's photograph.*

hymn tunes, including the melody now better known as "On Ilkley Moor baht 'at". Clark, however, defected from the Wesleyans, and by the time the census was taken had long worshipped with Baptists on the old Blackfriars site. A few yards away the Pepper-Box chapel was now used by another, more strictly orthodox, Baptist congregation. But this church was not rigid enough for some of its members: in 1845 they set up a rival 'Strict and Particular Baptist' chapel in a bastion of the city wall. Splits of this kind, reflecting lively debate as well as, perhaps, personal antagonisms, were not unusual in nonconformist circles.

The Victorian age was a great era of chapel building. In 1876 the Independents demolished their seventeenth-century building which had looked inwards to Dancing School Yard and built a new one on the same site, facing confidently onto Guildhall Street. One of their members, however, a Scotsman named John Fraser, decided to leave the congregation and erected a mission hall in Gas Street, which soon evolved into a Presbyterian church. The same year a congregation of 'Primitive Methodists', who had worshipped in a rented chapel since 1839, at last managed to raise enough money for a building of their own. Fundraising for new buildings – or to pay off debts on existing ones – was an important part of chapel life. Congregations organised concerts, bazaars, and spelling bees, and held special services with visiting speakers who not only inspired their hearers but also elicited large collections. Famous preachers attracted great attention, even adulation, in Victorian Britain: the guest preacher at

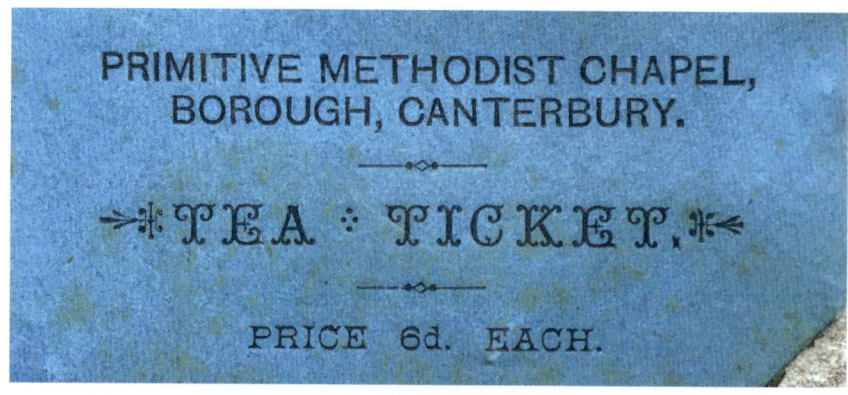

'Tea Meetings' were a popular way of raising funds. *Canterbury Methodist Church.*

the opening of the Prims' new chapel was a black ex-slave, Josiah Henson, the model for the title character in Harriet Beecher Stowe's best-selling novel *Uncle Tom's Cabin*.

Anglicans, like nonconformists, were busy building in Victoria's reign. Several parish churches underwent major refurbishment, but the most notable Church of England construction was a missionary college on the site of St Augustine's Abbey. By the early nineteenth century the monastic guest hall had become a brewery, and there were pleasure gardens where monks had once prayed. Such desecration appalled an idealistic twenty-

St Augustine's Missionary College, the finest surviving complex of Victorian buildings in Canterbury. *©Canterbury Museums and Galleries.*

four-year-old aristocrat, Alexander Hope (subsequently Beresford-Hope). Hope purchased the site in 1844 with the aim of restoring it to more appropriate use. A promising young architect, William Butterfield, was given his biggest commission to date and built the best surviving complex of Victorian architecture in the city. The buildings he designed were Gothic in style, evoking memories of the monastic past. The new college opened on 29 June 1848 and trained prospective missionaries until the Second World War. Many of its students were English but others, including an Inuit, Erasmus Augustine Kallihurua, came from further afield. Some never returned home. Jeremiah Libupuoa Moshoeshoe, the son of the king of Basutoland (present-day Lesotho), arrived in 1861 but died two years later of gastric fever. By contrast Gregory Ngcobo, a Zulu who enrolled in 1895 shortly before his nineteenth birthday, went back to Africa to work on the mission at which he had been converted. Two more 1890s students were local boys born only a stone's throw away from the college. On graduation Joseph Wilson Fogarty, the son of a Canterbury bootmaker, went to Canada, while his brother Nelson eventually became the first Anglican bishop of Damaraland (now part of Namibia). Other English graduates fared less well: Sydney Brooks was murdered in China in 1899, aged only twenty-four. The plaques on the walls of the college's memorial chapel show that many ex-students died abroad, often, like Brooks, only a few years after graduating.

A new synagogue was erected in Canterbury at the same time as the missionary college. There had been a Jewish community in the city from at least the 1760s, but its synagogue was demolished to make way for the Ashford to Canterbury railway line. The new building, which still stands in King Street, was constructed in the Egyptian style, in vogue in the early nineteenth century. Only a few synagogues followed this fashion, but a member of the Canterbury congregation, Jacob Jacobs, claimed that it was chosen in preference to the popular Gothic style which Jews associated with persecution and cruelty. Jacobs recognised, however, that his community's present position 'in this favoured land' was much better than that of earlier generations. Jews had been excluded from England until the time of Oliver Cromwell, but by Victoria's reign they were an accepted part of society. Donations for the new building were received from 'our non-Israelitish citizens' as well as from 'our brethren throughout the Empire'. When the cornerstone was laid on 23 September 1847, a number of civic dignitaries attended the ceremony. The chief rabbi came from London, travelling on the railway line which had displaced the old synagogue. Another person

Canterbury possesses a rare Egyptian-style synagogue. *Author's photograph.*

who was almost certainly present was Henry Hart, the fourteen-year-old son of a Canterbury pawnbroker. Henry subsequently became a leading figure not only within the Jewish community but also in the life of the city. A freemason and an alderman, he was even to serve three times as mayor – in 1869, 1870, and 1900.

Citizens of Canterbury may have been cordial towards Jews, but in the middle of the century they were still deeply suspicious of Catholics. A major outburst of anti-Catholic fervour erupted in 1850 when the Pope reintroduced Catholic dioceses and bishops into England for the first time since the Reformation. One newly appointed cardinal unwisely claimed to 'govern' the counties in his ecclesiastical area. Newspapers all over the land published letters of protest, some in the *Kentish Gazette* with headlines such as 'The Bishop of Rome hath no jurisdiction in this realm of England' and 'Protestants of the United Kingdom will ye suffer this?' On 26 November the editor gave pride of place to a long article reporting a 'densely thronged' public meeting in the Guildhall on 'Papal Aggression'. A Catholic priest who stood up to speak was greeted with a 'volley of hisses', but the mayor insisted from the chair that every speaker should have an impartial hearing. Catholicism had long been seen as a foreign faith: the reporter noted that the priest spoke in 'very imperfect English'. The meeting provided opportunity for the venting of other denominational antagonisms too. Some Anglicans lambasted fellow members of their own church who favoured practices reminiscent of Catholicism, while a nonconformist minister spoke disparagingly not only of the Pope ('an old gentleman far away in Italy') but also of the established Church of England. All but one attendant, however, backed a loyal address to the queen, which affirmed the meeting's

> zealous determination to rally round your Majesty and that glorious inheritance of freedom from spiritual tyranny which our martyred forefathers won, and bequeathed to us; and to resist … this bold endeavour to reduce our Protestant country to a state of abject submission to the see of Rome.

The meeting closed with three cheers for the queen and 'three groans' for the Pope.

One of the legacies of the Reformation was that there was no Catholic church within the city walls. The 1851 census recorded that 120 people attended Mass at Hales Place, a mansion a mile or so away, the home of the Catholic Hales family. A quarter of a century later, as a result of the unstinting efforts of an energetic priest, Father Richard Power, a church dedicated to St Thomas Becket was erected in the heart of Canterbury. The significance of the new building, which was situated only yards from the cathedral in which Becket had been murdered, was not lost on the wider Catholic community. Donations poured in from America, Australia, India, and France. The speaker at the opening service on 13 April 1875 was the country's leading Catholic, Cardinal Manning. The Pope sent a telegram. In contrast to the fervour of 1850 the *Kentish Gazette*'s report of the occasion was very measured. The census had revealed that Catholics were not sufficiently numerous in England to present a serious threat. There were, the *Gazette* noted, no more than two hundred Catholics in Canterbury. What annoyed the reporter about the occasion was the order in which toasts were proposed: it was 'unseemly' and 'disrespectful' that the Pope was honoured before the queen. Protestants remained seated during the papal toast, but it is unclear how many attended. The *Gazette* made no reference to any civic delegation of the kind that had graced the stone-laying at the synagogue.

One of the people present at the opening of St Thomas' was the ex-rector of St Margaret's parish church, Edward Harrison Woodall. Woodall, who served from 1841 to 1859, was a prominent figure in city life, much in demand as a lecturer. Like other well-to-do clergymen he used his wealth to help the needy, regularly supplying poor families with hundredweights of coal. In 1854 his parishioners presented him with a gift of plate in appreciation of his 'attention to the spiritual wants of the parish ... benevolence to the poor, and ... kindness to all'. Woodall even paid off a large debt incurred when the church was restored by the renowned architect George Gilbert

Scott. A year later, however, in 1859 he resigned his living. Woodall was part of a High Church movement which tried to reclaim for the Church of England practices jettisoned at the Reformation. While many men who thought as he did continued working for change within the national church, Woodall was one of a small number who made the difficult decision to convert to Roman Catholicism. His defection appalled and saddened both his parishioners and the wider society of Canterbury. In a sermon outlining the errors of Catholicism, the cathedral

St Margaret's church, where Woodall ministered, subsequently a visitor attraction, was restored in the 1850s by G. G. Scott. *Author's photograph.*

dean spoke of 'the passing of ... a pastor ... much beloved among us, under the dark shadow of the fearful apostasy of the corrupt church of Rome'. The *Kentish Gazette* lamented that someone so respected ('few men ... ever have lived more earnest or more sincere') should have plunged 'into the very depths of error'. The esteem in which Woodall had been held made his conversion all the more difficult for the people of Canterbury to comprehend.

There was further contention when a newly formed religious organisation, the Salvation Army, arrived in the city. With its military uniform and terminology the army was a deliberately un-churchy movement. It attempted to appeal to the lowest of the low (whom other denominations often failed to reach) by means of their own culture. Singing was accompanied by brass bands. The army also challenged accepted convention by its use of female preachers ('Hallelujah lasses'). A Salvation Army corps was established in Whitstable in 1885, and on 3 February 1886 'a Barracks capable of seating 800 people' was opened in an old rag store in Canterbury. The new citadel was very close to Biggleston's foundry, 'right amongst the poorest and roughest people'. The arrival of the army provoked riots in some towns, partly because of its opposition to drink. The *Gazette* reported that at the opening service in Canterbury there was 'some slight interruption caused by a few roughs', but a more serious altercation took place at the railway station: supporters returning to Whitstable were 'molested by the rabble', who threw mud and stones. The writer observed that 'several of the women and girls were struck' and noted 'a great deal of hooting and howling': 'Mr Fright (the esteemed station master) was pelted by the mob but fortunately escaped serious injury'. The *Gazette* was scathing of the city council's attempts to deal with the problem by restricting music and singing in the city: 'Probably nine-tenths of the citizens disapprove of the methods of the Salvationists, but ... nothing can be more disgusting or disgraceful than the conduct of rowdies who interrupt the services and attack the unresisting soldiers of "The Army"'. The only way forward was proper policing (which the council had failed to provide) and tough fines.

One of the topics which aroused a great deal of religious controversy in Victorian England was the provision of education. Canterbury had a large number of small private schools catering mainly for better-off pupils, but elementary education for the lower orders was almost entirely supplied by the churches. By 1870 Parliament realised that voluntary organisations such as churches lacked the resources to educate the nation's children: it ruled that, where insufficient places were provided by existing schools, local boards should be elected with the responsibility of setting up additional institutions. The 1870 Education Act caused uproar. Canterbury churchmen were appalled that the new 'board schools' would not be allowed to give any kind of denominational instruction, although simple Bible teaching would be permitted. To make matters worse, ratepayers would be required to finance this 'secular' education. The church party proposed that a fund should be established to increase accommodation in existing church schools, thus precluding the need for a school board. Nonconformists, for their part, were incensed that Anglicans were seeking to extend their hold on education. By this time there were seven parish, or 'National', schools in the city but only one nonconformist foundation, run by the British and Foreign School Society, along with an interdenominational 'Ragged School'. This meant that five sixths of elementary-school pupils received their education in Anglican institutions. There were complaints that parish clergymen exerted 'undue influence' over nonconformist children who, in the absence of alternatives, had little option but to attend Church of England schools. The opposing parties faced each other in a contentious public meeting chaired by the city's Jewish mayor, Henry Hart. This ended in disarray when the cathedral dean and other members of the church party stalked out, complaining that the chairman was partisan and had misjudged the number of hands raised for and against a particular measure. The town clerk calculated that the city needed 3,400 school places and that current provision fell 920 short of this. To the disgust of the church party, the city council voted to establish a school board. It also made education compulsory for children between the ages of five and twelve, and appointed an officer to chase up truants in board and church schools alike. These reforms, however, did not alter the balance of educational provision in Canterbury. The 'British School' was converted into a board school and was enlarged to cater for several hundred pupils, but no additional board schools were built. Instead, nearly six hundred additional places were created in denominational schools, a result of voluntary fundraising galvanised by the Act. The Wesleyans opened a school in 1871, and two new Anglican schools were established. Most primary-aged children in Canterbury continued to attend church-run schools.

Huge numbers of city children also attended Sunday school. On Sunday 20 June 1897 some two thousand pupils and their teachers gathered in the cathedral to celebrate the queen's Diamond Jubilee. The *Gazette* reported

Sunday School children processing to the cricket ground to celebrate Victoria's Diamond Jubilee. *Canterbury Methodist Church.*

that the nave was 'quite inadequate for the large numbers who wished to attend the service'. The reporter was delighted that nonconformists and members of the Church of England 'clasped hands on this occasion', but lamented that the Baptists, the Primitive Methodists, and the Roman Catholics declined to attend. Two days later, however, 4,241 Sunday school children from all denominations, along with 399 teachers, took part in a grand procession from the cathedral to the cricket ground. As soon as they arrived they were offered bread, butter, and cake 'thickly studded with currants'. After tea the children rushed around the site sampling various entertainments: a Punch and Judy show, an aerial railway, and, 'perhaps the most popular', Mr Julian's circus. By this time Canterbury also had a Boys' Brigade, one of a growing number of recreational organisations provided by religious bodies. Its band played during the procession and the lads gave a gymnastic display at the cricket ground: their use of dumb-bells, parallel bars, and a vaulting horse was greeted with 'unstinted applause'. As the jubilee celebrations showed, there was co-operation between churches as well as competition.

The most difficult relations had always been those between Catholics and Protestants, but cordiality seems to have prevailed when Hales Place was converted into a Jesuit-run college for French Catholic boys. The principal, Monsignor Stanislaus du Lac, visited the mayor in August 1882 to express his gratitude for the 'kind and generous way in which they had been received by the citizens'. In return the mayor paid a two-hour visit to the college and 'expressed himself well pleased with all he had seen'. Père du Lac kept up his connections with Canterbury even after he moved back to France, contributing to the retirement fund of the station master on the London–Chatham–Dover line. But anti-Catholic feeling was not totally eradicated. The *Gazette* carried advertisements for lectures organised by the Canterbury Protestant Union, such as a series on 'The Secrets of the Confessional', which Mrs Auffray delivered in January 1898 to a 'crowded audience of Ladies' in the Foresters' Hall.

Hales Place Jesuit College in the 1890s. It was demolished in 1928. *University of Kent Special Collections and Archives, Paul Crampton Photographic Collection.*

The Martyrs' Memorial in Martyrs' Field Road. The houses post-date the memorial which was originally surrounded by open land. *Author's photograph.*

On 10 June 1899 a new monument was unveiled commemorating the forty-one Protestants who were martyred in Canterbury under Mary Tudor. There had been some concern that this might 'recall ancient strifes and revive forgotten animosities'. Speakers at the opening ceremonies told stories of the martyrs in poignant detail, but they also took pains to stress how much times had changed. It was difficult, one said, to conceive of past despotism and tyranny 'at the close of the nineteenth century when the liberty of thought is so prominent a factor in both religious and civil life'. But he warned his hearers that the 'spirit of bigotry' had not disappeared. He urged them to emulate the martyrs' adherence to what they believed to be right while at the same time repudiating, in the present 'somewhat controversial' age, the intolerance which had led to their deaths.

15

'The Old Order Changeth'

30 November 1887

Alderman Henry Hart sits, frustrated, in a council meeting as his colleagues discuss whether to establish a telephone system. Some maintain that it would cost too much and isn't needed. Canterbury is a 'little stationary town,' says Mr Mercer; it can be crossed on foot in twenty minutes. Henry leaps to his feet. Canterbury is little, he argues, 'because there are little-minded people in it … narrow-minded people who will not go forward … That is what makes Canterbury little. I call Canterbury great, historically great and well-known.' His motion is rejected by nine votes to six.

In 1887 Henry Hart was in his mid-fifties. He had already served twice as mayor and had witnessed many changes in his native city. More were to follow in the remaining decades of his long life. The poet laureate Tennyson's words, 'The old order changeth, yielding place to new' had an obvious resonance as the queen, who had ruled as long as most people could remember, neared the end of her life. But many old attitudes and ways of life survived. In Canterbury as elsewhere change was both resisted and embraced.

As the councillors sat in the Guildhall talking about telephones, the city was being transformed before their eyes. Between 1885 and 1888 three substantial buildings were constructed further down the main street. Two

Entrance to 13 Best Lane, once a pawn-shop owned by Henry Hart.
Author's photograph.

imposing banks (which subsequently became Natwest and Lloyds) and an elaborately decorated, three-storey bootmakers (later taken over by Santander) were the work of John Green Hall and his pupils. Hall, who had been appointed city surveyor in 1866, had played a crucial role in improving Canterbury's sewage and drainage, but he was also the man primarily responsible for the city's changing appearance above ground. He designed Finn's department store, the Freemasons' temple, the Catholic and Congregational churches, and a double chapel for the new civic cemetery, where he was himself buried in May 1887. The grandiose Beaney Institute, the creation of one of his successors, A. H. Campbell, followed a decade later, the last of a series of commanding buildings reflecting the confidence and prosperity of the late-Victorian city.

Building erected in 1887 for Pool and Son, Boot and Shoe-Makers.
Author's photograph.

The Beaney Institute, opened in 1899. *Author's photograph.*

Architecturally, Canterbury had entered a new era, but in other respects it lagged behind the times. Politically it was still one of the most corrupt boroughs in England. The introduction of secret ballots in 1872 had not entirely eliminated traditional malpractice, and in the early 1880s a parliamentary commission enquired into electoral corruption in eight boroughs. The report on Canterbury revealed that Liberals had spent around £140 on bribery in the 1879 election and Conservatives some £400 in 1880. The amount expended on bribes was admittedly much smaller than in the middle of the century, but at least three past or future mayors were among those implicated. As a result of the commission's findings the two MPs elected in 1880 were dismissed, leaving the city without representation in Parliament until the next election.

Canterbury had been one of the first places to acquire a railway line, but some of its residents were loath to conform to 'railway time'. In the past individual towns had set their clocks according to the sun, but train timetables necessitated standardisation: the country's railway networks had operated according to Greenwich Mean Time since 1847. Public clocks were increasingly set to this 'London time', which in 1880 was legally extended to the country as a whole. The city council asked the dean and chapter to bring the cathedral clock into line, but they declined. They believed 'it was rather an advantage than otherwise that the town time should be in advance of railway time'. Canterbury Cathedral was to maintain its own time for years to come. In 1906 a *Kentish Gazette* correspondent complained that the clock, which often differed from railway time by four or five minutes, had recently been seven or eight minutes out: surely, he wrote, it should be within a minute or two of GMT 'and not dodge about in this eccentric manner'.

The dean and chapter might stick obdurately to old ways, but the city council tended to be more pragmatic. It discussed innovations vehemently and at length but eventually bowed to the inevitable demands of progress. The vote against telephones was soon reversed and between 1888 and 1889 the city's new exchange carried 127,808 messages. In the 1890s there were extended debates over the introduction of electricity – Hart, and others who had interests in the local gas company, wanted to delay this. Discussions were complicated by the thorny question faced by all councils at the time: should they fund an electricity generating station themselves or ask a private company to do so? Councillor Edward Lukey, the proprietor of the County Hotel, got tired of waiting for his colleagues to reach a decision and installed his own generator. In July 1895 some eight hundred excited citizens had the chance to look round his totally refurbished and well-lit premises. The council eventually opted for public rather than private ownership, and in March 1899 opened its 'Electric Lighting Works' (on a site subsequently occupied by Sainsbury's). Edward Lukey proposed one of the toasts: 'If Canterbury had been slow in the past,' he said, 'it did not mean to be behind other bodies in the future.' By March 1901, 280 street lights were lit by electricity, and 259 properties had been connected to the supply.

Developments in technology led to changes in transport. Mass production made bicycles increasingly affordable. In 1895 the police were alerted 'to the danger of furious riding by cyclists through the city'. A few years later newspapers started to report cases of 'furious driving' by motorists. The Motor Car Act of 1903 introduced licensing (and speed limits), and in the first four months of 1904 twenty-five cars and twenty-five motorcycles were licensed in Canterbury. George Barrett, an enthusiastic cyclist who had started to sell cycle and motor fittings a couple of years before, had an eye to the future when he renamed his St Peter's Street firm 'The West End Garage and Motor Works'. The proprietors of another new enterprise, the Canterbury Motor Company, were even more ambitious. Henry Dawson and his partner advertised four models of a 'Canterbury Car', ranging from an 8 horsepower two-seater to a 20 horsepower four-seater. These were manufactured between 1903 and 1906 just outside the city walls, at a works near the east station, but they failed to find much of a market. Production soon ceased and Dawson turned his attention to other things. His company advertised cars for sale or hire, and in 1909 acquired

The 'Canterbury Car'. *Catalogue of the Canterbury Motor Car Company, 1904.*

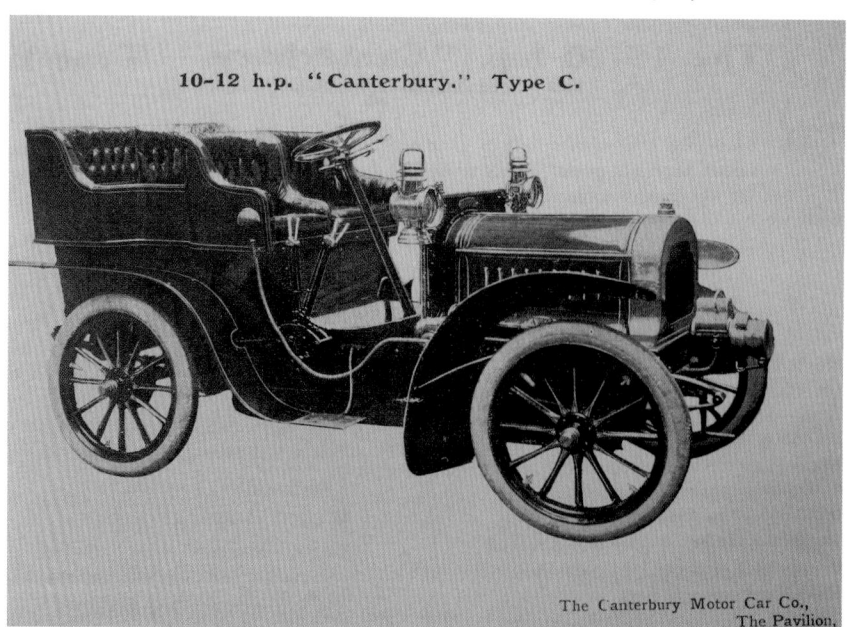

A double-decker bus in the High Street *c.* 1906, part of a short-lived service which preceded Dawson's. *Derek Butler Collection.*

a licence to run a motor bus service between Canterbury and Herne Bay. Dawson even tried his hand at aviation, but his light aeroplane, which was trialled on St Martin's Hill in June 1910, failed to rise more than a foot off the ground. A few weeks later early risers might have seen a plane navigated by John Moisant pass over the city at 5.30 a.m. on Tuesday 18 August. Even more may have watched another pioneer aviator, Cecil Grace, fly over Canterbury on the afternoon of 18 December. Both Moisant and Grace died in flying accidents before the end of the year.

The idea of travelling in a car, let alone an aeroplane, was beyond the dreams of most Canterbury residents. Many businesses relied heavily on horse-drawn transport, and the majority of citizens still went everywhere on foot. Each day Frank Honey, the schoolboy son of a foundry foreman, walked from his city-centre home to a grand mansion on the southern outskirts, where he worked from six to eight o'clock before walking back to school on the other side of town. Society was highly stratified, with different classes occupying different residential zones. Frank's life was far removed from those of the King's School pupils whose heavy brogue shoes he blacked as one of his houseboy jobs. But it was also far removed from those of boys who grew up in Northgate, an area shunned by working-class families which aspired to respectability. Working behind the scenes as a houseboy was acceptable, but Frank recalled that his father 'would never let me be a newsboy. That was undignified.' Mr Honey was determined

A horse-drawn cart on which pianoforte dealers, like other businesses, depended. ©*Robin Edmonds.*

that his son should learn a trade, and once Frank was fourteen his father apprenticed him to an electrician.

Most children left school between the ages of eleven and thirteen, but a few had the opportunity of extending their education. For centuries, sixteen poor boys had been nominated by the council to attend the Blue Coat School in the Poor Priests' Hospital, but old charitable foundations such as this had ceased to meet the needs of the age. It closed in 1879, and its endowments were used to fund two new 'middle' schools which opened two years later, one for 125 boys, the other for 75 girls. The governors were concerned that the designation 'middle' might fuel 'an erroneous idea' that the schools were 'intended solely for the middle class'. In 1887 the schools were renamed after a thirteenth-century benefactor of the Poor Priests' Hospital, Simon Langton. But the change of name did not alter their social composition. Each year around a dozen elementary-school children were awarded scholarships to the Langton schools, but the majority of pupils paid fees well into the twentieth century.

Many Canterbury inhabitants never moved far beyond the city of their birth, but a few young men travelled to the other side of the world to fight for their country in the Boer War. Among them were thirty-one old Langtonians, including Harold Gilham, who had been head boy in 1898. Canterbury had a close relationship with the Royal East Kent Regiment, the 'Buffs', and the mayor and corporation gave farewell banquets for each departing contingent. The local press published reports on the war and also letters which the young men sent home to their parents. In July 1902, after the war had at last ended, robed councillors attended by mace- and sword-bearers processed to the railway station to greet over 450 returning soldiers. Each was presented with a pipe and an inscribed tobacco pouch. Harold Gilham, however, never came back: he was killed in action on 11 June 1901. In May 1904 a war memorial was unveiled in the Dane John Gardens, commemorating Buffs who had lost their lives in the war through fighting or – all too commonly – through disease.

War was a matter for men. One of the arguments used against female suffrage at the time was that women, who could not fight, should not make decisions about warfare. Local government was a different matter, since it dealt with issues deemed to fall within the female sphere of interest. Women who satisfied certain criteria voted in municipal elections, but some maintained that they should also be allowed to choose members of Parliament. Canterbury's first petition in favour of female suffrage was presented as early as 1869, and meetings were held to promote the cause. At a gathering in the County Hotel, organised by the Conservative and Unionist Women's Franchise Association at the end of December 1908, the speaker maintained that female ratepayers should be enfranchised like their male counterparts – but she criticised the use of violence to achieve this end. Her complaint was directed against members of the militant Women's Social and Political Union (WSPU). At the time this had made little impact on Canterbury: in 1909 the *Gazette* reported that the city was one of only three places in Kent where cabinet ministers had addressed meetings without being disturbed by 'suffragettes'. Two of the movement's leaders, Mrs Pethwick-Lawrence and Mrs Pankhurst, visited Canterbury the next year. It is clear from *Gazette* reports that they delivered measured and reasoned addresses and answered questions satisfactorily. They did not ask for the vote to be given to all women, simply to those who qualified on the same basis as men by being householders. The reporter noted that, 'as is customary with this essentially up-to-date movement', the meeting on 21 April 1910, at which Mrs Pankhurst spoke, was well advertised, with directions chalked on city pavements. Four hundred people made their way to St Margaret's Hall, which was decorated in suffragette colours –

purple for dignity, green for hope, and white for purity. In the general election which followed a few months later, a motor car decked in purple, green, and white toured the streets, while ladies handed out flyers at polling booths urging electors to vote against the Liberal government, which seemed unwilling to admit women to the franchise. Their activity may have prompted the mobilisation of anti-suffrage forces. On 2 February 1911 a public meeting opposing votes for women was held in the Foresters' Hall under the chairmanship of the cathedral dean, Henry Wace. As WSPU violence mounted nationwide, the cathedral authorities decided to take precautions against female militancy. In 1913 they arranged for a policeman to be on duty whenever the cathedral was open for fear of 'outrages by women in connection with the "suffragette" movement'. According to a canon's daughter, a table was installed at the entrance, 'and everyone had to leave their handbags there and had to be searched before entering the building'. Unlike Dean Wace, some men sympathised with the women's cause. Fortescue West, a city draper and Justice of the Peace, proclaimed at one anti-suffrage meeting that if Queen Victoria could rule then so could other women. He also complained that women teachers were paid less than their male counterparts. Local debates and meetings on votes for women continued to be held in what appears to have been a well-mannered fashion.

Contests over the election of Canterbury's male representatives were far from well-mannered. The tenor of city politics in the Edwardian era was very different from that of late Victorian times, when power had rested unchallenged in the hands of a small group of men. John Henniker Heaton, who became MP for Canterbury in 1885 (the year in which parliamentary seats were redistributed and the city's representation was reduced from two to one), remained in post for the next quarter-century. He was returned unopposed at four successive elections. There was similar continuity in local government. Over a sixteen-year period from 1889 the office of mayor was held by just five men: two served double terms, while George Collard clocked up a remarkable total of ten years as mayor. In the early twentieth century, however, this concentration of power was challenged by an energetic and ambitious newcomer, Francis Bennett-Goldney. Born Francis Evans, Bennett-Goldney had changed his name as a condition of receiving an inheritance. He moved to the city in the late 1890s and, with private means and time on his hands, threw himself into its life. He was elected to the council in 1902 but quickly antagonised fellow Conservatives by scheming to replace Heaton as MP. The depth of ill feeling became evident in the 1904 mayoral elections. Bennett-Goldney defeated Henry Hart by ten votes to nine in a preliminary poll, but his colleagues refused to endorse his election. Normally a formal second vote would unanimously confirm the winner of the initial poll, but Bennett-Goldney was so hated that on this occasion George Collard was put forward as a rival candidate. Backed by Hart, Collard was elected by twelve votes to ten in what the *Gazette* called an 'unparalleled scene in the history of these elections'.

Francis Bennett-Goldney attracted fervent support as well as bitter enmity. Appreciative working men gathered at St Margaret's Hall to present him with a gold pocketbook case. His followers gained a number

Francis Bennett-Goldney (with a mayoral chain) and his mother, the lady mayoress, with French visitors, 1907. *Derek Butler Collection.*

Canvassers for the sitting MP, John Henniker Heaton, in the January 1910 election. *Derek Butler Collection.*

of council seats and, after his initial failure, Bennett-Goldney was elected mayor each year from 1905 to 1910. But he split the local Conservative Party. Antagonism was so intense that following a contretemps one New Year's Eve, two city councillors were taken to court, accused of lying in wait for a fellow Conservative and assaulting him on his way home. Bennett-Goldney's henchman and deputy mayor, Albert Anderson, was fined thirty-five shillings for the affray. What divided the party was not just antagonism between the old guard and the new, or even Bennett-Goldney's contentious personality, but his continuing attempts to displace Heaton as the city's MP. In the general election of January 1910 the Conservative mayor of Canterbury stood against the city's sitting Conservative MP. Calling himself an 'Independent Unionist', Bennett-Goldney came within twenty-two votes of defeating Heaton. There was a second election later that year, which Heaton did not contest, but in no circumstances would local Conservative leaders consider supporting Bennett-Goldney. John Howard was selected as the party candidate, and Bennett-Goldney once again campaigned against the official nominee. Since the two men had very similar views the contest was essentially one of personality and party loyalty. Canterbury had an electorate of 3,836, but non-electors as well as electors were involved in vigorous campaigning. Workers from Howard's mill in nearby Chartham were transported around the city in big wagons. Three large drayloads of George Beer's brewery employees trundled the streets cheering for Bennett-Goldney. Characteristically, Bennett-Goldney depicted himself as a man for the times: a model of a dreadnought was covered in the Bennett-Goldney colours, while an airship scene presciently portrayed Bennett-Goldney flying high above other competitors. General elections in Edwardian England always attracted high turnouts, and in December 1910 89.2 per cent of the Canterbury electors went to the polls. Bennett-Goldney was the clear winner.

Bennett-Goldney caused major controversy in Canterbury but he was also a generous benefactor who used his wealth and contacts to the city's benefit. In 1899 he obtained permission from the queen for the Beaney Institute to be called a 'Royal Museum'. He acquired mahogany display cases which the British Museum no longer needed at nominal cost. He also supplied many exhibits himself, including major art works by Van Dyck and Burne-Jones. Taking on the role of honorary director and curator of the museum, he continued to build up its collections, largely ignoring the governing committee, which was torn between gratitude for his beneficence and concern over his independent and high-handed behaviour. Like his eighteenth-century predecessor James Simmons, Bennett-Goldney took the initiative in providing gardens for public use, funding the laying out and planting the dry moat outside the city walls. In 1906 he secured the return of Stephenson's *Invicta* to the city, and when war broke out he lent his Canterbury home, Abbot's Barton, to be used as a hospital.

Francis Bennett-Goldney died in a car crash in August 1918, aged just fifty-three. He continued to cause controversy even after his death. Ancient city charters and objects which had once been displayed in the museum appeared in a catalogue of the London auctioneers who were disposing of his estate. The city council claimed that these items were corporation property and went to law to get them back. Judgement was passed in the city's favour, and the charters and other items which Bennett-Goldney had apparently purloined were returned to Canterbury.

Henry Hart survived a little longer, dying at the age of eighty-nine in 1921, just two years after retiring from the council which he had joined fifty-eight years before. Like Bennett-Goldney, albeit less dramatically, he had done much for Canterbury, a contribution recognised in 1905 when he was awarded the honorary freedom of the city. Since campaigning for a telephone exchange in 1887, Hart had witnessed the coming of electricity, motor cars, and even aeroplanes. Born in the year of the first parliamentary

The *Invicta* in the dry moat gardens outside the city walls. *Derek Butler Collection.*

reform act, he had lived into an age in which women demanded the vote. In his later years he had watched with distaste as Bennett-Goldney disrupted the city's political life as he had known it. He had seen young men leave to fight on the other side of the world and had welcomed some, but not all, of them home. All of this, however, paled into insignificance in the face of the war which dominated the closing years of his life, a war in which many more of the city's young men lost their lives and which led to even more extensive technological and political change.

16

THE DEMANDS OF WAR

4 August 1914

A young man applauds enthusiastically as Colin Blythe takes yet another wicket at the St Lawrence Cricket Ground. 'I always come when he's playing,' he confides to his companion, 'but there aren't so many people here today.' A neighbour raises his head from his newspaper: 'That's hardly surprising,' he says. 'There's going to be a war.' They do not know that they will never see Colin Blythe bowl again.

Colin Blythe *c. 1905.*
Wikimedia Commons.

On 4 August 1914, the day the United Kingdom declared war on Germany, the renowned Kent and England bowler Colin 'Charlie' Blythe took four wickets for thirty-eight runs. But a dark cloud hung over Canterbury Cricket Week that year. Never before, noted the *Whitstable Times*, had it been held 'under such disturbing and depressing influences'. Attendance at the St Lawrence Ground dropped to around fifteen thousand, under half that of 1913. Social events were cancelled and for the first time in seventy-two years, the city's amateur dramatic society, the Old Stagers, was unable to present its customary plays. These were called off on the opening night, the day before war was formally declared, since so many of the actors were involved in military preparations. Captain Gould apologised for withdrawing at the last minute but said that he was so 'hard at it clothing reservists and filling up countless documents ... that I see practically no chance of my getting away at all tonight from the Barracks'. Colin Blythe enlisted a few weeks later. He died at Passchendaele in 1917.

The presence of the barracks made war an immediate reality to the people of Canterbury. In the course of the first week, motor charabancs and lorries full of soldiers started to arrive in the city. As the barracks could not house the increased numbers some new arrivals were directed to private households. By the end of the week the *Kentish Gazette* was able to report that 'the houses at which troops are being billeted in Canterbury have chalk marks on the doors indicating the number and company of the men accommodated in each'. Subsequently soldiers were also quartered in public halls and in buildings, such as the roller-skating rink, which were adapted to new purposes. But much remained chaotic. Horace Reid, a recruit from Hertfordshire, ended up sleeping on a bench in the cathedral precincts. Meanwhile, householders who had German, Austrian, or Hungarian lodgers were required to notify the police authorities. A government vet arrived within days of the outbreak of war and requisitioned horses which he deemed suitable for military purposes: the owners rarely received the full price for their animals. Film screenings were advertised in the *Gazette* not only of scenes from the cricket ground but also of the mobilisation of local forces and of horses being commandeered in city streets.

The secretary of state for war, Lord Kitchener, owned an estate a few miles outside Canterbury, and on 7 August he called for 100,000 volunteers aged between nineteen and thirty to reinforce the regular army. Having achieved this target, he appealed again three weeks later for a further 100,000 aged up to thirty-five. Another local dignitary, Viscount Harris, sought to bring his message home to the people of Canterbury at a public

This 'War Horse', created by students and staff of Canterbury College, was erected in the cathedral precincts to mark the centenary of the First World War. *Author's photograph.*

meeting held in the city theatre on 1 September. As a front-line county, Kent had always been sensitive to threats of invasion: Viscount Harris drew on such fears by inviting his audience to imagine not only peaceful harvesting but also 'the smiling hills and dales that made Kent so beautiful being tarnished by the horrors of invasion'. Thirty-seven men enlisted on the spot. Others may have delayed until the harvest was over. There were complaints that the rural south produced fewer recruits per head of the population than more industrialised areas, but the *Gazette* maintained that it was unfair to stigmatise Kent for tardy recruitment. Local farmers had lost 'large numbers of men at a most inconvenient time, but to their credit … have been only too willing to help in persuading them to join the colours'. Harry Mount of Mount & Sons nurseries assured employees that their posts would be kept open for them if they enlisted, and other city firms followed suit. Almost all the eligible men who worked for Hunt & Sons drapers, furnishers, and tailors responded to the call to arms. Biggleston & Sons posted notices around their premises appealing for recruits and lost about a quarter of their workforce in the first few weeks of the war.

As men from Canterbury headed to the continent to fight, refugees from Belgium flooded into Kent. Some 18,000 arrived at Folkestone harbour within a month of the declaration of war and the number increased to over 100,000 in the weeks that followed. Proximity to the channel ports gave Canterbury people an early awareness of the human cost of war. On 19 September the *Kentish Gazette* reported that Mr and Mrs Herbert Mount had accommodated sixty to eighty refugees in tents on their farm – but that less exposed quarters were needed as the weather got colder. For years to come the town clerk's wife, Amy Fielding, threw herself into the task of organising local activity to support Belgian refugees.

Within weeks the refugees were followed by sick and wounded soldiers. Citizens gathered to cheer the men as they arrived at the railway station and gave them cigarettes and other gifts. Members of Canterbury Men's Voluntary Aid Detachment (VAD) were at hand to transport them to hospitals in the city. Some forty beds in the Kent and Canterbury Hospital had been allocated to the War Office to supplement those in the military hospital at the barracks, but far more were needed. For a few weeks St Augustine's Missionary College was turned into a makeshift hospital. After the students returned to their studies, two private houses were lent to be used as hospitals for the duration of the war. There were appeals in the *Gazette* for bed linen, bath towels, crutches, dressing gowns, brushes, and combs. The hospitals at St Augustine's, at Francis Bennett-Goldney's Abbot's Barton home, and at the Wightwick sisters' Dane John House were all staffed by members of the city's two female Voluntary Aid Detachments. Bertha Evans, a VAD nurse who cared for those taken to Abbot's Barton, was in her late teens when war broke out. The daughter of a master at the King's School, Bertha received basic training in first aid and home nursing but was then expected to carry major responsibilities, such as looking after men who had serious injuries, by herself, at night. Recording her memories in 1978, she stressed the contrast with her pre-war life, 'going to tea parties with my Mother, getting terribly bored'. Other women volunteered to help with the cleaning, cooking, washing, and mending. A young mother, Lilian Short of King Street, washed dishes at Dane John House three mornings a week, while Miss Tumber of Black Griffin Lane, a working woman in her late forties, cooked breakfasts from 5.30 to 7 a.m. before going to work.

Women who had been bred to assume responsibility were quick to take the lead. In September 1914 the wives of two cathedral canons, Catherine Spooner, a bishop's daughter, and Margaret Mason, whose father had been headmaster of the King's School, sent a letter to the *Kentish Gazette* which was co-signed by the mayoress, Hannah Mount. The three ladies invited women who wanted to help the war effort to send them 'flannel day-shirts' and 'full-size knitted socks'. By January they were able to report a generous response to their appeal. This was just the start of what became a major wartime enterprise. In the summer of 1915 the ladies formalised their ad hoc arrangements and established the Canterbury and District War Work Depot. They mobilised schoolchildren to make socks, mufflers, breeches, and shirts, and dispatched numerous parcels to soldiers at the front and to hospitals at home and abroad. The city council allocated them a room in the School of Art for the production of bandages and other surgical equipment. A local bank lent them a house in St Margaret's Street, where volunteers packaged clothes, bedding, bandages, and 'amusements'. The women took advantage of their cathedral connections to use the Chapter House for the manufacture of sandbags for coastal defence. By the time the government got round to appointing a retired civil servant to co-ordinate the country's voluntary activity, the Canterbury War Work Depot was well under way. Hundreds of receipts lodged in the cathedral archives, along with personal letters of thanks from nurses, commandants, and soldiers, testify to the scale of the work undertaken by the Canterbury ladies.

One of many appreciative letters received by the Canterbury War Work Depot. *Courtesy of the Chapter of Canterbury Cathedral.*

Meanwhile, as the months passed and casualties rose, more men were needed in the armed forces. In January 1916 the government took a previously unthinkable step and introduced compulsory military service for single men aged eighteen to forty-one. A few months later conscription was extended to married men, and for the last few months of the war the age limit was raised to fifty-one. Every family knew that male relatives would have to leave home and face the dangers of war. Some men sought to evade conscription by failing to respond when they received their call-up papers. Police and military officials conducted raids at cinemas and theatres to pick up these defaulters, and long lists of names were published in the *Gazette* of those the recruiting officer wanted to contact. Twice a week the mayor chaired a tribunal which heard applications from men who thought they had reason to postpone or be exempted from military service.

The tribunal reports reveal how severely the war impacted on the day-to-day work of the city. Only a handful of applicants appear to have appealed on grounds of conscience. Some men pleaded that they were the sole supporters of widowed mothers, but the majority of cases related to the demands of employment. Laundry proprietor Philip Hogg pointed out that, if he were to serve, the laundry would have to close and twenty-five to thirty people would lose their jobs. Many applications were made not by the men themselves but by a father or an employer. Walter Pearce, a nurseryman and greengrocer, stated that two of his sons had already enlisted; if a third, William, did so only a fourteen-year-old lad would be left and part of the business would have to shut down. William's case was backed by the commandant of the male VAD, which had already lost thirty men: he stressed that William Pearce was invaluable, since elderly and very young volunteers could not handle stretcher cases. Finn & Sons argued that none of the fifteen girls they had recruited to replace thirty-six men could cover twenty-four-year-old Albert Bailey's work. As it happened, the mayor, who chaired the tribunal, was a local physician: Dr Bremner knew that Bailey was unfit to serve as he had personally manipulated the man's dislocated shoulder back into place on five or six occasions. Some pleas were made on behalf of essential services. Morgan Fletcher, a dentist, was granted exemption when the tribunal learnt that three of his technicians had been called up and that he was working eighteen-hour days to meet the huge demand for dentistry. In May 1916 Mount & Sons asked for eight married men over thirty to be exempted from military service: the older men, women, and boys they employed were inadequate to farm 1,200 acres. The town clerk applied to the tribunal on behalf of three gravediggers.

Even the military representative on the tribunal agreed that the cemetery could not function with fewer than three men. Like many other applicants the gravediggers were given temporary certificates of exemption. The town clerk was told, notwithstanding his earlier lack of success, to go on advertising to replace them.

One obvious way of dealing with labour shortages was to enlist women to take over male jobs. A registration bureau was set up at the city's Chamber of Trade as early as December 1915 'to facilitate the employment of women in the place of men withdrawn for service with the military forces'. Some employers, however, were loath to contemplate the possibility of female workers. A farmer from the east Kent village of Elham went so far as to claim that 'cows will not put up with women milking them'. F. G. Coast, a Canterbury hairdresser, was equally opposed to the idea of women entering his profession. He applied to the tribunal on behalf of a male employee, claiming that it was neither practicable nor desirable to employ women: training as a hairdresser took years and women would not undertake it. Dr Bremner retorted that women were being trained as hairdressers in London and that his hair had been cut by a woman. But the tribunal recognised that there were limits to what women could be expected to do. Fifteen drivers from George Barrett's motor and taxi business had joined up early in the war. The company was training women in their place but did not send them out after eight o'clock at night. The tribunal granted a conditional exemption to one of Barrett's three remaining male drivers, thirty-eight-year-old Henry Hammond. Driving was one of several occupations which opened to women as a result of the male labour shortage. The crisis in agriculture was so severe that in March 1917 an advertisement was posted in the *Kentish Gazette*: 'Wanted immediately – Motor Drivers and Ploughmen (Male or Female)'. That same year St Augustine's College became a training centre for the Women's Land Army. Throughout the city girls took on jobs previously performed by men. Mabel, a participant in a later oral history project, recalled that at the age of sixteen or seventeen she was asked if she was 'interested in doing a post round because the postmen were having to go to the war'. For the next couple of years young Mabel was a 'postman'. Other women, employed by the Canterbury Motor Company, spent the war making munitions in its workshops.

As the war dragged on its impact on daily life became ever more marked. Defence of the Realm Acts curtailed pub hours and banned 'treating', since excessive consumption of alcohol by soldiers or workers was deemed harmful to the war effort. By mid-1916 drinking in Canterbury pubs was confined to two and a half hours at lunchtime and three hours in the evening, a marked contrast to pre-war arrangements when, according to the proprietor's young son, the Black Lion had been open from 6 a.m. to midnight. City shops had operated similarly long hours, but in October 1915 many agreed to shut early in the winter months lest their lights facilitate air raids: in future, they announced, they would close at 7 p.m. on Mondays, Tuesdays, and Wednesdays, at 8 p.m. on Fridays, and at 9 p.m. on Saturdays. (Thursday was early closing day.) British Summer Time was introduced on 20 May 1916 to maximise the use of daylight hours for agricultural production. Before the war Britain had imported 60 per cent of its foodstuffs. As this became more difficult prices had escalated, and by 1917 many basic commodities were in short supply. The *Gazette* reported that soon after 8.30 a.m. on 14 April 1917 a queue of over seven hundred people formed outside Pilcher & Chittenden's High Street greengrocery, which had received a large stock of potatoes: 'all classes of citizens were among the applicants and for some six hours there was a very large crowd waiting to be served'. Advertisers publicised alternatives to potatoes and bread, such as 'Taylors Dun Peas' or maize 'flaked or as flour for puddings and porridge'. Honey, molasses, syrup, and treacle were promoted

Queuing for potatoes in 1917. *Derek Butler Collection.*

as sugar substitutes. Posters urged restraint as a patriotic duty, and people were encouraged to eat food such as macaroni and salmon on 'meatless days'. Two hundred and forty-three allotments were created so that citizens could grow their own vegetables. A report to the council noted with satisfaction that 'the allotment holders represent both sexes, and all classes of society'; it was 'interesting to see a lady or professional gentleman working side by side with an ordinary working-class man each doing their best to increase the production of food'. Another scheme to maximise scarce resources was the creation of communal war kitchens, one in Castle Street and another in Northgate, from which customers could purchase cooked meals each day except Sunday: 'Save Coals, Bread, Money, Time. Bring your own Jugs and Basins.'

Food shortages were common to the country as a whole, but residents of east Kent had additional cause for anxiety since they lived in an area subject to enemy attack. Dover, Ramsgate, and other coastal towns were bombed, and there was fear that Canterbury might suffer too: one of the responsibilities of the city's male Voluntary Aid Detachment was to keep watch for air raids. Interviewees who looked back on their wartime childhood recollected Gotha bombers, whose approach could be heard miles away, and the occasional Zeppelin airship flying over the city. Shrapnel, fired at the airships from nearby anti-aircraft batteries, scared some children as much as the prospect of bombing. There was, however, excitement as well as anxiety. On 7 December 1917 a Gotha bomber crashed at Broad Oak, about a mile from the city centre. The rector of St Stephen's, who was a special constable, heard the noise and went to investigate. He told the three-man crew that they were his prisoners and searched them for weapons, but he also bound up their cuts and gave them cigarettes. In the days that followed, people from all over the district flocked to view the wreckage. There was a prisoner-of-war camp off Forty Acres Road which fascinated local children. One man recalled that 'us small lads used to go there Saturday mornings and make naughty gestures to them through the barbed wire'. For children who had known little else, war was normality. Part of the Simon Langton School was commandeered by the army, and pupils watched soldiers drilling in their playground. Young schoolboys played at being soldiers, while older ones learnt signalling and shooting in the cadet corps in preparation for their own call-up. But all this was a backcloth to the more immediate concerns of school life: 'Business as usual,' commented one lad in 1916. 'Men may come, and men may go, but lessons at home and at school go on for ever.'

A parade in the Simon Langton playground *c.* 1915. Most of the buildings shown here were destroyed in the 1942 blitz. *Derek Butler Collection.*

The war, which seemed as though it was going on for ever, eventually came to an end on 11 November 1918. Schools closed for the day and most firms suspended business. Flags were hoisted on public buildings, cathedral bells were rung, and crowds thronged the streets. Parading children beat kettles and any other utensils they could find. In the evening, lights were left on all over the city and celebrations continued, notwithstanding rain and mud. It was, the *Gazette* commented, 'like a delightful scene from Fairyland after the Stygian darkness of the past four years'. But the darkness was not over for everyone. Servicemen returned home with influenza, a rampant, potentially fatal disease which accounted for forty-five of the fifty-six admissions to the Dane John Hospital in November and December 1918. Some men who survived the war were haunted by what they had been through. One interviewee recorded that her husband 'used to cry and I used to have an awful job with him'; a doctor attributed the nervous breakdown he suffered years later to the after-effects of the war. Many other families grieved for those they had lost. Mrs Coley, who lived in Church Lane, mourned the death of three sons, the last of them barely a month before the armistice. In her Castle Street living room Mrs Mary Martin had a framed copy of a message from the king, sent in January 1915, expressing his gratification that she had seven sons serving in the navy and the army. Any pride she may have felt was seared with anguish: at least two of her sons never returned.

After the war there were long debates about how the dead should be honoured. Dr Bremner, who had served as mayor throughout the war, and Mrs Spooner, one of the formidable ladies who lived in the cathedral precincts, favoured a memorial hall in which groups such as the Canterbury Lads' Club could meet. Mrs Spooner even went so far as to claim that 'if those men who had died in the war could give their vote ... they would favour something which could be for the benefit of the young'. But the new mayor and Henry Wace, the cathedral dean, wanted a monument on which the names of the fallen could be recorded. Memorials were being constructed all over the country to ensure that the war dead were not forgotten. Like many others, the Canterbury war memorial was placed in a prominent position – in the middle of the Buttermarket, just outside the entrance to the cathedral. Deciding which names should feature on it was no easy matter, particularly when members of the memorial committee were faced with pleading letters from bereaved relatives. They did not want to cause hurt by omission, but they also had to judge whether a man had sufficient connection with the city to justify inclusion. An appeal by Mrs Burnap, whose son was born in a nearby village and enlisted in Dover, was refused on the grounds that he had never lived in Canterbury. Major Edward Mannock VC was not really eligible, but committee members succumbed to the *Gazette*'s insistence that the famous pilot's brief attendance at St Thomas' Catholic School made him 'a Canterbury product'. They also had to decide whether combatants who died after the war died because of it, men such as Private Archie Price (recorded on the monument as A. Price), who died in India in 1919. R. W. Simpson, who had served throughout the war, died of illness in Malta the same year. The committee acknowledged that 'according to our ruling he should not be included' but allowed compassion to prevail. They justified their decision on the grounds that 'his parents lived in Canterbury for forty-three years ... he was a native and his people are still here. He leaves a widow and a daughter.'

Compiling the list took so long that the memorial bore no names when it was unveiled by Earl Haig on 10 October 1921. Another year was to pass before bronze plaques were attached to it, inscribed with the initials and surnames of 'officers, non-commissioned officers, and men of Canterbury who gave their lives'. The use of initials obscured the fact that one of the names, E. F. M. Parker, was actually that of a woman. Ethel Parker, a member of the Queen Mary's Auxiliary Army Corps, worked as a waitress

Unveiling the war memorial, 10 October 1921. *Derek Butler Collection.*

serving soldiers in Abbeville: she was killed there in an air raid in May 1918. In all, 531 individuals who lost their lives in the First World War were commemorated on the memorial. For parents who had lost sons, sisters who missed their brothers, widows raising children alone, and children who never knew their fathers, as well as for young girls whose chances of marriage were now much reduced, life had changed in ways that would have seemed inconceivable a few years earlier.

17

THE 'INTERWAR' YEARS

14 December 1918

An injured soldier limps painfully towards the polling station. It is early, before eight o'clock, but already a couple of women are queuing, keen to cast their votes. He wonders what the future holds for them, for him, for the community to which they belong, now that the war is over.

The 'interwar' years were not just an interlude between two world wars. As 'the war to end all wars' drew to a close, people looked forward to a new, better, more peaceful world. Some hopes never materialised, but much was to change in the course of the next two decades. Canterbury in 1939 was a very different place from the city to which shell-shocked soldiers returned in the months following the armistice.

One major change was the extension of political rights to the population as a whole. Before the war fewer than four thousand Canterbury residents had been able to vote in general elections. But men who had fought for their country could no longer be excluded from the franchise, and in the election of December 1918 all men over twenty-one were allowed to vote. The work which women had done during the war gave grounds for giving them the same rights as men, but there was concern lest female voters outnumbered male. The 1921 census revealed that nearly 55 per cent of Canterbury's adult population was female. Women over thirty who satisfied certain property qualifications were enfranchised in 1918, but all the others had to wait until 1929 – only then did women receive the vote on the same basis as men. As a result of the 1918 changes the national electorate increased threefold, but boundary changes make it hard to assess how many people gained the vote in Canterbury. In 1918 the city lost its traditional status as a separate parliamentary borough and became part of a newly configured constituency which included Whitstable, Herne Bay, and surrounding villages. The election itself was a very low-key affair. The *Kentish Gazette* described it as one of the quietest on record. This was hardly surprising. In the aftermath of war there was little energy for the usual frenzied campaigning and nothing to get excited about: everyone knew that Ronald McNeill, a Conservative endorsed by David Lloyd George's coalition government, was going to win. His only opponent was a representative of the young Labour Party. The Liberals, loyal to their party leader Lloyd George, did not put up a candidate. Only 45 per cent of the electorate turned out to vote. Over four fifths of those who did go to the polls voted for McNeill.

The extension of the franchise was just one of the signs that people were entering a new world very different from the past. As soldiers returned from the front the government promised to provide 'homes fit for heroes'. Housing acts required local councils to build new houses and offered subsidies to help them do so. Canterbury City Council posted advertisements in the local press within weeks of the end of the war, seeking land which could be used for working-class homes. By 1929 438 'council houses' had been built on new estates in Thanington, St Martin's Hill, and Forty Acres Road.

This was just the start. Fourteen areas in the city were identified for slum clearance, some comprising just a few houses, others whole streets. The city's sanitary inspector produced detailed reports describing their condition: Jones' Cottages in Military Road (clearance area number 5) had two toilets for four houses, leaking roofs, damp walls, and inadequate foundations. In Knott's Lane (clearance area number 1) fifty properties were scheduled for demolition, but there were clear differences of opinion between the sanitary inspector and the owners. Whereas the former condemned numbers 6, 7, 9, and 10 as 'unfit for human habitation', Mrs Alice Alzapiedi, who let the four houses to tenants, maintained that they were 'in a very fair state of repair'. Number 8 Knott's Lane belonged to Gertrude Moyes, who told the council: 'I am a spinster and aged 65 years. It is very hard losing 9 shillings a week. I have spent a lot in the roof etc and I do object to having it pulled down.' There were protests, too, from residents who faced the loss of much-loved homes. Mr Willis, who described himself as a partial cripple aged sixty-five, had lived at 2 Woolpack Cottages for forty years; his house was 'a refuge from the traffic and would break our hearts to be turned out'. Such pleas were fruitless. The majority of clearance

Numbers 1–5 Woolpack Cottages where Mr Willis lived. *University of Kent Special Collections and Archives, Paul Crampton Photographic Collection.*

orders were confirmed by the Ministry of Health. A Housing Act of 1935 provided compensation for repairs made during the previous five years, but the actual demolition was the responsibility of the owners. Under pressure from the town clerk, Mrs Alzapiedi explained that she had not yet pulled down her Ryde Street properties because her husband (who had been ill) was busy demolishing houses elsewhere in the city. The loss of rental from twenty cottages had halved her income and she was not in a position to employ anyone else. Despite such delays, the pace stepped up in 1937 and 1938. By 1939 the council was able to inform the government that 128 houses had been demolished in designated clearance areas, along with 117 in other parts of the city. In total 741 people had been displaced. To house them more new council estates had been built in Thanington, along the Sturry Road, and in Reed Avenue. But these were on the outskirts of the city, and people who had always lived in the centre were sometimes loath to move out. Mrs Malpas, who ran a shop in Knott's Lane, claimed that relocation had destroyed her business, since she could not find suitable alternative premises. Her letter of appreciation for a couple of hundred pounds' compensation is but one item in the huge files of paperwork which testify to the complexities of the slum clearance programme.

The provision of adequate housing was only one of the problems facing councils in the post-war years. The American Wall Street Crash of 1929 helped trigger a worldwide depression which led to widespread unemployment. In some northern towns the majority of workers were left without jobs. The south of the country was nowhere near so badly hit, but even here the number out of work increased. In the cold winter months at the start of 1932 and 1933 more than nine hundred people living in Canterbury were unemployed, mostly men but some women and 'juveniles' aged fourteen to eighteen. Local trade unions helped them apply for means-tested benefits. They also urged the city council to create new jobs by speeding up its house-building programme – and complained bitterly when contractors brought in workmen from towns outside Canterbury. The council, for its part, authorised public works such as road repairs and the painting of railings to provide some additional employment. In conjunction with local businesses and the cathedral dean, it followed the example of other towns which had set up occupation centres for the unemployed. The Canterbury centre opened on 14 November 1932 in premises in Iron Bar Lane, which had been lent, rent-free, by auctioneer and estate agent F. J. Godden. Other local firms and residents supplied fittings and equipment such as benches and tools so that men who had no jobs could repair their families' footwear and furniture. The first annual report of the centre recorded that 857 pairs of boots had been mended at Iron Bar Lane. Card and waste paper were collected from city firms, sorted at the centre, and sold to a company in Essex which pulped it for boxes in an early attempt at recycling. In the first year over a hundred tons of paper were dispatched, yielding a return of £153 3s. 9d., which helped towards the centre's running costs. But these and similar well-meaning efforts to ameliorate the plight of the unemployed ran into difficulties, and the occupation centre closed in July 1934. Another project sought to enable poverty-stricken families to grow their own food. The council offered two and a half acres of vacant allotment land at Thanington, rent-free for the first two years, and as part of a nationwide scheme invited unemployed allotment holders to apply for free tools, seeds, and fertilisers. In comparison with other parts of the country (and even with neighbouring towns such as Whitstable, Herne Bay, and Faversham) unemployment in Canterbury was low – but this was no consolation to around a thousand city-dwellers who faced 1939 without work.

Dealing with unemployment, implementing large-scale slum clearance, and building council houses were all new challenges for members of the

Catherine Williamson, her three children, and her parents-in-law in the gardens of Tower House, 1932. *By kind permission of the Williamson family.*

city council. As in the past they were predominantly local tradesmen who had their own businesses to manage. Some, such as department-store keeper Charles Lefevre or miller Frank Hooker, had inherited established family firms, but others had risen by their own efforts: Councillor Stone ran a small tailor's shop in Palace Street and George Barrett had built up his substantial motor business from scratch. Their names were familiar to fellow citizens not only from fascia boards on their premises but also from lengthy, often verbatim, reports of council meetings in the local press. Men continued to dominate the council, but one of the most notable members in the later 1930s was a woman, Catherine Williamson. She was elected to the council in 1935 and three years later became the city's first female mayor. Under the heading 'Councillor Mrs Williamson makes History', the *Kentish Gazette* described her as a 'shrewd and telling speaker'. Like some of her colleagues she was an active nonconformist, a member of the Society of Friends. Charles Lefevre and Frank Hooker both belonged to St George's Baptist Church. Following the example set by James Simmons centuries before, they and their fellow councillors gave more than their time to the community. In 1936, following the death of her father-in-law

Tower House as it was when the Williamson family donated it to the city. The wing on the left, next to the old city wall bastion, has since been demolished. ©*Kent Messenger Group.*

who owned the flourishing Stour Street tannery, Mrs Williamson and her husband gifted the family home, Tower House, and its extensive gardens to the city. A substantial tract of land, Larkey Valley Woods, was among the donations made by Frank Hooker, while Charles Lefevre paid for wrought-iron gates for the Simon Langton schools.

Charles Lefevre's department store was one of the leading businesses in Canterbury. Many smaller concerns were also still owned and run by independent local traders. W. E. Pinnock was a coal merchant who diversified into road haulage. His son Kenneth wrote an account of *A Canterbury Childhood* which provides a vivid cameo of what life was like between the wars. Kenneth was born in 1919 into a world which bore many resemblances to that of the pre-war era. He recalled the constant sound of hoofs along St George's Lane, carthorses at a great granite trough 'refreshing themselves amid the petrol fumes', and blacksmiths who 'seemed to do nothing all day but shoe horses'. He remembered delivery men bringing goods to the house, the baker who hauled his bread round in a two-wheeled cart, and the milkman who ladled milk into his customers' jugs from a churn on a hand-pushed float. Since the city was 'peppered with shops', housewives could get everything they needed within yards of where they lived. Ladies would visit local shops to choose what they wanted and then go home to await the imminent arrival of delivery boys. There were, Kenneth recollected, 'battalions of tradesmen's bicycles, each with a large basket mounted on its handlebars', supplemented in the 1930s by a multiplicity of 'little vans scurrying everywhere'.

The increased use of motorised transport was a sign of the changing times. By the 1930s new-fangled 'traffic lights' were replacing the white-gloved policemen who had previously directed the traffic. In 1931 the city's first purpose-built car park was created on the site of the old Star Brewery (whose demolition exposed a long-hidden stretch of city wall). The volume of traffic was increased by motor lorries, which brought goods to a growing number of chain stores. Kenneth's parents refused to patronise these 'company shops', whose bulk purchasing threatened the livelihoods of independent traders. Inevitably, however, some family firms succumbed. Edward Bing & Son, pharmaceutical chemists and perfumers, sold out to a London company, to the regret of the young Pinnock, who lamented the

Delivery bicycle outside Wilkins of Dover Street, 1913. *Saunders postcard.*

A Model T Ford delivery vehicle used by a Canterbury store after the First World War. *Saunders postcard.*

disappearance of the fine Victorian shopfront and locally grown lavender toiletries. Lefevre's, too, changed hands. The shop was to retain the family name for decades to come, but from the mid-1920s the business was owned by Debenhams.

Just before he sold his shares Charles Lefevre commissioned a new building, a stylish art deco store on the site of the old Theatre Royal in Guildhall Street. This was but the first of many significant changes to the appearance of the city. In October 1933 the great six-storey Abbot's Mill, erected by James Simmons in the 1790s, was destroyed by a fire which was not quenched for several days. The *Kentish Gazette* caught the drama of the occasion: 'At half-past eight it still stood proudly, a landmark known in three centuries. By ten o'clock it was a roaring inferno of flame and was crashing to its doom.' A few years later another late eighteenth-century building, the Kent and Canterbury Hospital, ceased to be used for its original purpose. On 14 July 1937, after nearly a decade of fundraising, a new hospital was opened on a different site by the Duke and Duchess of Kent. The *Kentish Gazette* issued a special supplement to mark the occasion, celebrating the fact that the city now had a hospital with 181 beds and with outpatient and casualty departments capable of handling 40,000 attendances each year: 'Well Done, Canterbury'.

Pre-1933 postcard showing the great Abbot's Mill which towered over surrounding buildings. The mill was over a hundred feet high. *University of Kent Special Collections and Archives, Paul Crampton Photographic Collection.*

The Kent and Canterbury Hospital with the line of the Elham Valley Railway in the foreground, 1937. *©Kent Messenger Group.*

Further stimulus to new building came from changing patterns of leisure. Silent films were proving far more popular than live theatre, hence the decline and sale of the Theatre Royal. Canterbury's first purpose-built cinema, the 'Electric Theatre' in St Peter's Street, had been erected in 1910. In 1927 it was replaced by a new Central Cinema in St Margaret's Street capable of seating 735 people. But this was quickly outclassed by larger, lusher, picture palaces, such as the exotically named 'Granada' in Dover or the 'Troc' in Tankerton on the north Kent coast. To compete with these (and with each other) two state-of-the-art cinemas in the art deco style were opened in Canterbury on the same day, Saturday 5 August 1933. The mayor, Frank Hooker, performed the opening ceremonies at the Regal while his deputy, George Barrett, attended those at the Friars. These were conducted by the local MP, Sir William Wayland. The claims made by the respective speakers reflected not only the rivalry between the

The Regal Cinema (now the Odeon). The right-hand side was destroyed by bombing in the war. *King George V Silver Jubilee Celebrations: Monday 6 May, Canterbury* (1935).

two cinemas but also strong feelings of civic pride. The mayor described the Regal as 'the last word in cinema building': it could seat 1,700 people and its screen (24 feet by 18) was one of the largest in the county. The Friars had 1,300 seats but its screen, at slightly over 30 feet, was lauded as the biggest south of London. Both speakers commented on the speed of change. Mr Hooker recollected that forty-five years earlier he had ridden to school from the village of Chartham and had stabled his pony on the site of the new cinema. Sir William observed that it was only thirty-seven years since the first cinema show in the country; 'talkies' were a mere four years old. It was not just the novelty of talking pictures, however, which lured people to the cinemas. 'The air of luxury,' Kenneth Pinnock recalled, 'was staggering ... acres of wall-to-wall carpet, at a time when most people had to be content with chilly linoleum ... deliciously warm, banishing thoughts of ... unheated bedrooms ... gilded from floor to ceiling, and embossed with cunning plasterwork.' The Friars and the Regal gave their multi-class audiences access to a new, charmed world.

Talking pictures were just one of the new technologies which transformed life in the 1920s and 1930s. During the war the forces had used radios to send and receive messages. After the war the wireless was developed for civilian use. George Barrett's son, John, was an enthusiastic radio ham: in 1931 he and his father set up a shop selling gramophones, radiograms, and radios next door to their St Peter's Street motor business. Theirs was not the only such enterprise. Sydney Bligh ran a wireless shop in North Lane and Leslie Goulden stocked similar products in his High Street store. For a short time, before the big manufacturers started producing wireless sets en masse, small stockists made the radios they sold themselves, while some customers purchased kits to construct their own sets at home. The first radios were expensive, but as the 1930s progressed increased production brought prices down and listening to the wireless became affordable for more and more families. As well as building radios the technically inclined also made films. Bligh and Goulden were founder members of the Canterbury Cine Club, which was formed in May 1934 and met above Goulden's shop. The club's fifty keen amateur film-makers filmed their own dramas and produced documentaries of local events. Each year until the outbreak of the Second World War, Sydney Bligh compiled a ninety-minute newsreel of Canterbury life, featuring street scenes, floods, sports, fêtes, civic events, and visits of dignitaries to the city and the cathedral.

Canterbury Cathedral was not immune to the winds of change blowing through the post-war world. Henry Wace, who had been appointed dean in 1903, died in post on 9 January 1924 at the age of eighty-seven. He was succeeded by a man of vigour and vision less than half his age, forty-one-year-old George Bell. Bell was determined to make the cathedral more outward-looking. He abolished admission charges, sought to encourage visitors, and took the initiative in approaching the BBC to broadcast special cathedral services. One of his most remarkable achievements was the reintroduction of drama to places of worship, a practice which had died out at the Reformation. Bell commissioned a future poet laureate, John Masefield, to write a play which was performed in the cathedral nave on Whit Monday and Tuesday 1928. The staging of *The Coming of Christ*, with music by Gustav Holst, attracted nationwide attention. Over seven thousand people attended the five performances, including visitors from

Poster advertising 1936 Canterbury Festival. *Courtesy of the Chapter of Canterbury Cathedral.*

Margaret Babington in her Christ Church Gate office. *Courtesy of the Chapter of Canterbury Cathedral.*

London such as George Bernard Shaw and the director of the National Gallery. The *Daily Telegraph* announced that the church was indebted to Bell's 'courageous initiative' and maintained that his experiment was 'abundantly justified'. The play's success inspired the dean to establish an annual arts festival at the cathedral, which put the city on the national cultural map. More eminent authors were commissioned to write new plays, notably T. S. Eliot: the first performance of *Murder in the Cathedral* was in the Chapter House on 15 June 1935. A few years later Dorothy L. Sayers wrote *The Zeal of Thy House* for the 1939 festival. Local people were heavily involved in these productions: they made costumes and props, performed alongside professionals as actors and instrumentalists, and operated the lights. The success of the festivals owed much to the organisational skills of Margaret Babington, an indomitable woman whom some people likened to Boadicea. In 1928 Bell had appointed her steward of the Friends of Canterbury Cathedral, a society he had created to raise funds for building repairs. Miss Babington ran it for the next thirty years, enlisting six thousand members and raising £100,000. It was due to her that Bell's legacy was preserved – and extended – long after he left Canterbury in 1929 to become the bishop of Chichester.

Bell was succeeded in quick succession by two deans who were to become national figures. Dick Sheppard, who pioneered religious broadcasting, was subsequently to achieve further fame (and notoriety) as the founder of the pacifist Peace Pledge Union. But Sheppard only served as dean of Canterbury for eighteen months, resigning in 1931 because of ill health. His successor, the controversial 'Red Dean', Hewlett Johnson, remained in post from 1931 to 1963. Soon after arriving in the city Johnson invited Mahatma Gandhi to stay at the deanery. The *Gazette* reported that Gandhi wore a 'flowing national garment reaching to his knees' and brought goat's milk, which he liked to drink, with him. He met various civic and religious dignitaries, attended a service in the cathedral and, after rising at 3 a.m., toured the city at 5.30 with Hewlett Johnson. Some of the dean's colleagues were among those who disapproved of his support for an arch opponent of the British Empire. Worse was to follow. Hewlett Johnson was an enthusiastic traveller, hence a headline in the *Gazette* of 3 April 1937, 'Dean off again'. On this occasion he was visiting civil-war Spain, but he also went to the Soviet Union and made no secret of his admiration for 'the Russian experiment'. In July 1937 Sir William Wayland, the speaker at a garden party organised by the Canterbury Women's Conservative Association, complained of 'laymen, laywomen and also clerics' who travelled to places 'under the control of the Red government of Spain' where they were 'duped with stories about what has happened there'. No one in Canterbury would have had any doubt which clergyman he had in mind.

Dean Hewlett Johnson and Mahatma Gandhi in Canterbury, 1931. *University of Kent Special Collections and Archives, Hewlett Johnson Archive.*

Earlier that month Sir Oswald Mosley, the founder of the British Union of Fascists (BUF), visited Canterbury and addressed a meeting in the Foresters' Hall. The *Gazette* described the occasion as a 'Noisy Meeting which might have been Worse'. A renowned orator, Mosley spoke for an hour and a half and faced 'a barrage of written and verbal questions'. There was so much heckling and unruliness that the police had to be called. While there was clearly opposition to Mosley's views in Canterbury, some citizens were sympathetic, notably Richard Bellamy, who joined the BUF in 1933 and became a paid official. By 1939 he and his family were living at 6 St Alphege Lane, which was described in a local directory as a 'British Union of Fascists and National Socialists Bookshop'.

The threat posed by Hitler's National Socialist regime was one that was only gradually realised. At Easter 1936 a party of boys from Kent College, a Methodist school on the outskirts of Canterbury, visited Germany to play hockey against clubs there. A few weeks later Simon Langton Girls' School welcomed Fräulein Gloel and twelve of her pupils from the German city of Halle. The headmistress hoped that there would be many future exchanges, but it is not clear whether the planned visit of Langton girls to Halle the following year actually took place. By this time concern was mounting that Europe might once again be moving towards war. Throughout the spring of 1937 the *Gazette* carried letters on the fraught topic of 'Should we rearm?' The government told local councils that they must make arrangements for coping with air attacks. In June 1937 a training course in 'Air Raid Precautionary Duties' was held at Canterbury's Beaney Institute. At first relatively few people responded to requests to sign up as air-raid wardens, but numbers escalated during the Sudetenland crisis of September 1938: over 150 volunteered in the space of four days. Two hundred others offered to join the auxiliary firefighting service. Gas masks sufficient for the whole population were delivered to the city and distributed from ten depots to long queues of people. On 30 September the prime minister came back from Germany waving a piece of paper which he believed had secured 'peace for our time'. Churches in Canterbury, like those throughout the land, offered prayers of thanksgiving, but the reprieve was short-lived. On 3 September 1939 Chamberlain broadcast to the nation that a state of war existed between Britain and Germany. In 1914 people in Canterbury had learnt that war had been declared by means of telegrams posted in the windows of the *Kentish Gazette* offices. Twenty-five years later many of them heard the prime minister's sombre announcement on radios in their own homes.

18

BLITZ AND RECONSTRUCTION

Friday 1 September 1939

Catherine Williamson, the mayor of Canterbury, waits at the east station for a train bringing evacuees from the Medway towns. Children tumble out onto the platform, some excited and full of bravado, others anxious or tearful, all with name labels sewn onto their coats: Robert, Betty, Barbara, William, Shirley. For a moment Catherine thinks of their mothers returning to silent, empty houses. Then she steps forward to welcome them. There is work to be done.

At the start of the war Canterbury was regarded as a safe location, a suitable place to send children whose homes and schools, close to the naval dockyard at Chatham, might easily be bombed. The *Kentish Gazette* reported how, on Friday 1 September, train after train brought schoolchildren to the city, followed by mothers with toddlers (and prams) on Saturday. The influx continued until the following Tuesday. Elderly, disabled, deaf, and blind people were sent to Canterbury, along with fifty pregnant women, one of whom gave birth shortly after she arrived. Some evacuees were conveyed in coaches to nearby villages; others were taken by volunteer car drivers (including the bishop of Dover) to a reception centre at the Langton schools to be allocated billets in the city. In the first month of the war Canterbury became home to over 1,500 evacuees.

Plans for evacuation had been drawn up months before, clear evidence of how precarious Chamberlain's 'peace for our time' was deemed to be. As early as January 1939 canvassers had visited 7,141 city homes and identified 10,182 rooms in which children could be billeted. But Canterbury also prepared for the possibility of air raids. In response to a stream of governmental injunctions, trenches were dug and shelters constructed, enough by the time war broke out to accommodate 3,400 people. An underground control centre was set up at the back of the council offices and an air-raid siren was purchased. As a further precaution, buildings were identified for use as extra mortuaries, and timber was sourced for up to 5,000 coffins. Volunteers were recruited for a wide range of civil defence duties. One week in the spring, Mrs Williamson went each night to the two big cinemas to appeal for more offers of help. At the same time as preparing for war, however, she also performed all the usual mayoral duties. Her first year of office, she reflected later, was a 'double life … entertaining and being entertained on the one hand and on the other hand, making extensive and final preparations for a heavy arterial bombardment'.

There was some criticism of all this provision for a war which might never come, and objections continued even after the war started. In October 1939 the *Daily Mail* used Canterbury as an example of a town which was spending far too much on unnecessary arrangements: the city was deemed to be 'one of the safest' in the country, hence the presence of so many evacuees. Critics, including some councillors, complained that the emergency committee of four which Mrs Williamson chaired was autocratic and unaccountable. Others, however, appreciated her hard work, and in November she was elected to serve a second term. Criticism was also levelled at the dean and chapter of the cathedral. Soil was laid several feet deep in the choir to ensure that falling masonry did not crash down into the crypt below, which was to be used as a public air-raid shelter. Mrs Williamson's predecessor, Herbert Harrison, wrote to *The Times*, expressing horror that lorries and a horse and cart had been seen in the nave, depositing tons of earth. Cathedrals, he insisted, should be refuges where harassed people could rest and pray: 'The Dean … has prevented this and made Canterbury Cathedral of no avail for the high purpose with which it has been associated for the last eight hundred years.' Hundreds of people signed a petition claiming that 'air-raid precautions of the existing nature are entirely contrary to Christian teaching and practice'. The *Kentish Gazette* noted that no church question had roused so much feeling in Canterbury for a long time.

Preparing the cathedral for war. ©*Kent Messenger Group.*

Objections such as this were reinforced by the months of 'phoney war', but in May 1940 German bombs were offloaded onto open ground near neighbouring villages. Within days the Medway children were moved from Canterbury to a safer location in north Wales. Three Canterbury boarding schools, King's, St Edmund's, and Kent College, evacuated their pupils to Cornwall. Lone raiders dropped occasional bombs on the city, and on 21 August Canterbury suffered its first fatalities when four people were killed.

The bombing intensified in the weeks that followed as enemy aircraft, returning from London, deposited their remaining cargo. The *Gazette* reported that 'four or five warnings a day have become commonplace'. Some people moved to places they deemed to be safer, and in September 1940 orders were received to evacuate some others from the city. Meanwhile, householders were encouraged to erect air-raid shelters in their homes. A loudspeaker was mounted on the Guildhall, and precautionary advice was broadcast from the mayor's office: 'Should an air raid occur take refuge in your shelter at once or if you have not got a shelter protect yourself under the staircase'; 'Before you go to bed at night partly fill your baths with water'; 'If you have shelter accommodation to spare in your house, please put a notice on your gate.' New public shelters were planned, including one in Westgate Grove, but residents objected that this would obstruct their view of the Westgate Gardens. The location was changed to an adjacent graveyard. On the morning of 4 September Mrs Williamson and the sheriff went to the site to discuss exactly where to put the new shelter. They narrowly escaped death when three bombs fell just yards away. The mayor flung herself to the ground but the blast left her feeling quite unwell. Her health broke down and for months she was unable to work or to sleep. Carping criticism, constant stress, and two years of incessant work had taken their toll. Mrs Williamson declined to stand for a third term of office and spent much of the next year recuperating in the west country.

It was not only air raids that people in Kent feared. After the fall of France it seemed likely that England might be invaded. Kent was in the front line. Thousands of sheep were evacuated from Romney Marsh, posts were erected in fields, and old carts and cars were deposited on open ground to prevent enemy aircraft landing. A tank trap was constructed at Lady Wotton's Green, just outside the city walls, to impede the progress of German tanks. At the end of October 1941 an invasion exercise was staged to test preparations in Canterbury. This started with parachutists capturing the West Gate towers and ended with the 'blowing up' of Catherine Williamson's successor, Charles Lefevre, in the control room. According to a *Gazette* reporter, the dramatic effect was spoilt by photographers 'taking pictures of the death scene' and by pressmen who surged round to hear the mayor's 'last words'. There were also simulated gas attacks, designed to train and test decontamination squads and to remind people always to carry their gas masks. The emission of unpleasant fumes ensured that those who had no masks – or who removed them before handbells signified that all was clear – learnt an unpleasant lesson.

From the very beginning everybody's life was fundamentally changed by the Second World War. Compulsory blacking-out of windows and doors at night was imposed two days before war was declared. Conscription was introduced at once for men aged between eighteen and forty-one, and extended to those under fifty-one a couple of years later. At this time unmarried women and childless widows aged between twenty and thirty also became liable to call-up. Rationing of sugar, butter, bacon, and ham started in January 1940, and households were required to register with a butcher of their choice in preparation for meat rationing. In due course other foods, clothing, and footwear were added to the list of rationed items. People were urged to grow their own food and to 'dig for victory'. Advice on what, when, and how to plant filled many columns of the local paper. In March 1942, in response to government injunctions to economise on petrol and manpower, butchers and grocers stopped delivering within the city, announcing 'You must carry your parcels ... This is your contribution to help win the war.' Slogans such as 'Salvage with a Smile' and 'Hit Hitler in the Waste' stressed that everyone could help by saving reusable materials. A *Gazette* reporter described how, as part of 'War Salvage Week' in December 1941, decorated lorries drove down the main street, preceded by a tableau featuring 'a very charming Britannia who appealed for waste paper'. There was a tank made out of old drums and tins, and even a skeleton which danced about advertising the utility of old bones. On 20 April 1942 Canterbury was mentioned on the nine o'clock news for holding the first 'War Metal Week': citizens were invited to deposit old metal in 'victory piles' opposite the Post Office and at the end of St George's Terrace.

Another way in which ordinary people helped the war effort was by raising funds for weapons. Throughout the summer of 1940 the names of those who contributed to a 'Spitfire Fund' filled column after column in the *Kentish Gazette*. A year later, in 'Tank Week', citizens had the opportunity to view and even clamber on three great tanks in the Broad Street car park. The city's first 'War Weapons Week' took place in February 1941. Competitions were held for schoolchildren to produce posters and people paid to view the entries, which were displayed in Lefevre's restaurant. Social events such as films, dances, bridge, and whist drives brought in further funds, but by far the most productive way of raising money was through investment in 'National Savings', which was advertised with slogans such as: 'Invasion may be attempted. Resist with your savings'; 'The more you lend – the sooner the end.' A huge 'Progress Indicator' on the Corn Exchange depicted Hitler behind bars, and a new bar was added

Display of children's posters in Lefevre's restaurant in War Weapons Week, 1941. *Derek Butler Collection.*

The West Gate towers, erected at the time of the 1381 peasants' revolt, were used in 1941 to encourage the purchase of war bonds. A war-time look-out post can be seen on one of the towers. *University of Kent Special Collections and Archives, Fisk-Moore Studio, Paul Crampton Photographic Collection.*

for each £25,000 raised. The *Gazette*'s hope that 'by Saturday night Adolf will be completely grilled' was realised when over £500,000 was saved. By the summer of 1941 over three hundred savings groups had been formed in workplaces, shops, schools, social clubs, and streets throughout the district. In the second War Weapons Week the *Gazette* sought to mobilise competitive instincts by listing how much each group was aiming to raise and what the money would buy. Savers in St Stephen's Road hoped to cover the cost of a rubber dinghy, while the three Cherry Garden branches aimed to pay for a sailor's kit, a sextant, and a large mine. The published results showed that most groups substantially exceeded their targets.

Fundraising efforts helped boost morale in daytime, but many people suffered through lack of sleep. Hundreds of older men who served in the Home Guard spent one night in every six on guard duty, after which they performed a normal day's work. Each night firefighters kept watch on buildings throughout the city. Tom Hoare, who led a team stationed on the roof of the cathedral, recalled that there were sometimes as many as six alerts in one night. Even those who slept in their own beds suffered broken nights caused by the wailing of the city siren, 'Tugboat Annie', when enemy planes passed overhead.

The year 1941 passed with very little bombing in the Canterbury area, but in the spring of 1942 the Luftwaffe began attacking places of historic significance. The 'Baedeker raids', named after the guidebook which German tourists used when visiting Britain, were a retaliation for RAF assaults on towns such as Lübeck. Following attacks on Exeter, Bath, Norwich, and York, everyone knew that Canterbury would be targeted. Late on Saturday 30 May over a thousand British bombers took off for Germany. Shortly after midnight they inflicted devastating damage on the city of Cologne. Just twenty-four hours later, enemy planes deposited more than a hundred high explosives and several thousand incendiary bombs on Canterbury. They flew so low that Kenneth Pinnock, on fire duty at the Langton schools, said he 'could see their crosses'. The usual impenetrable darkness of the blackout was replaced by what onlookers described as a 'wonderful pink light', a 'huge cascade of the most beautiful flares floating down through the sky'. But the strange beauty was accompanied by a terrifying seventy-five minutes of ear-piercing noise, 'planes roaring and diving', the 'terrible scream of bombs', 'glass smashing, plaster falling on our heads'. The eastern end of the main street was flattened and landmark buildings such as the Corn Exchange were gutted. Of a long run of shops on the southern side of the street, only Marks and Spencer remained

St George's Street shortly after the 1942 Baedeker raid. *University of Kent Special Collections and Archives, Fisk-Moore Studio, Paul Crampton Photographic Collection.*

standing amidst a sea of rubble. In the New Dover Road thirteen-year-old Leslie Andrews watched as flames devoured his family's four-storey house, totally destroying his father's accountancy business. Gwen Bates, who was ten at the time, emerged from a Morrison shelter in her Querns Road home to find that the back wall of the house had been blown out and the bedroom floor was tipping at a dangerous angle. The rabbits they kept in the garden had been 'blown to bits', 'all the bits of rabbit hanging up in the tree'. The following morning, architect Anthony Swaine climbed to the top of the cathedral and risked prosecution by illegally taking photos of the smoking ruins of the city. As young Ted Chappell cycled to school he saw 'molten lead from the roofs that had fallen in' and 'fires still smouldering'. When he reached the Simon Langton School, 'there it was – gone! ... There was exercise books and papers, people's notes, broken glass, lead, and this great dusty burning smell everywhere.' The cathedral precincts were peppered

Dean Hewlett Johnson outside the 'grand and unhurt' cathedral. *University of Kent Special Collections and Archives, Hewlett Johnson Archive.*

with craters from bombs which had destroyed some King's School buildings, several houses, and the cathedral library. But the damage could have been worse. Medieval stained glass, valuable books, and documents had been removed to safety long before. A few days later the dean noted that the 'cathedral itself, though all the windows are blown out, stands up grand and unhurt', newly visible across the devastated city.

Given the severity of the raid the death toll was low, just fifty people. Many of the bombs had dropped on the central commercial area, which was fairly empty at night. One of the men who died was the town clerk, George Marks, who as head of the city's civil defence had done so much to help prepare Canterbury for such an eventuality. His house was one of over three hundred destroyed in the raid. Some 2,500 others were damaged. The mayor had long urged fellow citizens to make contingency plans to stay elsewhere in the city if their homes became uninhabitable, and many families went to live with friends or relations. Others were given temporary accommodation in the Technical Institute before being billeted in neighbouring villages and towns. Schemes to issue emergency clothing coupons and replacement ration books were implemented immediately, but other losses had not been foreseen. Some people had left their spectacles and false teeth by their beds as they fled to the safety of shelters. It took them some time to get replacements. First of all, however, survivors needed to assure their relatives that they were still alive. Special tables were set up outside the Post Office to cater for the crowds who came to write telegrams. Since there was no school, Ted Chappell and his friend spent the rest of that first day working as volunteer messenger boys, delivering numerous telegrams which poured into the city from anxious relations who had heard on the 7 a.m. news that Canterbury had been bombed.

There were two further bombing raids that week, but stalwart attempts were made to re-establish 'business as usual'. Schools were reopened and shopkeepers whose premises had survived intact lent floor space to enable less fortunate neighbours to continue trading. Hundreds of workmen were drafted into the city from elsewhere in Kent to help with emergency repairs. There was no possibility of major renovation as long as further raids were likely, but gaping roofs were covered with some three thousand tarpaulins. Buildings which were deemed dangerous were demolished. Meanwhile, barrage balloons attached to thick steel cables were launched to impede low-flying aircraft. But citizens remained fearful. Some took to sleeping in public shelters, while others sought safety in the countryside and spent warm summer nights under hedges and haystacks. A few even took their bedding to the railway tunnel on the Canterbury–Whitstable line. The next attack, however, took place not at night but in daytime. At 5 p.m. on Saturday 31 October 1942 Canterbury was full of shoppers, and a long queue of people waited outside the Regal Cinema to see *Gone with the Wind*. The barrage balloons were grounded for repairs, so enemy planes were able to swoop low over the city, strafing the streets with machine-gun fire. One of the bombs they dropped demolished part of the cinema. After a few hours' respite, people were woken at 1 a.m. as bombs rained down once again on their homes. Thirty-five people were killed in the two raids, and over a hundred were injured.

These were the last major assaults on Canterbury, but in 1944 fear of flying bombs, 'doodlebugs', caused many to spend their nights once again in air-raid shelters. The *Kentish Gazette* tabulated the suffering inflicted during five years of warfare up to 30 September 1944: there had been 2,477 alerts and 35 bombing raids. In total, over 10,000 incendiaries had been dropped on Canterbury, 455 high explosives, and one flying bomb. One hundred and fifteen people had lost their lives and 380 had been injured. Eight hundred and eight properties had been destroyed and 6,738 damaged. Many other towns had experienced similar devastation, but images of Canterbury were widely disseminated through Michael Powell's evocative mystery film *A Canterbury Tale*. Its world premiere took place in the Friars Cinema on 11 May 1944. At the end of the screening Powell introduced some of the film's famous stars to the excited audience, before taking them across the road to a civic reception in the County Hotel. According to the *Gazette*, it was 'Canterbury's most important social occasion since the outbreak of war'.

Planning for the future started long before the war ended. On 4 July 1942, just over a month after the Baedeker raid, a letter from the mayor, the cathedral dean, the archbishop, and his predecessor was published in *The Times*. The four leaders called for 'artists of real vision' to be involved in the redevelopment of Canterbury and urged that private interests be subordinated to the good of the whole. The Blitz acted as a catalyst to national planning of a type never attempted before. Throughout the country, architects engaged in enthusiastic discussion, relishing the opportunity to think long term and to design city centres as whole entities rather than piecemeal. A Ministry of Town and Country Planning was created in 1943, and the following year Parliament gave councils of blitzed towns huge powers to purchase the land needed to make the new schemes work. A prizewinning architect, Charles Holden, who had designed the University of London's Senate House as well as many underground stations, was engaged to devise a plan for Canterbury. The scheme which Holden submitted to the council in March 1945, like the designs which fellow architects produced for other towns, was bold and extensive. Holden proposed a great double-lane boulevard some seventy feet wide, leading from a new civic centre by the Dane John Gardens to

Artist's impression of the new 'Civic Way' proposed by Charles Holden.
Canterbury's Problem: the answer is your responsibility (c. 1945).

the heart of the city. He aimed to reduce traffic congestion by constructing outer and inner ring roads, as well as a new city-centre road parallel to the High Street, which would therefore become one-way. Mrs Williamson was enthusiastic, describing the Holden plan as 'gallant' and 'beautiful'. Others, however, were far from convinced, and Canterbury became one of several cities in which proposed redevelopment met with vociferous opposition. Letters poured into the *Gazette* from people signing themselves 'a lover of Canterbury', 'one born in this city', 'lifelong Canterburian' and, significantly, simply 'ratepayer'. Critics complained about the cost of the scheme, particularly the expense of the new 'Civic Avenue', and protested that the development was out of scale with the rest of the city: it would destroy its traditional character and 'the charm and intimacy' of its narrow streets. A 'Citizens' Defence Association' (CDA) was formed to oppose the Holden scheme.

The CDA brought together a diverse group of people with contrasting concerns. There were conservationists such as Anthony Swaine, who was horrified that the imposing facade of the Corn Exchange had been taken down within weeks of the Blitz. Looking back years later, Swaine wrote: 'Many buildings, though damaged, were ... capable of repair; however, while the ashes and cinders were still warm, the evil act of matricide was about to begin.' Swaine was to spend the next seventy years fighting tirelessly to save and restore buildings in Canterbury and other Kentish towns. Other CDA members had different worries. They were businessmen who wanted to resume trade as quickly as possible. They believed that this would best be achieved if they were allowed to rebuild their own premises along old street lines, an approach which precluded major redesign of the city centre. The Holden scheme assumed that the council would acquire some seventy-five acres of privately owned land, a proposal described by one *Gazette* correspondent as 'sheer nationalisation in our time'. Compulsory purchase of bombed sites was a contentious issue in all blitzed towns, with owners protesting that the projected reimbursement at 1939 values was inadequate. Moreover, councillors who had financial interests in areas designated for compulsory purchase were barred from voting. In consequence, momentous decisions about the future of Canterbury lay in the hands of just six individuals, a situation denounced by the *Gazette* as a 'municipal farce'. The CDA's most vocal leader, W. J. Jennings, appealed to fellow citizens:

> Unless you wish to see this old city turned into a mongrel from an architectural point-of-view, develop into a white elephant economically and yourselves condemned to live in subservience to numbers of municipal bureaucrats, rise up and make your stand before it is too late.

The influence of the men and women who had steered the city through the trauma of war was now much reduced. In the general election held in July 1945, Mrs Williamson contested the Canterbury seat on behalf of the short-lived Commonwealth Party – and lost her deposit. A few months later Charles Lefevre, who had served as mayor from 1940 to 1944, suddenly died. The editor of the *Gazette* articulated the city's sense of shock and loss: 'In the time of our direst need, Alderman Lefevre was to Canterbury what our great war leader, Winston Churchill, was to the nation.' But as the nation rejected Churchill as peace-time leader, so the people of Canterbury rejected the plans which Mrs Williamson, Mr Lefevre, and their colleagues had proposed for their city. Twelve council seats came up for re-election in the autumn of 1945 and CDA candidates won them all, helped by the fact that no Conservatives opposed them. Mrs Williamson lost her seat.

Charles Lefevre. ©*Imperial War Museum (D 5010)*.

The new councillors faced the same problems as their predecessors: how to take advantage of the opportunity to remodel the city while also enabling traders to resume business as quickly as possible. Like their counterparts throughout the country, they were constrained by new government regulations and dogged by a shortage of building materials, which were desperately needed to replenish the housing stock. Grandiose schemes were not feasible in the straitened financial circumstances of the post-war era, and many towns had to modify their redevelopment plans. Holden's original design for Canterbury was scaled down and then replaced by a more modest scheme, drawn up by architect and planning officer Hugh Wilson in 1951. Wilson rejected Holden's proposed boulevard, with its vista of the cathedral, and produced a plan which he believed was more in keeping with the city's medieval character. This too, however, necessitated the compulsory purchase of bombed land, albeit less than half the amount proposed by Holden. CDA councillors accepted that some compulsory purchase was unavoidable, but the *Gazette* criticised them for repudiating the mandate on which they had been elected. The editor feared ever-increasing council control, and warned that traders outside the compulsorily purchased area would enjoy greater freedom than those operating within an 'Iron Curtain'.

Temporary pre-fabricated shops, erected in 1947, survived until the second half of the 1950s. *University of Kent Special Collections and Archives, Fisk-Moore Studio, Paul Crampton Photographic Collection.*

Even Wilson's modified scheme was not fully implemented. Houses were demolished to make way for a ring road, but only part of this ever materialised. Plans for a new civic centre within the city walls were dropped, as was any idea of building a new road parallel to the High Street. To the dismay of conservationists, however, redevelopment still involved the destruction of a number of medieval buildings. After years of debate the tower of St George's church, with its landmark clock, was saved, but the church itself, which Holden had planned to retain, was demolished. Part of the problem for the council was the sheer cost of repairing damaged buildings. In the late summer of 1950, work to restore the ancient Guildhall was suspended in the face of serious structural defects. The mayor wrote to *The Times* explaining that the council was not prepared to ask ratepayers to cover the high cost of reconstruction. Mrs Williamson urged fellow citizens to contribute towards a restoration fund, and the *Gazette* vainly hoped that people from the Empire and the United States might help, but in 1955 the surviving walls of the Guildhall were demolished. Conservationists lobbied hard to preserve what remained of the medieval Fleur de Lys inn in the High Street, but in 1958 it too disappeared.

The reconstruction of Canterbury, like that of many other cities, took far longer than anyone had expected. Temporary prefabricated shops, erected in the Longmarket in 1947, were not demolished until the late 1950s. For years after the war, blitzed areas of the city remained wastelands of rubble in which buddleias flourished: local historian Paul Crampton dubbed the late 1940s 'the Buddleia Years'. The flattened land gave archaeologists a chance to investigate the city's past. An excavation committee was set up in July 1944, before the war ended, and from time to time exhibitions were held displaying Roman, Saxon, and medieval finds. The summer of 1951 provided an opportunity for a more extensive celebration of the city's heritage. After much debate about expenditure, Canterbury became one of twenty Festival of Britain cities. A substantial exhibition on bombed wasteland in the heart of the city depicted 'all that is typical of Kent' – from gypsy caravans to oast houses – alongside the illustrious history of Canterbury itself. On 18 July robed mayors from more than twenty local towns attended a special cathedral service. A fortnight later a colourful procession of floats from all over east Kent displayed characters and events from the county's past. Several amateur film-makers captured the scenes for posterity. 'Who would have thought,' asked John Clague in the soundtrack to his film, 'that bombs which fell nearly ten years ago would have cleared the site for an exhibition in which the city of Canterbury could display so magnificently the treasures of its past and the hopes of its future?'

19

UNIVERSITY CITY

11 October 1965

An eighteen-year-old girl gazes curiously across the campus of the University of Kent, at the place which will be her home for the next three years. There is mud everywhere, a few very new buildings, and in the distance the great cathedral looming over the city below. Some of her friends said she was crazy to come to a new university but she thinks it will be exciting. She picks up her suitcase and steps forward into her new life.

Students arriving at the University of Kent, October 1965. *University of Kent Special Collections and Archives, University Collection.*

The coming of higher education transformed Canterbury. Hewlett Johnson had mooted the idea of a university during debates on post-war reconstruction, but no such development was possible in the austere years following the war. By the 1960s, however, the national economy had recovered and hordes of young people, born since 1945, were approaching university age. A government report published in 1963 recommended a massive expansion of higher education, including the creation of several new universities. There was much debate where these should be situated. A number of places in Kent – Thanet, Chatham, and Folkestone – had started to develop schemes for local universities, but the county council believed that an application made at county level stood greater chance of success. In the discussions that followed, Canterbury emerged as the favoured location: a regional centre, not too close to London, with historic associations and an environment attractive to potential staff and students. The new University of Kent at Canterbury (UKC), like others which received their charters at the same time, was built on a campus on the outskirts of its host city. In October 1965 it welcomed its first cohort of 460 students. A few years earlier another higher education institution had opened in Canterbury: Christ Church College, a Church of England foundation for the training of teachers. In 1964 its students took possession of a new campus appropriately located on the site of St Augustine's Abbey, which thirteen centuries before had been an internationally renowned centre of teaching and learning. Education was once again to become a major feature of the city's life.

When the first undergraduates arrived in the mid-1960s, Canterbury was a small, provincial market town with a population of around thirty-two thousand. It was still full of little shops: a 1966 trade directory listed thirty-five grocers, twenty-two fruiterers or greengrocers, twenty butchers, and thirty-nine tobacconists and confectioners. There were thirty-one outfitters, tailors, or clothiers, at least eighteen of them in the main street. For centuries, farmers from the surrounding region had brought their animals to the city's cattle market, and this continued to function, albeit since 1955 in a less central location, as the old site was needed for a new dual carriageway. To students from other parts of the country, Canterbury seemed a long way from anywhere. The train journey from London took at least an hour and forty minutes, often longer, with stops at numerous intervening stations. Anyone who travelled by car benefited from the recent opening of the Dartford Tunnel and the M2, but drivers then had to negotiate the narrow twisting A2 through the villages of Boughton and

Harbledown, which were not bypassed until 1976. When they reached the city it was obvious that the planned post-war rebuilding was not yet complete: the dual carriageway round the southern walls and the new buildings which would line it were still under construction.

One major development in Canterbury, as everywhere else in the country, was the creation of vast new housing estates to cater for an ever-increasing number of young families. The post-war boom in births necessitated more schools, and so primary schools were erected on each out-of-town estate. The bombed Langton schools were rebuilt on the outskirts of the city, and several new secondary schools were established, including one named after Frank Hooker, who had served nineteen years as chair of Canterbury's education committee. (The school's name was changed in 1990 to 'Canterbury High' as part of a rebranding exercise, which had the added advantage of sparing female pupils the embarrassment of being nicknamed 'hookers'.) Secondary schools had previously been single-sex.

A new housing estate at Hales Place under construction, 1957.
©*Kent Messenger Group.*

It was a mark of the changing times that the Frank Hooker and other new foundations of the 1950s and 1960s were co-educational.

The baby boom, followed by the later influx of students, made young people a visible presence in Canterbury, but it was many decades before a flourishing youth culture developed. Teenagers born in the city complained that there was little to do, while students who came from larger, more bustling towns grumbled about the lack of nightlife. Ironically, however, this quiet provincial town nurtured a group of future professional musicians who played a part in the development of pop music. In the mid-1960s old schoolfriends from the Simon Langton started a rock band, the Wilde Flowers, whose distinctive style of music set them apart from other such groups. Some members moved on to other Canterbury-based bands, such as Soft Machine and Caravan, both of which gained international reputations. Their highly original fusion of jazz and rock, characterised by unusual chord changes, extended improvisation, and abstruse lyrics, became known as the 'Canterbury Sound'.

The Wilde Flowers, March 1965. ©*Kent Messenger Group.*

Other Canterbury residents made significant contributions to children's entertainment. Mary Tourtel, who had been educated at the Simon Langton Girls' School and Sidney Cooper's School of Art, was an interwar illustrator who created a *Daily Express* newspaper strip featuring the much-loved Rupert Bear. Mary died in Canterbury in 1948, but her bear, in his distinctive red jumper and yellow checked trousers, proved so popular that Rupert annuals continued to be produced decades after her death. In 1959 two pioneers of TV animation, Oliver Postgate and Peter Firmin, moved to east Kent and set up a workshop in an old cowshed in Blean, a couple of miles outside Canterbury. Here they filmed handmade figures and recorded soundtracks in ways that later generations would regard as laughably primitive, but the characters they created proved as endearingly memorable as Rupert Bear: Ivor the Engine, Noggin the Nog, the Pingwings, the Clangers, and an ultimate triumph, Bagpuss. The story of the saggy pink-and-cream cloth cat (he was supposed to be ginger but the dyeing company made a mistake) topped a 1999 BBC poll as the most popular children's programme of the century. Another children's favourite – at least among little girls – was also produced in Canterbury. From the early 1960s to the late 1980s there was a toy-making factory in Market Way. Initially it produced model battleships and the like for boys, and then

Bagpuss. ©*Firmin/Postgate.*

soft toys, but its claim to fame came from assembling the best-selling Sindy doll. Sindy's success generated a wide array of accessories and companion dolls, such as 'Canterbury Patch'. The Sindy range proved so popular that at the height of production the factory employed over four hundred people.

Notwithstanding the baby boom, the coming of light industry, and the introduction of higher education, Canterbury remained a small town. Its population at the time of the 1971 census was just over 33,000. Nevertheless, it possessed an unusual degree of administrative autonomy, dating back to the fifteenth century when it had been designated a county borough. County councils were created in 1888, but Canterbury survived, independent of Kent, as the smallest county borough in the country. This meant that it ran its own services and was therefore England's smallest education authority. All this came to an end when an act introducing major changes to local government was implemented in 1974. Even cities as large as Bristol, Nottingham, Leicester, and Hull lost the right to run their own schools, libraries, and social services. Canterbury was brought under the jurisdiction of the county for the first time in over five hundred years, and decisions about schools, and much else besides, were thereafter made at the county headquarters in Maidstone. One of the aims of the act was to ensure that all units of local government were large enough to be viable. Kent was divided into fourteen district councils. There was some protest about this, but only Gillingham, which was nearly three times as big as Canterbury, managed to stave off amalgamation with smaller bodies. The county borough of Canterbury was merged with the two urban districts of Whitstable and Herne Bay and the rural district of Bridge-Blean. The varied character of this new council inevitably led to conflicts of interest. Canterbury residents complained that decisions about their future were now made by councillors who neither lived in nor understood the needs of their city. On the other hand, villagers and people from the coastal towns sometimes felt that they were treated as mere appendages of Canterbury, a feeling reinforced by the fact that the new authority was called 'Canterbury City Council'. Its offices were in Canterbury and in 1978 a redundant church in the city was converted into a new council chamber.

The pre-eminence of Canterbury reflected not only its position as the main town of the region but also the importance of its cathedral. Long before the sixteenth-century break with Rome, the archbishop of Canterbury had been recognised as the chief archbishop in England, superior to the head of the northern province of York, an arrangement which continued when England became Protestant. Church of England missionaries took their faith to other countries, and by the late Victorian period the archbishop of Canterbury was recognised as the spiritual head of a worldwide Anglican communion. To this day, people around the globe regard Canterbury as their spiritual home. Roughly every ten years, bishops from Anglican churches across the world come to England at the archbishop's invitation for a 'Lambeth' conference. Since 1978 this has met not in London but on the campus of the University of Kent at Canterbury.

One of the most momentous events in the history of the cathedral took place on 29 May 1982, when Pope John Paul II and Archbishop Robert Runcie knelt together on the spot where Becket had been murdered over eight centuries before. This was the first time a pope had visited England since the Reformation, and the ecumenical 'Celebration of Faith' in Canterbury Cathedral was the symbolic highlight of his tour. The papal helicopter landed in the grounds of the Frank Hooker School, and the Pope then travelled with Archbishop Runcie in a 'popemobile', past waving crowds who lined the streets. The city council had anticipated that attendance might reach six figures but, in the event, numbers were fewer than expected. Around 25,000 people gathered along the Pope's route. Shopkeepers who had hoped for a boom in takings found that their shops were deserted, and some recorded their worst Saturday for years. Also

Pope John Paul and Archbishop Runcie in the 'popemobile', May 1982. ©*Kent Messenger Group.*

disappointed were some of the spectators who stood for hours in the hot sun without ever seeing the Pope: a gas leak in the main street led to a last-minute alteration of his return route through the city. By contrast, some of those who watched the Pope walk through the cathedral precincts were thrilled that he actually spoke to them. Twins John and Kentigern Hawkins had reason to remember their eighth birthday, since they broke away from the crowds to give a posy to the pontiff, who blessed them and patted their heads. Thirteen-year-old Karolina Krynicki, a Simon Langton pupil whose father taught at the university, attracted the Pope's attention by wearing the red and white of her – and his – native Poland: when she offered him a bouquet of red and white carnations, the Pope responded 'Thank you, daughter of Christ. Pray for me.' A number of Canterbury residents would remember the day they met the Pope for the rest of their lives.

Four years later, on 12 February 1986, another significant international event took place in Canterbury, when the prime minister, Margaret Thatcher, and President Mitterand of France signed the Channel Tunnel agreement. The choice of Canterbury was controversial, since there was vociferous opposition to the tunnel in east Kent. The editor of the *Gazette* feared 'scars across the county, village life ruined, job losses, opportunities for terrorists. It would be nice to be proved wrong. The Garden of England must not become the Backyard of Europe.' Five east Kent councils, including Canterbury, issued a joint statement with the county council urging the government to ensure that 'Kent reaps the benefits – not just the drawbacks – from having the project on our doorstep.' There was anxiety that the tunnel would harm the environment, that property prices might soar to the detriment of local inhabitants, and that jobs, particularly those associated with seafaring and the ports, might be lost. Opponents included groups such as the Campaign to Protect Rural England and the Women's Institute, which included many normally loyal Conservatives in their membership. Canterbury's Conservative mayor, Hazel McCabe, noted that councillors across the political spectrum voted against the project by forty-five votes to four. The local MP, David Crouch, another Conservative, told the transport minister that while he personally supported the tunnel, he could not carry his constituents with him.

Since the treaty was signed only sixteen months after the Provisional IRA had bombed Mrs Thatcher and fellow Conservatives at their party conference in Brighton, even greater security precautions were taken than for the papal and royal visits. Police frogmen searched city sewers, dogs sniffed for explosives, and armed officers patrolled snow-covered roofs.

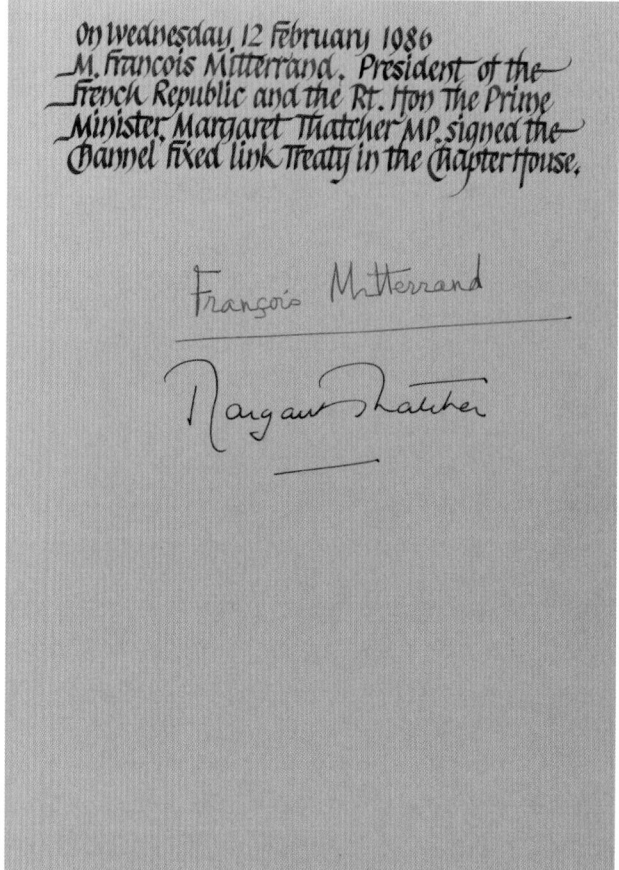

On Wednesday, 12 February 1986
M. Francois Mitterrand, President of the
French Republic and the Rt. Hon The Prime
Minister, Margaret Thatcher MP, signed the
Channel fixed link Treaty in the Chapter House.

François Mitterrand

Margaret Thatcher

Entry in Canterbury Cathedral Visitors' Book. Courtesy of the Chapter of Canterbury Cathedral.

Happily, the event took place without major incident. Jeering, banner-waving protesters lined the road along which the prime minister and the president travelled, and the odd egg was thrown, but according to a local reporter the police seemed 'to have more problems keeping back curious King's School pupils clutching cameras than would-be troublemakers'. The most dramatic protest was that made by Mrs McCabe: given 'the feelings of the majority of the people of the district of which I am mayor', she refused to witness the signing of the treaty. (She also objected to the use of the cathedral for such a purpose on Ash Wednesday, a significant day in the church year.) The mayor deemed it her duty to welcome the visitors to the city and she dined with them, but she sat outside in her car while they did their business in the Chapter House.

In her address Mrs Thatcher acknowledged the concerns of the people of Kent. She promised that her government would help ease environmental and infrastructure problems, but she maintained that it was right for the treaty to be signed in Canterbury. She reminded her audience that the Chapter House in which they were meeting was part of a great Benedictine monastery, revived and reorganised by Lanfranc, the first Norman archbishop of Canterbury. The cathedral was built of French stone from Caen, and a Frenchman, William of Sens, had played a major role in its construction: 'Our surroundings are thus rich in associations with France stretching back over centuries. What more fitting place could there be to sign this treaty which takes those associations forward into the 21st century.' President Mitterand predicted that future generations of schoolchildren in Britain and France 'will have a new date to remember: February 12 1986 – the Treaty of Canterbury'.

Whether or not they were aware of the treaty which bore the city's name, increasing numbers of children, both British and French, came to Canterbury on school trips in the decades that followed. Arguably, more French was heard on city streets than at any time since the Huguenot influx of the late seventeenth century. Tourism boomed worldwide in the last few decades of the twentieth century, and Canterbury was one of the beneficiaries. Its proximity to the channel ports, a major asset throughout its history, meant that school parties from Germany and the Low Countries, as well as France, included it on educational visits to England, sometimes staying in the city. Young people of many nationalities converged on language schools in south-east England, and some Canterbury families made a little extra money by providing accommodation for them. Improvements in transport made the city more accessible than ever before. At the end of 2009 high-speed trains were introduced on the Canterbury West line, reducing the journey from London to under an hour. This made it easy for overseas visitors who were staying in the capital to spend a day in Canterbury. To the disappointment of city traders, keen to maximise their profits, most of the tourists who came to Canterbury did not stay overnight, but were just day trippers.

Over the decades, returning visitors witnessed major changes to the city streets. Once the dual carriageway to the south of the city was completed in the late 1960s, the main thoroughfare became one-way and was subsequently pedestrianised. As in other towns, butchers, grocers, greengrocers, and other small shops gradually disappeared from the city centre. In 1984 a big Sainsbury's supermarket opened on the site of the old electricity generating plant, one of several superstores built on the outskirts of the city with large car parks to cater for people who now did a weekly food shop by car. Concerned that retail parks such as those which had already developed in Ashford and Bluewater might lure even more shoppers away from the city centre, the council approved the demolition of 1950s and 1960s buildings on the old Whitefriars site and their replacement by a new, more modern, shopping centre. This opened in 2004, but only a few years later everything began to change again with the growth of internet shopping. High streets everywhere went into decline, populated increasingly by eateries and charity shops. As a major tourist centre Canterbury suffered less than many places, but boarded-up shops could be seen in its streets too.

While some visitors from east Kent may have come to Canterbury to shop, tourists from further afield were attracted, as in the past, by the city's heritage. In 1988 the cathedral, St Augustine's Abbey, and St Martin's parish church (the oldest in continuous use in the country) became a three-centre 'World Heritage Site'. But the costs of maintaining places which were deemed to be of 'outstanding universal value' were considerable, exacerbated in the case of the cathedral by the wear and tear caused by the huge press of tourists. The cathedral received no state or church aid, and on average visitors donated only a few pence each.

The ancient St Martin's church and the cathedral, part of Canterbury's World Heritage site. *Oosoom, Wikimedia Commons.*

In 1995 the dean and chapter concluded that they had no option but to reintroduce admission charges, which George Bell had abolished in the late 1920s. This was controversial, but the fees reduced visitors to a more manageable number (around a million a year) while also contributing towards the maintenance of the building. Further income was provided by donations which Anglicans across the world made to the mother church of their communion. In acknowledgement of American generosity, a new wooden-clad auditorium was named after George Clagett, a seventeenth-century mayor whose family had emigrated to Maryland. This was part of an international study centre and hotel erected in the cathedral precincts at the turn of the century. The old Victorian missionary college had ceased to function during the Second World War, and a replacement had closed in the 1960s for lack of funds. As its twenty-first-century successor, the new study centre gave people of different nationalities – seminarians, newly ordained priests, trainee bishops – the opportunity to spend a few weeks living and learning together in Canterbury.

Educational institutions were Canterbury's primary employers. In 2011 schools, colleges, and universities provided employment for a fifth of the city's working residents. The University of Kent was by far the largest

Newly-appointed bishops on a course in Canterbury, 2008. *Courtesy of the Chapter of Canterbury Cathedral.*

employer in the district, way ahead even of the health service. By 2017 it had a workforce of 3,400. Over the decades Christ Church College had expanded and diversified beyond teacher training, and in 2005 it too became a university. Sidney Cooper's School of Art and a number of other south-eastern art colleges had evolved into the University of the Creative Arts, and one of its four campuses was situated in Canterbury. There was a huge expansion of higher education in the early twenty-first century, and this had a marked impact on Canterbury, which was much smaller than many university towns. The city contained far more eighteen- to twenty-four-year-olds than most places and had one of the largest concentrations of students, relative to the resident population, in the country. Houses which had been built in the 1950s, 60s, and 70s for young families had long been purchased by buy-to-let landlords, and whole streets (particularly those near the universities) were occupied predominantly by students. Other university towns suffered in the same way, but by 2018 Canterbury had the lowest rate of owner-occupation in the UK, just 43 per cent. In the general election of June 2017 the parliamentary constituency produced a shock result which hit the headlines: the Labour candidate, Rosie Duffield, won the previously safe Conservative seat by 187 votes. Her success was widely attributed to effective social-media lobbying among the city's many university students.

The preponderance of students affected the town in other ways too. The days when Canterbury was criticised for a lack of nightlife were long past: from late evening the city centre became the domain of the young. At the same time, however, the existence of the universities encouraged the provision of a range of cultural facilities from which all ages could benefit, with the result that Canterbury was better served in this respect than many communities. In the 1980s one of the old Art Deco cinemas was converted into a theatre, which was replaced a quarter of a century later by a state-of-the-art building on the same site. The new Marlowe Theatre, which opened in 2011, was large enough to accommodate performances such as Glyndebourne operas, which needed a bigger stage and orchestra pit than had previously been available. Now Canterbury audiences could see nationally acclaimed productions such as *War Horse*, West End musicals, Royal Shakespeare Company plays, and dance of all kinds, without travelling far from home. A smaller, more intimate theatre, the Gulbenkian, had been provided on the University of Kent campus as early as 1969, and in 2012 a wood-lined concert hall was constructed alongside it, with

Canterbury Christ Church University Library, Augustine House, was opened in 2009, across the road from the old city wall. *Author's photograph.*

acoustics that delighted visiting musicians. Many of the most striking new buildings in the city were financed by schools and universities. Members of the public had the opportunity to attend lectures, concerts, and a variety of other activities in facilities such as Kent College's Great Hall and Christ Church University's plate-glass Augustine House.

As Canterbury developed, its population continued to expand. By the time of the 2011 census some fifty thousand people lived in the city and its immediate suburbs. In comparison with many other towns, however, it remained a small place, characterised by an intimacy which larger conurbations lacked. Walking down the main street, residents regularly met people they knew. They also, of course, encountered visitors and students from all over the world. Some grumbled as noisy school parties crowded the streets by day and as exuberant undergraduates talked outside pubs at night. But Canterbury's economy depended on tourists and students, and their presence gave the city a vibrancy which belied its small size.

Epilogue

Much has changed in Canterbury since 1500. In the sixteenth century it was one of the largest towns in the country. By Victoria's reign it was dwarfed by conurbations throughout England and overtaken even within its own county. Over the years the base of its economy has altered. A centuries-old tourist industry came to an end when Becket's shrine was demolished in 1538. Silk-weaving flourished in the late seventeenth century, but a hundred years later there were hardly any weavers in Canterbury. Even as a religious centre the city's importance waxed and waned. In 1500 the cathedral attracted eminent guests from across Europe as well as many pilgrims. A few centuries later Canterbury was held in such little regard that some archbishops did not even come to the city to be enthroned. Gradually, however, the cathedral regained its significance, and by the twenty-first century it regularly welcomed bishops from all over the world, along with millions of tourists.

Like every generation before them, present-day residents of Canterbury face an unpredictable future. The long-term effects of the Covid-19 pandemic and of British withdrawal from the European Union are yet to unfold but may well lead to further reshaping of the city's economy and to adjustments in the lifestyle of its inhabitants. As the pace of change has quickened, children are born into a society their parents and grandparents could never have imagined. But whether they realise it or not, they live with the legacy of earlier generations. The city's heritage surrounds those who walk its streets today.

Despite the destruction of many old buildings in the bombing raids of the Second World War and through the earlier dissolution of the monasteries, much survives from the past. Narrow lanes, distinctive roof lines, and hundreds of listed buildings serve as reminders of what Canterbury was like in earlier times. The monument commemorating James Simmons, one of several major benefactors, still towers over the Dane John Gardens which he laid out in the 1790s. Marlowe, Chaucer, and Becket, along with more recent archbishops, are commemorated in the names of the theatre, a care home, pubs, and numerous roads. Meanwhile, archaeological digs, which precede much new building, constantly modify and extend our understanding of Canterbury's history.

As pilgrims neared the end of their journey five hundred years ago, their first glimpse of their destination was the great Bell Harry Tower soaring high above the surrounding buildings. Despite everything that has happened, that same sight still greets twenty-first-century visitors, a witness through the ages to the ever-evolving story of Canterbury and its people.

The Bell Harry Tower soars above the city. *Author's photograph.*

BIBLIOGRAPHICAL ESSAY

Abbreviations

AC   *Archaeologia Cantiana*

CCA   Canterbury Cathedral Archives

CHAS Canterbury Historical and Archaeological Society:
www.rockhost.co.uk.

CPL   Canterbury Public Library

KCC   Kent County Council

KG   *Kentish Gazette*

ODNB *Oxford Dictionary of National Biography*

RCHM *Royal Commission on Historical Manuscripts, 9th Report:
Appendix* (HMSO, 1883)

UKC University of Kent at Canterbury

WT   *Whitstable Times and Herne Bay Herald*

1. Becket's City

Erasmus' reflections on his visit to Canterbury can be found in 'A Pilgrimage for Religion's Sake' (1526), https://www.degruyter.com/document/doi/10.3138/9781442659964-041/pdf. The Becket cult and visits to his shrine are discussed in P. Collinson, N. Ramsay, & M. Sparks (eds), *A History of Canterbury Cathedral* (Oxford University Press, 1995), pp. 135ff., and in B. Nilsen, *Cathedral Shrines of Medieval England* (Boydell, 1998). See also J. Zeiger, 'The Survival of the Cult of St Thomas in the Later Middle Ages' (UKC M.A. thesis, 1997) and essays by T. Tatton-Brown and P. Roberts in C. Morris & P. Roberts (eds), *Pilgrimage: The English Experience from Becket to Bunyan* (Cambridge University Press, 2002).

Canterbury's socio-economic situation is examined by M. Mate, *Trade and Economic Developments, 1450–1550: The Experience of Kent, Surrey and Sussex* (Boydell, 2006) and by P. Clark, *English Provincial Society from the Reformation to the Revolution: Religion, Politics and Society in Kent, 1500–1640* (Harvester, 1977). A wider context is provided by A. Dyer, *Decline and Growth in English Towns 1400–1640* (Cambridge University Press, 1995). Local government is analysed by J. Palmer, 'Politics, Corporation and Commonwealth: The Early Reformation in Canterbury' (UKC Ph.D. thesis, 2016). Lists of city traders can be found in two privately printed books by J. Meadows Cowper: *Roll of the Freemen of Canterbury 1392–1800* (1903) and *Intrantes: A List of Persons Admitted To Live And Trade Within The City* (1904). On fairs, see S. Letters, *A Gazetteer of Markets and Fairs in England and Wales to 1516* at https://archives.history.ac.uk/cmh/gaz/gazweb2.html (accessed 15 Jun. 2022).

The various religious orders in Canterbury are described in *Victoria History of the Counties of England: Kent*, ii (St Catherine's Press, 1926), which also lists benefactors and people buried in their churches. Sheila Sweetinburgh explores gifts to hospitals in 'The poor, hospitals and charity in sixteenth-century Canterbury', in R. Lutton & E. Salter (eds), *Pieties in Transition* (Ashgate, 2007). On parish church expenditure, see her essay in A. Foster & V. Hitchman (eds), *Views from the Parish* (Cambridge Scholars, 2015). Arrangements at St Dunstan's are described by M. Caiazza, 'The Parish Church of St Dunstan's Canterbury and its Fraternities *c.* 1485–1540' (UKC M.A. thesis, 1999) and by A. Hogarth, *The History of St Dunstan's Church Canterbury* (Oyster Press, 2009).

Battles between religious institutions and the city are examined by R. Warren, 'Conflict, Compromise and Co-Operation: The Civic Government's Relationship with the Church in Late Medieval Canterbury' (UKC M.A. thesis, 2010), and by D. Grummitt, '"Stond Horeson and Yeld Thy Knyff": urban politics, language and litigation in late medieval Canterbury', *The Fifteenth Century*, xvii (2020). See also CCA-CC-J/Q/299, CCA-DCc-ChAnt/C/1232/15, 20, 23, and CCA-DCc-ChAnt/C/1236. The story of the Marching Watch and St Thomas Pageant is told by J. Brigstocke Sheppard (*AC*, xii (1878)) and S. Sweetinburgh (*AC*, cxxxvii (2016)). Corporation expenditure on this event and on gifts for visitors is detailed in *RCHM*.

2. Dissolution and Demolition

Elizabeth Barton's career and significance are discussed in *ODNB*, in D. Watt, *Secretaries of God* (Brewer, 1997), and in E. Shagan, *Popular Politics and the English Reformation* (Cambridge University Press, 2003), ch. 2. See also *The Story of Oaten Hill in Canterbury* (Oaten Hill & S. Canterbury Association Local History Group, 2018). The sermon preached against her is reproduced by L. Whatmore in *English Historical Review*, lviii (1943). There are many references to 'the Nun' in *Letters and Papers foreign and domestic of the reign of Henry VIII* (HMSO, 1961–5), iv–vii. Volumes ix to xiv contain material relating to the closure of religious houses and the demolition of the shrine.

Detailed accounts of what happened in the city during the 1530s can be found in Palmer's thesis (cited in ch. 1) and in an unpublished paper by M. Sparks & T. Tatton-Brown, 'Religious Houses in Canterbury and the Dissolution' (1988, CCA Pamph.28/33). The atmosphere of dissolution is evoked by G. Moorhouse in *The Last Office* (Phoenix, 2008), an account of Durham, another cathedral priory. A record of the dismantling of St Augustine's is transcribed by D. Sherlock in 'The account of George Nycholl for St Augustine's 1552–53', *AC*, xcix (1984). See also R. Gem (ed.), *St Augustine's Abbey* (English Heritage, 1997) and www.canterbury-cathedral. org/heritage/archives/picture-this/canterburys-16th-century-deer-park/ (accessed 15 Jun. 2022) The state of the Augustinian Friary prior to dissolution is discussed by S. Sweetinburgh in J. Burton & K. Stöber (eds), *Monasteries and Society in the Later Middle Ages* (Boydell, 2008). For the dig on its site, see A. Hicks, *Medieval Town and Augustinian Friary* (Canterbury Archaeological Trust, 2015). The demolition of Becket's shrine and legends surrounding it are discussed by P. Roberts (cited in ch. 1) and by J. Butler, *The Relics of Thomas Becket* (Pavilion Books, 2020). The cost of putting Friar Stone to death is detailed in *RCHM* and in CCA-CC-FA/13 folio 69v–70r.

3. From Catholic to Protestant

Churchwardens' accounts have been transcribed by J. Meadows Cowper, *AC*, xvi and xvii (1886–7) (St Dunstan's) and by C. Cotton, *AC*, xxxii, xxxiii, xxxiv, and xxxv, 1917–21 (St Andrew's). Contemporary statements derive from information collected during Cranmer's investigation of the Prebendaries' Plot. The original register is preserved at Corpus Christi College, Oxford, but much is reproduced in *Letters and Papers*, xviii (cited in ch. 2). Good modern accounts which make use of this material are E. Shagan, *Popular Politics* (cited in ch. 2); E. Duffy, *The Stripping of the Altars* (Yale University Press, 1992); P. Collinson, *The Birthpangs of Protestant England* (Macmillan, 1998); and M. Zell (ed.), *Early Modern Kent 1540–1640* (Boydell, 2000), chs 6 and 7. For battles between clergy, see B. Hogben, 'Preaching and the Reformation in Henrician Kent', *AC*, ci (1984).

John Twyne, John Mychell, John Bland, Thomas Wyatt, James Hales, Nicholas Harpsfield, John Bale, and John Foxe all have entries in *ODNB*. See also A. Watson, 'John Twyne of Canterbury', *The Library*, viii (1986), and W. Sessions, *John Mychell: Canterbury's First Printer* (Ebor, 1983). The story of Bland and other Kentish Protestant martyrs is told by P. Collinson in E. Duffy & D. Loades (eds), *The Church of Mary Tudor* (Ashgate, 2006). A biographical list of those who died is provided by Zell (cited above). The dismissal and reappointment of clergy is charted in C. Buckingham, 'The movement of clergy in the diocese of Canterbury', *Recusant History*, xiv (1978). On continuing support for traditional practices, see A. Willis, *Church Life in Kent: Church Court Records of the Canterbury Diocese* (Phillimore, 1975) and E. Baskerville, 'A religious disturbance in Canterbury June 1561', *Historical Research*, clviii (1992).

Accounts of city politics and religious change in this chapter are indebted to theses by J. Palmer (cited in ch. 1) and by A. Le Baigue, 'Negotiating Religious Change: The Later Reformation in East Kent Parishes 1559–1625' (UKC Ph.D. thesis, 2019). These challenge P. Clarke's older emphasis in *English Provincial Society* (cited in ch. 1) on continued conservatism and factional fighting.

There is a brief description of the Canterbury militia in W. Urry, *Home Guard for Canterbury 1588* (Canterbury Local History pamphlet no. 1, Kent County Library, abridged from *Good Books*, i, Royal Museum and Public Library, Canterbury, 1947).

4. Citizens, Strangers, and Community Life

Accounts of French-speaking Strangers are provided by F. Cross, *History of the Walloon and Huguenot Church at Canterbury* (Huguenot Society of London, 1898) and by A. Oakley, 'The Canterbury Walloon congregation from Elizabeth I to Laud' in I. Scouloudi, *Huguenots in Britain* (Macmillan, 1987). An extensive archive is held at CCA-U47/N. Other newcomers are discussed by P. Clark, 'The migrant in Kentish towns 1580–1640' in

P. Clark & P. Slack (eds), *Crisis and Order in English Towns 1500–1700* (Routledge, 1972).

Much material relating to life in the city can be found in G. Durkin, 'The Civic Government and Economy of Elizabethan Canterbury' (UKC Ph.D. thesis, 2001), a work which suggests that Strangers constituted a smaller percentage of the population than is generally assumed. Other sources include *RCHM* pp. 154ff.; J. Bower, 'Kent towns, 1540–1640' in Zell (cited in ch. 3); and P. Clark, 'The social economy of the Canterbury suburbs', in A. Detsicas & N. Yates (eds), *Studies in Modern Kentish History* (Kent Archaeological Society, 1983). A history of almshouses is provided by D. Ingram Hill, *The Ancient Hospitals and Almshouses of Canterbury* (Canterbury Archaeological Society, 1969; 2nd edn with additional chapter by M. Lyle, 2004). On Thomas Stransham, see *AC*, lxxv (1961). There are articles on William Watmer, including material on plague deaths, in *AC*, lxi (1948) and cii (1985). Information about the theatre and other forms of recreation can be found in J. Gibson (ed.), *Records of Early English Drama: Kent: Diocese of Canterbury*, i (University of Toronto Press, 2002). Marlowe, Lyly, and Gosson all feature in *ODNB*. The city in which they grew up is well delineated by cathedral and city archivist William Urry in a posthumously published study, *Christopher Marlowe and Canterbury* (ed. A. Butcher, Faber & Faber, 1988). On early city maps, see www. canterbury-cathedral.org/heritage/archives/picture-this/the-canterbury-map/ (accessed 15 Jun. 2022).

5. Disputes, Departures, and Discord

The 1608 charter (CCA-CC-A/A/56) is discussed in *Cathedral Archives and Library News*, xlv (2010) and at www.canterbury-cathedral.org/heritage/archives/picture-this/illuminating-nature-canterburys-james-i-charter (accessed 15 Jun. 2022).

Many of the men mentioned in this chapter feature in *ODNB*: Isaac Bargrave, Richard Culmer, Henry Finch, John Finch, William Laud, Thomas Scott, John Tradescant, Thomas Wilson, and Edward Wotton. Information about elections and city MPs can be found in the History of Parliament Online, at www.historyofparliamentonline.org (accessed 20 Jun. 2022). On Thomas Scott, see also P. Clark, 'Thomas Scott and the growth of urban opposition to the early Stuart regime', *Historical Journal*, xxi (1978); C. Cuttica, 'Thomas Scott of Canterbury (1566–1635)', *History of European Ideas*, xxxiv (2008); and R. Cust, *The Forced Loan and English*

Politics, 1626–1628 (Clarendon, 1987) pp. 175–85. Scott's 1626 'Report on the Canterbury election in which he was lawfully elected but injuriously rejected by the Tyrannical Sheriff' is held at CCA-U66/1, and Isaac Bargrave's *Sermon preached before King Charles March 27 1627* at CCA ChekerBox 2/15. The king's 1625 visit is discussed by M. Toynbee, 'The wedding journey of Charles I', *AC*, lxix (1955). Information relating to ship money levies can be found in *Calendar of State Papers Domestic: Charles I*, http://www.british-history.ac.uk/cal-state-papers/domestic/chas1/1634-5/ p. 581 and http://www.british-history.ac.uk/cal-state-papers/domestic/chas1/1635-6/ pp. 204 and 397; see http://www.british-history.ac.uk/cal-state-papers/domestic/chas1/1635-6/ p. 164 for the attack on precincts housing (all accessed 8 Aug. 2022). The Burghmote minutes record the city's response to the levy of eighty men to fight the Scots: CCA-CC-SuppMs/21/9, pp. 485–6. On Thomas Belke's mobilising of a volunteer force, see *House of Lords Journal* (17 Aug. 1642), https://www.british-history.ac.uk/lords-jrnl/vol5/pp297-300 and *House of Commons Journal* (14 Sept. 1642), https://www.british-history.ac.uk/commons-jrnl/vol2/pp765-767 (both accessed 6 Aug. 2022).

Religious antagonisms are covered by A. Bateman, *The Mayflower Connection* (privately published, 1997) and R. Cushman & M. Paulick, 'Robert Cushman, Mayflower pilgrim in Canterbury 1596–1607', *Mayflower Quarterly*, lxxix (2013). The 1625 defacement of the cathedral Bible is detailed in *Manuscripts of the House of Lords*, n.s. xi (1514–1714) (Historical Manuscripts Commission), p. 204. Canterbury emigrants to New England feature on a list dated 9 June 1637 of passengers certified to travel from Sandwich (Sandwich Year Book 1637, Kent History and Library Centre, Maidstone, Sa/AC). See also E. Putnam, 'Two early passenger lists 1635–37', *New England Historical and Genealogical Register*, lxxv (1921), amended lxxix (1925). An account of Laud's dealings with the Strangers is provided by A. Oakley, 'Archbishop Laud and the Walloons in Canterbury' in W. Jacobs & N. Yates (eds), *Crown and Mitre* (Boydell, 1993). Richard Culmer's view of Laud's religious changes is given in his *Cathedral News from Canterbury* (1644, 1649 edn with postscript, CCA ChekerBox 4/21). His son, another Richard, defended Culmer in *A Parish Looking-Glasse for Persecutors of Ministers* (1657).

6. Civil War and its Aftermath

Detailed overviews of the Civil War in Kent with accounts of what was happening in Canterbury can be found in A. Everitt, *The Community of Kent and the Great Rebellion, 1640–1660* (Leicester University Press, 1966) and in J. Eales, 'Kent and the English Civil Wars, 1640–1660' in H. Lansberry (ed.), *Government and Politics in Kent, 1640–1914* (Boydell/ KCC, 2001). Canterbury is unusual in that its 1641 poll tax records have survived; see https://www.canterbury.ac.uk/arts-and-humanities/school-of-humanities/history/research/1641-poll-tax/home.aspx (accessed 20 Jun. 2022).

Attacks on the cathedral are described in Collinson, Ramsay, & Sparks (eds), *History of Canterbury Cathedral* (cited in ch. 1); in M. Aston, *England's Iconoclasts*, i (Clarendon, 1988); and in J. Walter, 'Abolishing superstition with sedition', *Past and Present*, clxxxiii (2004). On Culmer, see ch. 5 above and J. Eales, *Community and Disunity: Kent and the English Civil Wars* (Keith Dickson Books, 2001). For the sale of Lady Wotton's property, see C. Young, '"The Gentry are Sequestered All": A study of English Civil War sequestration' (Royal Holloway, University of London Ph.D. thesis, 2019), p. 227. The disciplining of clergy is discussed by J. Eales, 'The clergy and allegiance at the outbreak of the English Civil Wars: the case of John Marston', *AC*, cxxxii (2012), and by G. Ignatijevic, 'The Parish Clergy in the diocese of Canterbury and archdeaconry of Bedford in the reign of Charles I and under the Commonwealth' (University of Sheffield Ph.D. thesis, 1986). See also A. Matthews, *Walker Revised: being a revision of John Walker's Sufferings of the Clergy during the Grand Rebellion 1642–60* (Clarendon, 1988). The story of Dean Bargrave's royalist son is told by M. Brennan, 'The exile of two Kentish Royalists during the English Civil War', *AC*, cxx (2000).

A contemporary account of the Christmas riots can be found in *Canterbury Christmas or a true relation of the insurrection in Canterbury on Christmas Day last … written by a citizen there, to his friend in London* (1648). The list of those arrested is at CCA-CC-J/Q/447/iv. For the 'Declaration of Many Thousands of the City of Canterbury', see CCA ChekerBox 4/29.

The minute book of Canterbury's first Independent (Congregational) Church is held at CCA-U37. On Durant, see M. Jones, 'The Divine Durant: a seventeenth-century-independent', *AC*, lxxxiii (1968). New congregations are discussed by R. Acheson, 'The Development of Religious Separatism in the Diocese of Canterbury, 1590–1660' (UKC Ph.D. thesis, 1983) and by

G. Draper, 'Some Aspects of Quakerism in Kent, 1655–1690' (UKC Local History Diploma, 1991). See also the latter's articles in *AC*, cxii (1993), and cxv (1995).

Much information about city life can be gleaned from the Burghmote minute books (CCA-CC-A/C). There is a useful abridgement, thematically arranged, by an eighteenth-century alderman, Cyprian Rondeau Bunce (CCA-CC-SuppMs/21/9); some entries are reprinted in *RCHM*. In addition to court cases mentioned in these sources, see *Calendar of Assize Records: Kent Indictments 1649–1659* (Public Record Office, 1989).

7. Legacies of War

There is a contemporary account of the king's stay in Canterbury in E. Hyde, *History of the Rebellion and Civil Wars in England* (1702–4) and details of the cost in *RCHM*. Letters written by Charles from Canterbury can be found in *Calendar of State Papers Domestic,* http://www.british-history.ac.uk/cal-state-papers/domestic/interregnum/1659-60/ p. 446 and examples of requests for jobs and alms at http://www.british-history.ac.uk/cal-state-papers/domestic/chas2/1660-1/ pp. 139 and 303 and http://www.british-history.ac.uk/cal-state-papers/domestic/chas2/1661-2/ p. 229 (all accessed 8 August 2022).

On the Somner brothers, see William Urry's introduction to W. Somner, *The Antiquities of Canterbury* (1703 edn, republished EP Publishing, 1977) and articles by D. Wright in *AC*, cxl (2019) and cxli (2020). Somner's rescue of the font is discussed in www.canterbury-cathedral.org/heritage/archives/picture-this/observing-by-the-way-the-story-of-canterbury-cathedrals-font/ (accessed 20 Jun. 2022) and his role in restoring the cathedral in Collinson, Ramsay, & Sparks (eds), *History of Canterbury Cathedral* (cited in ch. 1). CPL holds a copy of *A True Relation of the Accompt of the Whole Procedure between the Corporation at Canterbury and Mr John Somner, concerning the new market-house there* (1666).

Clergy who lost their jobs at the Restoration are listed in A. Matthews, *Calamy Revised: being a revision of Edmund Calamy's account of minsters and others ejected 1660–2* (Clarendon, 1988). For accounts of dissenters, see works cited for ch. 6; R. Watson, 'Presbyterian Canterbury', *Journal of the Presbyterian Historical Society in England*, xiii (1967); and G. Nuttall, 'Dissenting churches in Kent before 1700', *Journal of Ecclesiastical History*, xiv (1963), an essay which contains details of the 1669 episcopal returns. A transcription of the Canterbury General Baptist church book for 1660 to 1695 by J. Creasey & L. Maguire is held at Dr Williams's Library, London. The Quaker 'Book of Sufferings' for Kent can be consulted at the Kent History and Library Centre, Maidstone, N/FQz1 and 2. Letters of complaint about 'fanatics' and protestations of loyalty from dissenters can be found in *Calendar of State Papers Domestic: Charles II*, http://www.british-history.ac.uk/cal-state-papers/domestic/chas2/1661-2/ p. 541; http://www.british-history.ac.uk/cal-state-papers/domestic/chas2/1663-4/ pp. 177 and 208; http://www.british-history.ac.uk/cal-state-papers/domestic/chas2/1665-6/ pp. 42, 47, and 463; http://www.british-history.ac.uk/cal-state-papers/domestic/chas2/1675-6 p. 68; http://www.british-history.ac.uk/cal-state-papers/domestic/chas2/1680-1 pp. 433, 479, 505; http://www.british-history.ac.uk/cal-state-papers/domestic/chas2/1682 pp. 227, 250 (all accessed 9 August 2022). Colin Lee drew heavily on such material to argue that dissenters dominated the Canterbury Burghmote, a view I challenge: see his '"Fanatic magistrates": religious and political conflict in three Kent boroughs 1680–84', *Historical Journal*, xxxv (1992). On Huguenots, see Cross (cited in ch. 4). Numbers are estimated by R. Gwynn, 'Distribution of Huguenot refugees in England', *Proceedings of the Huguenot Society*, xxi (1970).

On council activity during the Restoration, see Bunce's abridgement of the Burghmote minute book (cited in ch. 6), which contains lists of aldermen and councillors and details of dismissals and reinstatements. 'The Case between the Mayor and Aldermen of Canterbury and Mr Sergeant Hardres their late Recorder' is reproduced in 'Alderman Gray's Notebook' (CCA-CC-SuppMs/6). The surrender and reissue of charters is outlined by E. Hasted, *The History and Topographical Survey of the County of Kent*: Volume 11 (1800), British History Online http://www.british-history.ac.uk/survey-kent/vol11 and in the addenda of Volume 12, British History Online http://www.british-history.ac.uk/survey-kent/vol12 (accessed 16 August 2022). A summary of council events (relying heavily on Lee) can be found at www.historyofparliamentonline (accessed 20 Jun. 2022) which also provides biographies of Paul Barrett, Sir Edward Hales, Thomas Hardres, Francis Lovelace, and Sir William Rooke (in an entry on his son George). On Hales, Hardres, and William Somner, see also *ODNB*. Biographical notes about John Whitfield and other Canterbury figures can be found on the CHAS website.

8. An Eighteenth-Century Town

Urban developments discussed in this chapter are set in a wider context by P. Borsay, *The English Urban Renaissance* (Clarendon, 1989) and by A. Everitt, 'Country, county and town', *Transactions of the Royal Historical Society*, fifth series, xxix (1979), reprinted in P. Borsay (ed.) *The Eighteenth-Century Town* (Longman, 1990). A helpful overview is provided by R. Sweet, *The English Town, 1680–1840* (Longman, 1999). The rise of Tunbridge Wells is outlined by A. Savidge, *Royal Tunbridge Wells* (Oast Books, 1995).

Contemporary descriptions of Canterbury can be found in C. Morris (ed.) *The Journeys of Celia Fiennes* (Cresset Press, 1947), D. Defoe, *A Tour Through England and Wales*, i (1724), and the *Gentleman's Magazine*, xxxiii (1763). For the Great Storm of 1703, see D. Defoe, *The Storm* (1704, Penguin edn, 2005). W. Gostling, *A Walk in and about the City of Canterbury*, first published in 1774, went through many subsequent editions which can be read on Google Books.

Letters and petitions from silk-weavers about threats to their industry can be found in CCA-U47/H/4/55–72; see item 58 for claims about cheap Indian production and item 69 for the number of looms in the city. The 1766 charter establishing a hop market can be seen at CCA-CC-A/A/61 and a 1768 map by John Andrews and Matthew Wren depicting hop fields at CCA-DCc-PRINDRAW/3/A/3. The city's manufactures, along with many other aspects of its life, are detailed in volume xi of Hasted (cited in ch. 7). Information about the growth of luxury trades can be gleaned from A. Bartlett (ed.), *Canterbury Masters and their Apprentices* (Harrington Family Miscellany Record Publication, 1978) and from lists of Canterbury freemen compiled by S. Corpe & A. Oakley (UKC, 1982 onwards). For further discussion of Canterbury as a commercial centre, see A. Armstrong (ed.), *The Economy of Kent, 1640–1914* (Boydell/KCC, 1995). The city's transport networks are discussed by F. Panton, 'Turnpike roads in the Canterbury area', *AC*, cii (1985). For timing of journeys from London see *Gentleman's Magazine*, xxxxi (1771), p. 167.

James Abree's story is told by D. Shaw & S. Gray, 'James Abree (1691?–1768), Canterbury's first modern printer' in P. Isaac & B. McKay (eds),*The Reach of Print* (Oak Knoll Press, 1998). See also articles by D. Shaw on his distribution network in J. Hinks & C. Armstrong (eds), *Worlds of Diversity in the Book Trade* (British Library Publishing Division, 2006) and on the serialisation of *Moll Flanders* in *The Library: The Transactions of the Bibliographical Society*, seventh series, viii, 2 (2007). The *Kentish Post* itself can be read on microfilm in the British Library and (in part) in CPL. References to the paper in this chapter are largely drawn from three sets of sample years: 1738–40, 1750–2, and 1764–5. An analysis of adverts is provided in *Kent References: The Kentish Post 1750–52* (International Research Publications, 1970).

Copies of *A Panegyrical Poem* (1718) can be found in CCA and CPL. For Urry's comments, see CPL, 'Scrapbook' xxxix, item 2659. There are accounts of assemblies in G. Hampshire (ed.), *Elizabeth Carter, 1717–1806: Some Unpublished Letters* (University of Delaware, 2005). Theatrical advertisements are reproduced in D. Manners, *Canterbury Stage by Stage* (privately published, 2011). On Marsh, see *ODNB*, *The John Marsh Journals* (Pendragon Press, 1998), and 'The harmony of heaven: John Marsh and provincial music' in J. Brewer, *The Pleasures of the Imagination* (HarperCollins, 1997), a work which contains a wealth of information about the social mores of the time. Catch Club archives are held at CCA-CC-W/7. See also C. Price, *The Canterbury Catch Club 1826: music in the frame* (Cambridge Scholars Publishing, 2019). S. Gray writes about 'William Flackton, 1709–1798, Canterbury bookseller and musician' in P. Isaac & B. McKay (eds), *The Mighty Engine: The Printing Press and Its Impact* (Oak Knoll Press, 2000). The Mozarts' visit to the Canterbury races is mentioned in E. Anderson (ed.), *The Letters of Mozart and his Family*, i, 2nd edn (Macmillan, 1966). My thanks to Lady Juliet Tadgell of Bourne Park for the information that the young Mozart was unable to perform. On cricket at Bourne Park and elsewhere, see J. Goulstone, 'Some cricket grounds and clubs in Kent', *Cantium*, ii (1970). Lists of printer/booksellers can be found in R. Goulden, *Biographical Dictionary of Those Engaged in the Book Trade in Kent, 1750–1900* (privately published, 2014), and libraries are detailed at www.scribd.com/doc/63097781/Robin-Alston-Library-History-England (accessed 20 Jun. 2022). There is an account of James Callaway on the CHAS website. For the Society for the Cultivation of Useful Knowledge, see A. Barber, *Uncovering the Beaney Backstory* (Bene Books, 2013).

9. Governing the City

Information in this chapter derives largely from 'Alderman Gray's Notebook' (CCA-CC-SuppMs/6) and from Alderman Bunce's abridgement of the Burghmote minute book (CCA-CC-SuppMs/21/9). Further summaries of the Burghmote minutes can be found in Hasted (cited in ch. 7). There are articles by F. Panton on city finance and government in *AC*, cix (1991), cxii (1993), and cxx (2000), on the Court of Guardians (*AC*, cxvi (1996)), and on the courts of justice (*AC*, cxviii (1998)). See also his thesis, 'Finances and Government of Canterbury Eighteenth to Mid-Nineteenth Century' (UKC Ph.D. thesis, 1998). Roch's criticisms of the council were published in his *Proceedings of the Corporation of Canterbury: Shewing the Abuse of Corporation Government* (1760) and *An Address to the Electors of the City of Canterbury* (1761) (CCA Chekerbox 6/15 and 6/17).

For Canterbury elections and MPs, see History of Parliament Online (cited in ch. 5). A 1734 manuscript poll list for Canterbury is held by the British Library (Add Ms 28014). Copies of the printed *Poll of Electors* for 1790 and 1796 are lodged at CCA. Freemen and trading companies are discussed by S. Corpe, 'Canterbury Freemen 1700–1750' (UKC Local History Diploma, 1982) and the range of businesses by A. Bartlett (cited in ch. 8). R. Tittler, *Townspeople and Nation* (Stanford University Press, 2001), devotes a chapter to Sir Thomas White. Sir John Hales' death is recounted in M. Pennington (ed.), *A Series of Letters between Mrs Elizabeth Carter and Miss Catherine Talbot 1741–70*, i (1809), pp. 48–9.

10. James Simmons and the Remodelling of Canterbury

Material for this chapter has been largely drawn from F. Panton, *Canterbury's Great Tycoon*, revised edn (Canterbury City Council, 2007) and from his Ph.D. thesis (cited in ch. 9). For Pavement Commission votes, see D. Gardiner, *Canterbury*, new edn (Sheldon Press, 1933), p. 113. Canterbury's new theatre is set in a wider context by J. Baker in 'Theatre in the Provinces in the Late Eighteenth and Early Nineteenth Centuries, with Special Reference to Sarah Baker in Kent' (UKC Ph.D. thesis, 2000) and in *Sarah Baker and her Kentish Theatres* (Society for Theatre Research, 2019). Theatre advertisements and commentary relating to what was happening in France are taken from *KG* 1790 and 1793. The early history of the hospital is recounted in F. Hall, R. Stevens, & J. Whyman, *The Kent and Canterbury Hospital, 1790–1987* (Kent Postgraduate Medical Centre, 1987). Contemporary accounts of the young boy's accident, of the great freeze of 1795, and city dealings with the militia can be found in the 'County Intelligencer' sections of *The Kentish Register and Monthly Miscellany*, i–iii (1793–5). See also C. Cooper, 'The Impact on the County of Kent of the French Revolution, 1789–1802' (UKC Ph.D. thesis, 2004). On Canterbury barracks, see the CHAS website. Any estimate of population in the early nineteenth century must be tentative; I have drawn on parish returns printed in the *Victoria County History of Kent*, iii (1932), adding figures for the parishes of St Dunstan's, Holy Cross, St Gregory, and Staplegate to those listed for the city.

11. Into the Victorian Era

Much of the detail for this chapter comes from local newspapers: the *Kentish Gazette*, the *Kent Herald* (both CPL microfilm), and the *Kentish Chronicle* (British Library microfilm). Copies of *KG* for the years 1768 to 1873 can also be viewed online through the British Newspaper Archive. For analysis of the local press, see K. Eaton, 'Newspapers and Politics in Canterbury and Maidstone 1815–50' (UKC M.A. thesis, 1972).

The story of Canterbury's first railway is told in B. Hart, *The Canterbury & Whitstable Railway* (Wild Swan Publications Ltd, 1991) and I. Maxted, *The Canterbury & Whitstable Railway* (Oakwood Press, 1970). Many other topics, including the Swing Riots, feature in Lansberry (ed.), *Government and Politics in Kent* (cited in ch. 6). The riots have been the subject of detailed research by C. Griffin, whose article in *Southern History*, xxii (2000), focuses on east Kent. For eyewitness accounts of burning farms and the attack on the archbishop, see R. Cowtan, *Passages from the Autobiography of a 'Man of Kent'* (1886, reprinted Nabu Press, 2010).

My discussion of parliamentary and municipal reform is indebted to J. Young, 'Aspects of Local Government in Canterbury, *c.* 1820–1870' (UKC M.A. thesis, 1985). There is a useful historical survey of how Canterbury was governed in *Reports from Commissioners on Municipal Corporations in England and Wales: Appendix* (HMSO, 1835). For electoral corruption, see *Report of the Commissioners … into the Existence of Corrupt Practices in the City of Canterbury* (HMSO, 1853). Poll books for this period are held at CCA-CC-R/P. There are summaries of voting in the History of Parliament Online (cited in ch. 5) and in F. Craig, *British Parliamentary Election Results 1832–1885* (Parliamentary Research Services, 1989). As for the colourful 'William Courtenay', the best account is by B. Reay, *The Last Rising of the Agricultural Labourers* (Clarendon, 1990), but note also an older narrative: P. Rogers, *Battle in Bossenden Wood* (Oxford University Press, 1962).

12. Work and Recreation

The Oaten Hill and District Society Local History Group has published a number of informative pamphlets, including *The Bigglestons of Canterbury* (1996) and *The Holmans of Canterbury* (1992). On occupations, see contemporary directories: *Stapleton and Co's Topographical History and Directory of Canterbury* (1838), S. Bagshaw, *History, Gazeteer and Directory of the County of Kent* (1847), *The Post Office Directory of the Six Home Counties* (1878), G. Stevens, *Directory of Canterbury and Neighbourhood* (1882), and Bedwell & Co, *Canterbury and District Directory* (1888–9). Occupational information from censuses can be found at www.histpop. org (accessed 4 Jul. 2022). For population figures, see ch. 10. For child involvement in hopping, see transcripts of logbooks of the Wesleyan and St John's schools, held respectively at St Peter's Methodist Church, Canterbury and CPL. The development and impact of the railways are usefully explored by F. Templeman, 'Canterbury and the Coming of the Railways' (UKC extended essay, 1970) and F. Andrews, 'The Effect of the Coming of the Railway on the Towns and Villages of East Kent, 1841–1914' (UKC Ph.D. thesis, 1993). On Finn's, see G. Pike & M. Crux, *History in a City Street* (Oyster Press, 2008), and on Lefevre's, see A. Bateman in *Bygone Kent*, ix (1988). City pubs are described by E. Wilmot, *Inns of Canterbury* (privately published, 1988) and *Eighty Lost Inns of Canterbury* (privately published, 1992). The Westgate Temperance Hotel, Baker's Temperance Hotel, and Slatter's Temperance Hotel feature in late 1890s directories. For the number of pubs, see Stevens' 1882 directory, which also lists Friendly Societies. Membership cards and rule books for the various orders can be consulted at CCA-U520/8. The Wesleyan Mothers' Minute Book for 1881 to 1949 is held at the city's Methodist Church. Reports and catalogues relating to the Literary and Philosophical Institution can be found in CPL. Halls are described in Manners, *Canterbury Stage by Stage* (cited in ch. 8) and Dickens' visit in P. Brown, S. Hutchinson, & M. Irwin, *Written City*, revised edn (Yorick Books, 1990). For William Masters' Exotic Nursery, see the CHAS website. Details of Blondin's performance, cheap excursions, temperance activities, burial societies, concerts, talks, swimming, circuses, and fairs derive from *KG* and *WT*. On Cricket Week, see the *Illustrated London News*, 13 Aug. 1881. A bound volume of student essays of variable merit, 'Living in Victorian Canterbury as Portrayed in Historical Sources', can be found in UKC and KCC libraries.

13. Drains, Disease, and Destitution

The *British Medical Journal* contains articles by and about Rigden: on public health in Canterbury in 1861 (13 Dec. 1862), on epidemics in the city (17 Apr. 1869), and an obituary (9 Apr. 1904). A transcript of his 1847 report is lodged at CCA Pamph.129/8. The Nuisance Inspector's books (1855–71) can be found at CCA-CC-Q/LB/S/F. There is a copy of Pilbrow's 1867 report in CPL; see www.gracesguide.co.uk/James_Pilbrow (accessed 4 Jul. 2022) for his obituary (1894).

Most of the material for this chapter has been gleaned from *KG* and *WT* reports. These provide fuller and more vivid accounts of meetings and disputes than the council minutes which are held in CCA. Other papers consulted were the *Kent Herald* (30 Jan. 1840) and the *Illustrated London News* (11 Nov. 1882). For local government changes, see J. Young (cited in ch. 11) and A. Bateman, 'Public Health in Mid-Nineteenth-Century Canterbury' (UKC Local History Diploma, 1988). Public health looms large in Bateman's *Victorian Canterbury* (Barracuda Books, 1991), a book which needs to be handled with care as it contains a mass of fascinating but miscellaneous and disorganised information. An overview of the poor law and of public health is provided in N. Yates, R. Hume, & P. Hastings, *Religion and Society in Kent, 1640–1914* (Boydell/KCC, 1994). See also R. Scott, 'The Administration of the Poor Law in Canterbury' (UKC extended essay, 1979). City charities are detailed at CCA-CC-S/21/1, CCA-U36/3, and CCA-U483. On the hospital see F. Hall *et al.* (cited in ch. 10).

Sidney Cooper's life and work is detailed in *ODNB* and in his autobiography, *My Life* (Richard Bentley & Son, 1890). A room in the Beaney House of Art and Knowledge is dedicated to his work. For Beaney's early life and disputes over his will, see M. Blackamore, 'The Life and Times of James George Beaney' (UKC MPhil, 1996). Articles on Cooper, Beaney, Rigden, and the Wincheap waterworks can be found on the CHAS website.

14. Communities of Faith

Religious census returns for Canterbury places of worship are reproduced in M. Roake (ed.), *Religious Worship in Kent: The Census of 1851* (Kent Archaeological Society, Kent Records, xxvii (1999)). On nonconformist congregations, see A. Taylor, *The Free Churches of Canterbury* (1929), J. Vickers, *The Story of Canterbury Methodism* (1961, reprinted 1970), and W. Harvey, *Thomas Clark of Canterbury, 1775–1859* (1983). Josiah Henson is discussed in Brown, Hutchinson, & Irwin's *Written City* (cited in ch. 12). There are articles on Clark, Henson, and Beresford-Hope in *ODNB*. The establishment and construction of the missionary college is described by L. & M. Lyle, *Canterbury and the Gothic Revival* (History Press, 2013). A large archive from the college is held at CCA-U88. For Jacob Jacobs' account of the erection of a new synagogue, see D. Cohn-Sherbok, *The Jews of Canterbury, 1760–1931* (Yorick Books, 1984). Henry Hart features in www.jtrails.org.uk/trails/canterbury/articles (accessed 4 Jul. 2022). Contemporary descriptions of the arrival of the Salvation Army can be found in *KG* and in a centenary number of *Contact*, lxii (Jun. 1986) at CPL. Information on all other topics covered in this chapter has been gleaned from *KG* and *WT*. See also the pamphlet version of a *KG* report, *Canterbury Martyrs' Memorial: Influential Meeting at the Guildhall* (1898). To set these events in national context, see D. Rosman, *The Evolution of the English Churches, 1500–2000* (Cambridge University Press, 2003), chs 7–8.

15. 'The Old Order Changeth'

For Henry Hart, see ch. 14. There is an article about John Green Hall on the CHAS website, which also contains material on telephones and electricity, and on Henry Dawson and the Canterbury car. The history of George Barrett's firm can be found at http://www.barrettskent.co.uk/about-us/history/ (accessed 4 Jul. 2022) and details of car registration in Armstrong (ed.), *The Economy of Kent* (cited in ch. 8). I have drawn heavily on *KG* and *WT* for first-hand accounts of transport and utilities, the cathedral clock, aviation, the Boer war, and suffrage meetings. See also E. Crawford, *The Women's Suffrage Movement in Britain and Ireland: a Regional Survey* (Routledge, 2006) and L. Probert, *Women of Kent Rally to the Cause* (Millicent Press, 2008). Frank Honey's story is told by M. Winstanley, *Life in Kent at the Turn of the Century* (Dawson, 1978) and that of the Langton schools by L. Lyle, *To Be Continued … A History of the First Hundred Years of the Simon Langton Schools* (KCC, 1981). For Harold Gilham, see https://www.thelangton.org.uk/app/uploads/2017/09/October-2014-1.pdf (accessed 4 Jul. 2022).

Corruption in Canterbury elections is placed in its national context by H. Hanham in *Elections and Party Management* (Harvester Press, 1978). Transcripts of interviews with local people are included in the *Report of the Commissioners Appointed … to Inquire into the Existence of Corrupt Practices in the City of Canterbury* (House of Commons Sessional Papers, 1881, xxxix). Background political information is provided in Lansberry (ed.), *Government and Politics in Kent* (cited in ch. 6) and in N. Yates (ed.), *Kent in the Twentieth Century* (Boydell/KCC, 2001). These works do not deal with the controversies surrounding Francis Bennett-Goldney, which can be found in *KG* and in A. Bateman, *The Magpie Tendency* (self-published, 1999). On his predecessor, see A. Porter, *The Life and Times of Sir John Henniker Heaton* (Bodley Head, 1916).

16. The Demands of War

CCA holds a wealth of material relating to the First World War: see www.canterbury-cathedral.org/heritage/history/remembering-world-war-i/ (accessed 4 Jul. 2022), which contains articles about cricket, the War Work Depot, and the war memorial. Patterns of recruitment are explored in M. Connelly, *Steady the Buffs!* (Oxford University Press, 2006). The arrival of Belgian refugees is discussed at www.kent.ac.uk/ww1/news.html?view=159 (accessed 4 Jul. 2022). On the work of Voluntary Aid Detachments, see two works by H. Basford: 'Kent VAD: the work of Voluntary Aid Detachments in Kent during the First World War' (UKC MPhil, 2004) and 'Bertha Stapley (née Evans), a Canterbury VAD' (typescript lodged in CPL). Women's life in the cathedral precincts was described by a canon's daughter, Ruth Spooner, in 'Memories' (1968), available in typescript in CPL. Other material for this chapter, including tribunal reports, derives from *KG*. This was also a primary source for A. Bateman, *Wartime Canterbury 1914–1918* (self-published, 2003) and for a student research project, 'Life in Kent during the First World War' (UKC, 1975). Interviews with people who were children during the war have been collated by A. Pope, *Tell Us About When You Were Young: Living in Canterbury and Its Villages, 1900–1939* (Canterbury Environment Centre, 1997). For details about the munitions work in which one of Pope's interviewees was involved, see M. Worthington Williams 'The Canterbury Car', *Kent Life*, vi, 2 (1967). I am indebted to D. Evans, 'How Far Were the Lines Between Frontline and the Home Front Blurred in East Kent (Canterbury) during the Great War 1914–1918?' (UKC M.A. thesis, 2016), for the use of unpublished material relating to the Langton schoolboys. On the 1918 flu epidemic, see the admission and discharge book of the Dane John Hospital (CCA-CC-W/26/A/3). The post-war movement to remember those who died in the war is examined by P. Donaldson, *Ritual and Remembrance: The Memorialisation of the Great War in East Kent* (Cambridge Scholars Press,

2006). City trails featuring the activity of individual residents during the war can be found at http://kentww1.com/trail-files/canterbury-booklet.pdf (accessed 4 Jul. 2022). A comprehensive list of sources and sites is provided by H. Basford & K. McIntosh, *Gazetteer of East Kent in the Great War* (East Kent Branch of the Western Front Association, 2008).

17. The 'Interwar' Years

The main sources for this chapter are the *Gazette* and K. Pinnock, *A Canterbury Childhood* (Robert Hale, 2009). Voting figures for elections can be found at https://commonslibrary.parliament.uk/research-briefings/cbp-8647/ and population figures at http://www.histpop.org/ohpr/servlet/ (both accessed 4 Jul. 2022). For reports and correspondence on slum clearance and house building, see CCA-CC/BB/290, CCA-CC/A/SC/62/1, and CCA-CC/A/SC/64/1–4. The numbers unemployed are listed in records of the Canterbury and District Trades Council (CCA-U75/3–4a). Information about the occupation centre is given in papers of the Unemployment Committee (CCA-CC/BB/393 and CCA-CC/A/SC/3223/1–2). On Catherine Williamson, see her book *Though the Streets Burn* (1949, reprinted Merlin Press, 1966) and the CHAS website. Small neighbourhood shops are described in publications of the Oaten Hill Society, such as *Dover Street Remembered* (enlarged edn, 1993) and *Ivy Lane Remembered* (1994). There are accounts of Lefevre's store on the CHAS website and in *Bygone Kent*, ix (1988). Cinema provision before 1933 is described by T. Thompson in *Bygone Kent*, vi (1985). Films shot by Sidney Bligh and other Canterbury Cine Club members have been preserved by Tim Jones of the School of Media, Art and Design, Canterbury Christ Church University. Extracts including the burning of Abbot's (Denne's) Mill can be viewed at https://blogs.canterbury.ac.uk/cafa/dennes-mill-fire/ (accessed 4 Jul. 2022). On cathedral developments, see Collinson, Ramsay, & Sparks (eds), *History of Canterbury Cathedral* (cited in ch. 1), pp. 308ff.; K. Pickering, *Drama in the Cathedral: The Canterbury Festival Plays, 1928–1948* (Churchman Publishing Ltd, 1985); E. Bliss, *The Urgent Miss Babington* (Canterley Publishing, 2018); and J. Butler, *The Red Dean of Canterbury* (Scala Publishers Ltd, 2011). There is an essay on Richard Bellamy and other Canterbury fascists on the CHAS website.

18. Blitz and Reconstruction

Much of the detail in this chapter derives from Catherine Williamson's recollections of the war years in *Though the Streets Burn* (cited in ch. 17). Her predecessor's protest about lorries in the cathedral was printed in *The Times*, 22 Sept. 1939. Eyewitness accounts of the bombing of 31 May/1 June 1942 are quoted in A. Pope, *Memories of the Blitz* (Canterbury City Council Museums, 1992) and in *The Story of Oaten Hill in Canterbury* (cited in ch. 2). Information about the damage caused by the bombing and about redevelopment plans is provided in invaluable photograph collections compiled by P. Crampton: *The Blitz of Canterbury* (1989), *Canterbury after the Blitz 1942–1945* (1993), *Canterbury in the Late 1940s: The Buddleia Years* (1995), and *Canterbury Then and Now: The Lost Scenes and Buildings 1950–1975* (1991), all published by Meresborough Books. Note also his *Canterbury 1945–1975* (Tempus Publishing, 2002) and *Canterbury's Lost Heritage* (Sutton Publishing, 2006). On Anthony Swaine, see the CHAS website and obituaries in the *KG* (11 Apr. 2018) and at http://ihbconline. co.uk/context/130/index.html#6 (accessed 4 Jul. 2022). John Clague's film of the 1951 festival can be viewed at https://player.bfi.org.uk/free/ film/watch-festival-celebrations-in-canterbury-1951-online (accessed 4 Jul. 2022).

19. University City

Recollections of first-generation UKC students can be found at https:// www.kent.ac.uk/50/pride-in-our-past/index.html (accessed 4 Jul. 2022). There is an account of the founding of the university in G. Martin, *From Vision to Reality* (UKC, 1990). For parliamentary discussion of A2 bypasses, see https://api.parliament.uk/historic-hansard/commons/1973/ jun/28/a2-brenley-corner-dover (accessed 4 Jul. 2022). Lists of traders can be found in *Kelly's Directory of Canterbury* (1966). Wikipedia contains material on the Canterbury Sound (or Scene), https://en.wikipedia.org/ wiki/Canterbury_scene (accessed 4 Jul. 2022). There is an entry on Mary Tourtel in *ODNB*. For images of Rupert, see https://followersofrupertbear. co.uk/rupert-annuals-2/ (accessed 4 Jul. 2022). The creation of Bagpuss and his predecessors is discussed in Oliver Postgate's autobiography, *Seeing Things* (Sidgwick & Jackson, 2000). The history of local government is summarised in Appendix ii of Yates (ed.), *Kent in the Twentieth Century* (cited in ch. 15). Detailed coverage of the papal visit can be found in

KG, 4 Jun. 1982. For attitudes to the Channel Tunnel, see the *Gazette*'s leading article on 24 Jan. 1986. The signing of the treaty was reported on 14 February 1986 under the heading 'The Deed is Done'. There are transcriptions from an interview with Hazel McCabe on pp. 95–7 of E. Darian-Smith, *Bridging Divides* (University of California Press, 1999). The impact of students on the community is set in a national context in https://www.theguardian.com/education/2018/sep/23/town-v-gown-is-the-student-boom-wrecking-communities (accessed 4 Jul. 2022). On the new Marlowe Theatre and its predecessors, see https://marlowetheatre.com/about/what-we-do/our-history/ (accessed 4 Jul. 2022).

INDEX